TECHNIQUE IN JUNGIAN ANALYSIS

THE LIBRARY OF ANALYTICAL PSYCHOLOGY

TECHNIQUE IN JUNGIAN ANALYSIS

Second edition
with a new introduction by Judith Hubback

Published for
THE SOCIETY OF ANALYTICAL PSYCHOLOGY
LONDON
by

Karnac Books
London 1989

First published 1974

Second edition 1989 published by
H. Karnac (Books) Ltd
58 Gloucester Road, London SW7 4QY

ISBN 0 946439 64 8

Printed in Great Britain by BPCC Wheatons Ltd, Exeter

Contents

An asterisk at the end of a reference indicates that the paper is also published in the present volume.

Introduction to the Second Edition

This collection of papers by members of the London Society of Analytical Psychology is being republished as it has proved to be of continuing interest and value to the growing number of people qualified both in the established and the new training societies for analysts and therapists, or studying to enter them. It is likely that much of its appeal stems from the fact that in it theory and practice are closely interwoven: in only two of the nineteen papers is there no case material. The collection demonstrates, as does any presentation of scientific or therapeutic research or practice, how theories and models emerge both from the study of earlier, pioneering, publications and from day to day experience, and are tested time and again in the process of a group of practitioners accepting them as viable. So backing up concepts and theories with clinical descriptions is considered very important in showing how the writers work – or worked, since Ruth Campbell, William Kraemer and Kenneth Lambert have died since the book first appeared.

Although *Technique in Jungian Analysis* is certainly neither a text-book nor – heaven forbid – a handbook on technique and on how to work with transference and counter-transference, it draws together many of the major tenets of contemporary analytical psychology, which have developed on the foundations laid by Jung. While all his work has continued to be of central importance, the emphasis given to certain aspects of it has changed over the years, in some centres more than in others. Jung died in 1961; even before his death various individuals and groups of analytical psychologists were finding that some of his concepts and ways of working appealed to them either more, or less, as the case might be, than others. Moreover Jung himself favoured a flexible use of his concepts. As Plaut writes (page 155, below): 'Jung, throughout his writings, eschews anything that savours of a technique; the idea of a blueprint is abhorrent to him'. So for us Jung's work offers guidelines and an inspiration rather than being a pattern indelibly etched into us during training. When Jung left Freud he was both developing from, as well as reacting against, certain features of psychoanalysis as it was then, in the early years of the century. It will be seen that the contributors of the papers chosen for this book have not been defensive against making use of the writings of analysts trained along different lines: only three of the nineteen reference lists are exclusively Jungian. That is typical of the 'London School', whose members treat many patients who seem to need an approach which incorporates the findings of psychoanalysis and which is also in keeping with some of Jung's early work, either because of their being still in the first half of life (emotionally and/or in terms of their age), or because of their psychopathology.

Some of the member societies of the International Association of Analytical Psychology maximise the importance of technique and others minimise it. Not only does the particular style or way of working vary as between each analytical psychology association, society, group or centre, but individuals who differ considerably from each other can be found in any of them. Some favour an emphasis on the art, and others on the craft, of our shared discipline. One of Lambert's contributions to the present volume, 'The personality of the analyst in interpretation and therapy', shows how there can be no question of relying simplistically on theories relating to technique. But it can also plausibly be said that the book in its entirety rotates round Fordham's paper, 'Technique and counter-transference', where he poses the question: 'Is it possible to formulate a concept of technique'? (page 270, below). And he writes: 'Technique, which I shall identify mainly with interpretation . . . comes to depend upon the analyst's having achieved a sufficient range of experience and maturity' (*Ibid.*). In commenting on that paper, Plaut links Jung's use of the term 'personal equation' with the modern analyst's use of 'style': and considering that to some extent modern psychologists and modern physicists discover that they function in similar ways where subjectivity and objectivity are concerned, it is interesting to learn also that

Jung's favoured term was coined by the astronomers at the Greenwich Royal Observatory in 1796 (page 292, below).

In the practice of modern analytical psychology it has become of central importance to recognise, analyse and interpret projections and introjections of many sorts, the patient's transference, the analyst's counter-transference, and the dialectical interaction between the two, which is descriptively termed transference/counter-transference. Transference and counter-transference evoke each other; the patient's gradual acceptance of the analysis of those processes and his growing consciousness of the way they influence his relationships are facilitated by the analyst who can successfully blend his knowledge of archetypal forces, images and symbols with his experience of developmental factors.

This collection of papers describes and defines many aspects of the difficulties arising in clinical practice with respect to three considerations. The first is as to how much emphasis should be given to comments or interventions which concentrate, perhaps exclusively, on the 'here and now' of the patient's current life and his relationship with the analyst. The second is the use of interpretations which link the present with the past, thereby enabling the patient to understand how his earlier experiences, fantasies and interactions are still dominating his current life. The third is for each analyst to study how the mutative process of freeing the patient from those now inappropriate attitudes and ways of life can be set going.

In reading again the papers now being reissued, I have been struck by their impressive blend of the characteristics which this profession demands of its practitioners, subsumed under the suggestive words: head and heart. No long or learned terms will ever replace them. And as analysts we hope, through personal work and the study of the work of others, to pass on that creative blend or combination to those who seek our professional help.

JUDITH HUBBACK
September 1988

Editorial introduction

In this, the second volume of the Library of Analytical Psychology, a further set of papers by members of the London Society of Analytical Psychology is brought together to demonstrate the results of some twenty years of work upon certain themes related to technique in Jungian analysis. These are considered more in terms of macro- than micro-analysis, and specially refer to the problems of transference and counter-transference. That the two themes are inter-connected has become sufficiently clear, for although transference and counter-transference are known to be constantly present in the psychotherapeutic process, their development and the elaboration of their therapeutic potential are bound up with questions of setting, management and technique.

It seems likely that both Jung and Freud agreed about the importance of transference, and probably counter-transference, and indeed it was Jung who proposed the analysis of analysts as part of their training. Nevertheless, despite these and other areas of agreement, their differences of viewpoint, more clearly revealed after Jung's separation from psychoanalysis, have often been emphasized and regarded as largely opposing and irreconcilable rather than complementary or mutually enriching. London Jungian analysts have been concerned for some years to reinvestigate and in some way to repair this situation. There are two main reasons. First, many of the wide variety of patients seeking their aid seem to need the kind of approach that has become linked with psychoanalysis and with the methods described by Jung and considered in his earlier writings to be appropriate to such cases. Second, Jungians in London have been exposed to the stimulus and criticism of psychoanalytical and other colleagues, both in connexion with everyday clinical work and on the meeting ground afforded by the Medical Section of the British Psychological Society.

It is hoped that the results of this work will be apparent to the reader of these essays, many of which have already appeared in the *Journal of analytical psychology*, and some in the *British journal of medical psychology.* This volume has also been organized as an attempt to show something of the historical development of ideas and experience in the realm of transference and counter-transference that has taken place during this period.

Accordingly the papers have been arranged in the historical sequence of their publication. Some have been revised, though most not to any great extent. To his rather early paper on 'The dangers of unrecognized counter-transference', however, William Kraemer has appended an addendum describing his present-day reaction to a paper written by him so long ago. In addition, Ruth Strauss has introduced into the text of her early paper on 'Counter-transference' some comments from her present position.

Historically viewed, it seems fair to say that the recognition and analysis of transference as such was the first subject to become a central one for clinical preoccupation in the London group. Then, as anxiety about this began to diminish with the acquisition of increased skill and experience, counter-transference became a subject that could be tackled. The analyst could then see it less as a focal point of response overdetermined by delusion or illusion on his part and more as a source of important information about his patient's transference. Finally, more recent experience and theoretical development have established that, at a central point in the dialectical process between patient and analyst, the transaction involved is most suitably termed transference/counter-transference. In other words, transference and counter-transference at this point evoke each other. It is then the task of the analyst to increase his ability to help the patient towards the greater consciousness of such processes that undoubtedly facilitates growth towards both individuation and the realization of the self.

Another problem in transference/counter-transference that has received increasing attention is concerned with the relative weight to be given to 'here and now' interpretations on the one hand and, on the other, to interpretations that include re-construction of earlier patterns of relationship. These latter often remain unchanged and overdetermine the patient's relationships in his adult life, rendering him subject to affective responses totally disproportionate to the reality of the 'here and now' relationship situations in which he finds himself. Especially is this the case in his relationships with his analyst. Some

Jungians have tended to lay emphasis upon Jung's criticism of reconstructive interpretations as 'nothing but' and so 'merely' reductive. They have therefore concentrated on 'here and now' transference interpretations, mainly in archetypal terms. Others, remembering that Jung in other parts of his writings was much less critical of reductive interpretations, feel that these two emphases are not necessarily incompatible. Interventions that look like 'here and now' interpretations are often revealed, upon examination, as mainly descriptions or definitions. To include reconstruction within the transference/counter-transference is, in this view, considered most likely to produce an analytic intervention that deserves the term 'interpretation', for this procedure both links the patient with his past in a meaningful way and can begin the mutative process of freeing him from being fixed in it for the rest of his life.

Furthermore, the handling of transference/counter-transference is decisively affected by two developments among psychoanalysts in London. First, the work of Klein on unconscious infantile fantasies links up in an amplifying way with the work of Jung on archetypes. Secondly, the emphasis among London psychoanalysts upon 'internal objects' and 'internal part-objects' has been found very useful by Jungians in understanding some of the complicated and dynamic interplay between archetypal processes in the early life of the individual and his personal environment—experienced as depriving, validating, facilitating, enabling or destructive of the individuation process. Naturally these studies have arisen out of transference/counter-transference experiences and, in turn, shed light upon them in all their complexity and multi-dimensionality.

One of Jung's emphases has always been upon the personal analysis and integrity of the analyst as a central factor in the therapeutic process. Accordingly a paper has been included that stresses the analyst's need to be aware of his own real personal involvement in the analytic process, through which he may develop the capacity to use his growing consciousness of the transference/counter-transference situation to the benefit of his patients' individuating and integrative processes.

In connexion with technique, a small selection has been made of essays that deal mainly with management problems seen in the large rather than in detail. It is hoped that further volumes, both by single authors and in the form of collections of essays by several authors, may examine in greater detail problems of technique in micro-analysis.

References to Jung's writings in this volume are taken from the *Collected works*, which is abbreviated '*Coll. wks.*' followed by the volume number. Dates refer to the first publication in whatever language and not to the English translation.

We thank Diana Riviere and John Lucas for their professional assistance in preparing this volume for press.

Acknowledgements are also due to the British Psychological Society and the authors for permission to reprint articles by Michael Fordham, Alfred Plaut and Ruth Strauss originally published in the *British journal of medical psychology*.

PART I

Technique

The symbolic attitude in psychotherapy*

JUDITH HUBBACK

1969

Introduction

The intention in this paper is to study some aspects of psychotherapy, as distinct from analysis, with a view to finding out
what happens; to examine the value of the therapist's having
an active attitude to the developmental possibilities inherent in
various kinds of symbols and symbolic occurrences; and to
show that the nature of effective interaction is the same
whether the treatment is labelled analysis or psychotherapy.

The analyst pays attention to what he is doing, to what the
patient is doing, and to the psychodynamics of what is happening. In this work, actions and interactions are of even greater
interest than are concepts. Concepts distract from actions
through turning them into things; they can be used defensively
against experiencing and understanding the patient as a person.
Without neglecting the careful consideration of nouns we have
to be even more closely acquainted with verbs.

Over the years interest has gradually deepened in the theoretical bases of the various types of treatment. Jung, in 'Problems of modern psychotherapy' (1929, p. 72), says: 'The
doctor is as much "in the analysis" as the patient.' In 'Medicine
and psychotherapy' (1945) he says (p. 89): 'The real point is
the treatment of the whole psychic human being.' In 'Fundamental questions of psychotherapy' (1951) he says (p. 116):
'The intelligent psychotherapist has known for years that any
complicated treatment is an individual, *dialectical*, process' and,
later in the same paper, 'I therefore consider it my main task
to examine the manifestations of the unconscious . . . but . . .
the symbols produced by the unconscious derive from archaic

* First published in the *Journal of analytical psychology*, **14**, 1.

3

modes of psychic functioning' (p. 123). These considerations are theoretical statements arrived at through clinical experience. They apply in brief as well as in long therapy.

In his paper 'Analytical psychology and psychotherapy', originally published in 1949, Fordham writes: 'In stating that analytical psychology can contribute to the theory of psychotherapy it is necessary to point out that analytic concepts can be applied whether the procedure under consideration be long or short. Therapy is basically not a question of time, but of how the needs of a patient can best be met' (p. 169). The psychoanalyst Szurek, in attempting to differentiate between analysis and therapy, discusses the question of whether the similarities between the two are the factors that account for improvements in the patient, and asks whether the differences are matters of nature or of degree. He also wonders whether psychotherapy is a special application of the same basic theory as psychoanalysis and queries whether an analytic situation is possible with fewer than five sessions each week. He comes perhaps a little closer to Fordham's view, quoted above, when he makes use of Freud's discovery that the question 'How can, must, or shall, I treat the patient?' was the wrong one, and that a better one to ask is 'What can I do *with* the patient?'

Another psychoanalyst, Edward Glover, reviewing the theory of psychotherapy in the United States and in Great Britain (Glover, 1960), comes to the conclusion that 'it is doubtful whether the principles of general psychotherapy have changed much since the period following the First World War', but he is willing to add that 'the move towards character analysis' and 'the complications of ego-analysis' do not alter the 'fundamental factor of transference' and 'the approaches to the unconscious'. He writes, moreover, that 'the prerequisite of a coherent theory of psychotherapy is a theory of mind that will account for both normal and abnormal manifestations' (p. 75).

The increasing attention given to symbols, to symbol formation, to object relations, to transference and to countertransference in their totality, are all gradually contributing to the understanding of what happens in all personal relationships, of which therapy is one, and to the theory of minds in action. The constituent theories, and the possible general one, have to be seen against the background of various current social facts. An important one for the purposes of this paper is that there is a rising demand for therapy, as compared with full analysis, which analytical psychologists are trying to meet, in a variety of settings.

Where a theory of mind is concerned, there are distinctions but there are no hard and fast lines either between normal and abnormal, or between therapist and patient, or between analysis and psychotherapy. The therapist uses the same tool—himself—whenever he meets a patient (or tries to meet a patient who is frightened of meetings) even though he uses this tool in varying ways with different people, in different settings and at different times. In his *Study of brief psychotherapy* Malan shows, most convincingly, what others have perhaps discovered independently for themselves, that it is necessary to tackle the patient's negative feelings and the mourning and separation problems inherent in the end of even brief treatment. The other finding of importance is the influence of enthusiasm: 'Perhaps the intense interest of any worker new to this field engenders a corresponding heightened excitement in the patient, with the result that repressed feelings come easily to the surface and are experienced with such intensity and completeness that no further working through is necessary. Subsequently this excitement can never quite be recaptured, nor can its effects' (Malan, 1963, p. 13).

The study of work that has been done in long analyses on the integrating aspects of the functioning of symbols 'has much to offer if it can be related to current knowledge of how symbol formation comes about' (Jackson, 1963, p. 156). And more recently Plaut (1966), being concerned with ego development, linked transference preparedness, and the lack of it, with trust and with the inability to trust, and with the capacity to make and to use images.

Psychotherapy

The term psychotherapy will be used here to denote what is commonly thought of as brief work: a matter of months, not usually years. The experiences of sixteen particular patients in therapy, and mine with them, provide the background, individually and cumulatively. Three will feature in detail to substantiate some of the processes I want to describe. Nine came once a week only: they were university students. Seven

5

used to come, or are at present coming, twice a week; fourteen of the sixteen are under thirty years old; ten are under twenty-five. Of those who pay for their therapy themselves only one could at present afford to come frequently. They are a group of patients who, by and large, come to the number of sessions that are considered sufficient for psychotherapy, but not for analysis; they are in this position for reasons of age, and geographical reasons, or because they are students earning nothing, or people with very small incomes.

Therapy once or twice a week is not miniature analysis, in the sense of frequent sessions over a long period, dependency, and a very considerable investment of libido on the part of analyst and patient. There are many features in a long intensive contact that can only rarely be discerned in the work described here, but a strongly experienced involvement can occur in the therapist which, if well understood, contributes most valuably to the patient's development and to the integration of previously damaging unconsciousness.

When I think of the course of treatment with each of these patients, and try to discern which factor was crucially important, it seems to me that it was their use of a symbol or of a symbolic event that on each occasion led to ego-development. They were people who were amenable to therapy, meaning that their personalities predisposed them to being able to make use of it, and most particularly of its symbolizing component. Certainly many people who are referred for therapy turn out not to have this capacity.

Symbols and the Symbolic Attitude

In spite of the great amount of work done, and the consequential vast literature written, on the subject of symbols, there is as as yet no consensus of opinion that satisfies a variety of analysts on how to use the word. In the present state of the controversy, and for the present purpose, symbol is being used as a descriptive word for any idea, thing, action or event representing in the present any such item that existed previously. The item in the past is, as a result of repression, relatively unknown in the present; the symbol is, at the time of its occurrence, the best possible representation. 'Whether a thing is a symbol or not depends chiefly upon the attitude of the consciousness considering it . . . it is quite possible for a man to produce a fact which does not appear in the least symbolic to himself, although profoundly so to another' (Jung, 1921, p. 603). A symbol 'manifests itself spontaneously in a symbolical effect upon the regarding subject' (ibid.). And the therapist's symbolic attitude (still following Jung) 'is the outcome of a definite view of life endowing the occurrence, whether great or small, with a meaning to which a certain deeper value is given than to pure actuality' (ibid. p. 604).

The therapist is responsible for discerning the prospective meaning of the phenomenon being used as a symbol by the patient. On the basis of his greater consciousness he can, with a symbolic attitude, make possible an experience of transition from lesser to greater awareness of the previously unconscious forces at work, which are distorting current events and behaviour. It follows that in even brief therapy the patient can be seen to be using unconsciously a wide range of possible ways of conveying to the therapist essential information about pathogenic facts in his earlier life. The particular activity of the symbol that is used in therapy is its activation of ego-development, as a result of unintegrated past experiences being brought together with present ones, in the transference, so that something happens.

In the popular world outside most consulting rooms there are a number of new terms that have swum into my orbit in the last year (they have probably been current longer) and one of them is 'a happening'. This is not necessarily the same as a 'love-in'; a 'happening' is a generic term, of which a 'love-in' is one instance. Unless a therapy hour has at least some of the same essence as a 'happening', the loss of tempo, impetus, interest and libido will be serious. And this is of greater importance in once or twice a week therapy than when the contacts are more frequent.

In considering happenings in therapy, it is worth being thoroughly acquainted with what attitude is, and the power it exerts. Jung defined it as 'a readiness of the psyche to act in a certain direction . . . an attitude always has an objective; this can be either conscious or unconscious' (1921, p. 526). In 'attitude' are also included the concepts of aptitude, fitness, a posture and a gesture adapted to some purpose. In cases where, for whatever reason, less frequent rather than more frequent therapy is undertaken, the first basic attitude must be to accept the limitations imposed by the reality, and deciding to adapt oneself to the maximum within that frame.

In treating those who can come only once or twice a week, I find it essential to try to keep in mind that if I can manage to adapt to them, this is more than likely to foster in them the growth of a capacity to adapt in the various ways that each individual is going to need. In so far as 'attitude' is a synonym for readiness, the analogy of the mother being ready for a particular baby to give her indications of its individuality from the earliest possible moment, and her readiness to respond partly as *a* mother but also as *the* mother that *that* baby requires —this is the sort of thing that happens in the less-frequent just as much as in the more-frequent therapies.

It is necessary to be ready for almost anything to become an image representing, in therapy, earlier events, experiences or attitudes to others and to the patient himself; and to be ready to bring out the symbolic potential in such images. If they are left, rather than picked up, there is more likelihood in once- or twice-a-week therapy that they will not recur. When I am reflecting on the course of a particular hour with a patient who comes infrequently and I find that I failed to notice something that had an image and a symbol-potential, then I think more has been lost than when this occurs with a patient in full analysis. This is inherent in the conditions of work, although it may also be an example of excessive super-ego domination.

The Illusional Transference

Images, illusions and delusions can be examined in conjunction with each other. An image, in therapy, is a more straightforward presentation or representation of material than is an illusion or a delusion. The root word in 'image' is the Latin *imitor*, meaning 'I imitate'. The root in 'illusion' and in 'delusion' is *ludo*, 'I play'. In 'illusion', the image plays in with the subject; in 'delusion', the image plays him down, and mocks at him.

The important happening in therapy is the interplay between therapist and patient, on the basis of the fact that play and interplay between the mother and the infant set the tone of his later interplay and interaction with other people. In a deep analysis there may well be a long stage, or a short phase, in which the patient's transference onto the analyst takes on a delusional quality, particularly when it has become essential for paranoid anxieties to be worked through.

I have not yet found that a situation of that depth or quality has developed in once- or twice-a-week therapy (and it is tantalizing to have a patient who would quite likely be able to benefit by such a difficult experience, who most likely needs it if he is to be enabled to achieve a hopeful amount of healing, but who, at the current stage of his life, is financially debarred from the possibility), but short of the fully experienced delusional transference and the regression to symbolic equivalence, which is what happens then, the rather less extreme illusional transference develops, and the therapist plays in with this.

A small example may illustrate what I have in mind. One of my twice-a-week patients, who uses the couch, is very knowledgeable and leads an active and full life; in therapy, also, he uses almost every available instant of his time. He is decidedly observant. His dreams, as well as being vivid, accurately recalled and physical in content, also contain jokes. On occasions he has thought that I will not believe him, that I will think he has invented them, cleverly, and perhaps especially for me. For weeks on end he needs to have the illusion of feeding me, which he does in many other ways as well as the dreams with jokes.

He can easily tell me about his overt envy of me, but the unconscious envy (which is what he defends himself against in reversing the rôles and trying so often to feed me) only emerges through an actual and startling experience of an illusion. This happened after he had been coming for some months, a few sessions after he had told me that his friend's analyst supplies *his* patients with a rug. The friend had been in analysis nearly six years, going five times a week. I just managed not to fall into what looked like a trap set to catch me out in not feeding him adequately, in which case he would have continued in his fantasy of always being the feeding one: I made no comment on the fact that there was, and always had been, a rug on the couch. It seemed better to wait until he had noticed it himself. Over the weekend his envy of the friend and also of myself dropped in intensity, and at the next session the moment he arrived he saw the rug, and the illusion was dropped to the tune of much amusement on his part.

Unfortunately, I felt, the side-effect of the incident was to reinforce his idealization of my powers and his conviction of my being 'a clever one'. But it is possible that he still needed that illusion, and that in time it will come within reach of experience and interpretation. The rug incident made it possible for him to start getting over his very considerable deprivation in childhood with two fussily obsessional and anxious parents, who apparently never joked at all; the patient thought he had to impress them with cleverness so that he became excessively keen to be 'bright' and to succeed intellectually. In therapy he grew able to allow himself to make unintellectual punning jokes. It seemed important not to be heavy-handed in commenting on jokes: that would have represented, within the transference, a pompous parent's status-conscious frown, or an irritable mother's slap. So I took up the act of joking, with the element of playful attack, rather than the content of the jokes.

With patients who can come only once a week, and who are, many of them, very much aware of their frustrated wishes to come more often, the particular feature of their earlier lives that they found it most difficult to tolerate, and that was perhaps most potent in inhibiting normal development, may have to be discovered in just as actual a way, and just as much enacted in the transference, as would be the case with those who are in full analysis.

In this connection I think of a very uncheerful young man whose presenting symptom was an apathetic inability to work. Among the first things he told me about himself were how he could not get up in the morning, how he fell asleep when working and how much he enjoyed being sarcastic. He had enjoyed friendships with a small group of rather clever boys at school, but his teachers had labelled him lazy. He had failed the first part of his university course, and had been demoted from working for an honours degree to doing the general one. His manner was in some ways passive and yet already in the first session there were, I felt, cutting attacks going on somewhere, so that it looked as though there might be a serious risk of unmasking a depression such as cannot be properly treated in once-a-week sessions.

I decided not to try to fit him into a morning appointment, even though that might perhaps have resulted in his getting up, so that he might then have attended his college at least for the remainder of one day a week, and then possibly it would have helped him to re-acquire the taste for work. This would have been a practical approach, but I thought it would be less therapeutic than an afternoon session. He held the view that he could not get up in the morning merely because he stayed up so late with friends. After a few weeks it emerged that from the age of about seven onwards, his mother being out at work, he stayed in bed every Saturday until she came back in the afternoon, and also much of Sunday, because neither she nor his father ever did anything with him. On weekdays, when he had to go to school, she used to bring him his breakfast in bed (he told me this consisted solely of bread and margarine—he did not want anything else) and he never said 'thank you' (his mother never required this of him, and she did not mind).

This régime continued until he was sixteen, when his mother had to go to hospital, and she died, after an operation for cancer. He remembered sitting by her bed during the visiting hour, with nothing to say at all. He was, of course, very often silent in therapy; but this went with an ability, surprising in the circumstances, to express himself well and accurately when he felt comfortable. He gradually became able to make good use of his time, when he had worked through the fantasy that during these silences I was having scathing and sarcastic thoughts about him, and then another, alternative fantasy that I was not thinking about him at all, but using the time to think of something else.

When I pointed out that these fantasies contained considerable attacks on me, he said he preferred to imagine that I was being critical, as that would make me more like him, and less like his mother, who never had anything to say to him and did not seem to mind that he had nothing to say to her. Another fantasy was connected with his stepmother (his father had remarried): breaking one of the silences, he said he had been fearing that I was thinking up an attacking kind of remark, like the stepmother, who invariably upbraided him for never saying 'thank you'. Fairly soon after this he said that he hid from people, in silence or in bed, in order to try to force them to fetch him, but that he hoped at the same time that they would leave him in peace.

This revealing information did not come about as a result of verbal interaction, but through an incident in which, instead of as usual coming first to my door to see if it was open at the time for a session, he had gone off to the waiting room. I was waiting for him and he was waiting to be fetched. As he had been coming for over four months, I thought he knew the routine. But it turned out that there was another routine, dating from earlier in life, that he knew in a different way. After a bit, I went to look for him, to fetch him; and I left it to him to start.

He said: 'My grandmother once told me that my mother believed in feeding by the clock. If I cried before the right time, she wouldn't fetch me. I've spent all these weeks trying not to tell you that, because I want to be different from other people: I didn't want you to use your textbook knowledge with me, and tell me everything that goes wrong is due to what happened in the cradle; I want to be able to do things *I* decide on, rather than always have things happen to me, as a result of other people's actions.' Then he added: 'To be honest, I must say, too, that I've been spinning out therapy by not telling important things, because you seem to care, and I like coming.'

After this session the amount of work he did increased (although it did not become exactly impressive); he had the sense to seek advice from his academic tutor, which he had until then avoided doing because, in the same way as he had needed to treat me in fantasy as a non-communicating and non-caring mother, so the tutor was being forced into the rôle of the semi-absent father. Not long after, he sat his finals, and obtained a degree. He wrote to tell me that he had and also described his future plans. He ended the letter by saying: 'Anyway, I keep so cheerful it amazes me, for which I thank you (or me, or psychotherapy, or luck).'

I suggest that, in a case such as this, the improvement factor lies in the therapist's holding the attitude that, within the transference, there was growth potential. The waiting incident had the characteristics of a symbol and it was fully within the transference, so that ego-growth resulted. The interaction in the transference/counter-transference projections was representative of the archetypal mother-infant relationship, and it was also individual and specific to that patient.

His behaviour had some of the quality of acting-out (avoiding verbal or non-verbal experiences with the therapist and inter-acting unsuitably with members of the environment) but what is more important is that it did the work of a symbol. The patient had to work through the illusion, which developed an almost actual quality, of me being like a mother who decides by the clock when to pick him up, and then to discover me as more like one who waits until he is ready, or goes to fetch him when he is. The imagery and the illusion were in the silences and then in the waiting; the transcendent or developing quality of the experience was in the fact that imagery occurred as a result of factors in him and in me; there was, I think, communication at an unconscious level; his sarcasm turned out not to be too destructive, nor his scepticism too strong, for him to pick up and to use just enough of my view that libido could be reached and set free from the 'laziness' which had held it captive.

Adolescent Depression and the Illusional Transference

Patients who are depressed, or whose symptoms are very clearly defensive substitutes for admitting to being depressed, can present very considerable difficulties in psychotherapy. One way of tackling the work with them is to aim first at trying to find out which aspect of feeling depressed is the one round which the others cluster. If there is improvement in that limited area, the ego may be strengthened, and in late ado-lescence enough growth may be set going for the therapist to retire from the situation and leave the patient to do the rest.

In this connection one of Ernest Jones's remarks in 'The theory of symbolism' (1948) is a useful one: 'The order of development seems to be: concrete, general, abstract.' Marion Milner's work on the rôle of illusion in symbol formation, with the key idea that 'this word (illusion) does imply that there is a relation to an external object of feeling' (Milner, 1955, p. 86) is also helpful in experiences with a depressed patient between, say, eighteen and twenty-five years old, even if it only shows why treatment failed. Such a patient, when he was an infant or a child, had certain experiences that were concrete in the sense of actual. The therapist has learned how to derive the general from the particular concrete experience; he abstracts and selects from his generalized knowledge what is of immediate use to the individual patient. He becomes the new external object who can represent the parent symbolically, the parent who should have been there enough, and who steps out of the way when he is not needed. That applies particularly to adolescents. There must, if possible, be real happenings within the transference, experienced with feeling by the therapist as well as the patient. The patient learns from the concrete experience with the therapist to generalize in his experiences with other people, and can abstract from therapy what he needs in the rest of his life.

The work I was able to do with a certain depressed young man, although at the time it was only minimal and now can only be outlined, illustrates the value of a constructive illusion. The patient looked saturnine, gauche, and fierce. I had been told that he hated his parents, particularly his father, who was withdrawn and hostile, and that he had been quarrelling with his flat-mates. He objected to being referred for therapy, saying that it would do him more harm than good, but that he had no alternative but to comply. In manner he was cynical and aggressive. He was obviously frightened. The persecutory element behind the depression seemed very pronounced. He had very dark eyes, and thick eyebrows. He had a hare-lip. On first meeting him I assumed that, whatever were the hidden roots of his depression, the hare-lip would feature in therapy.

But in the twenty sessions that he allowed himself before deciding to carry on independently, he mentioned it only once. The occasion for this was when he had given me an opening for pointing out that his mind, which he talked about most intelligently, was *in* his body, and he responded by saying that *perhaps* his hare-lip was *partly* a cause of his difficulties. This remark rang true; it became clear to me that it was not the lip by itself but the interpersonal aspects of it that provided the persecutory basis of the current depression. It is tenable that the worst aspect of early persecutory fears is the terror of annihilation, death just at the beginning of life. He seemed to be having, at the crisis of growing up, entering adult life, a recurrence of such persecutory fears.

He started therapy one January, and he told me of a fearful

experience he had had in the recent Christmas vacation, in which he had had a terrifying feeling of being senile. He could do nothing, for several days, but sit by the fire, like a very old man. He had days in therapy when his fear of me was quite patent: he spoke with his mouth almost shut, but just managed to say that he was certain I was going to open him up. During most sessions his arms would gradually stiffen, and most of his body followed. I pointed out that this was happening, and each time that I interpreted the stiffness in terms of his preventing himself from in any way attacking me, improvement followed in the form of greater ease, and he reported better contacts with his workmates.

The crucial session was one in which he finally allowed personal feelings to emerge naturally: he said that I did not like him personally, and that I knew he was afraid of intimacy but, because this was my work, I would try to get him out of his hermit-like defensive retreats. If this had been analysis I should have thought of the transference projection behind his statement that I did not like him as delusional in quality and I should have assumed it would take quite a time to resolve. But in this instance I treated it as if it were an illusion, on the grounds that he had shown he had enough ego-strength to tolerate the fact that I had never given him any overt indication of liking, as it is usually conveyed in ordinary social contacts, and it looked as if I could trust to his being able to discover that, in fact, I did like him.

So in the session referred to just now, all it was necessary to do, in response to the remark I have reported, was to keep looking at him. He gradually opened his eyes a little wider, the scared, suspicious and saturnine expression altered very slowly, and he ended up with a look that I can only describe as amused. He concluded the session by saying that he couldn't expect people to like him unless he was likeable. This may sound too crudely logical to be a felt remark, but at the time it was said there was an impressive and convincing simplicity about it. The simplicity became an interesting event to me, as I felt that its truth was crucially connected with his having had to experience the illusion of my having had an essentially non-personal attitude in work, and then discovering that the facts were different.

The illusion that had gripped him earlier in life (and revived

15

in the crisis of late adolescence) seemed to be of himself as basically unlikeable, damaged, quarrelsome, defensively aggressive, irrevocably set on the path towards becoming an objectionable old man like his father.

As therapist I was 'the external object of feeling' (in Milner's words) that had temporarily been fused with that illusion. In the transference, the past where this had originated was brought together with a present quite opposite in quality. There was in this instance no idea or single event that could be called a symbol, but he benefited by experience in therapy as a direct result of being able to use the symbolic attitude on which I was functioning. I think that symbolization occurred, in this case, in the fact of discovering he was liked: this disposed of his current version of the original persecutory terror and made it possible for him to make the remark with which he opened the next session: 'Now that I've found out my main problem, it's up to me to do something about it, and this means I've decided to make definite efforts to become more likeable'.

Conclusion

With the patients described here, the issue often focused upon the need each of them had to attack in safety. This sometimes involved a need to feel, within the transference illusion, that he or she was counter-attacking defensively, and to discover that the incidents that brought this impulse to light were actual and present-day, concrete events, which could perhaps be made into something else.

In attempting to convey the feel of some psychotherapy sessions, I have given material from three patients, with the intention of showing in action the influence and effect of the symbolic attitude: the experience of constructive illusions from which ego-development may proceed.

The commonly perceptible themes in the process by which an image develops into a transforming symbol emerge in a more sketchy form if patients can be seen only once or, better, twice a week than they do in analysis. But, to use some of Milner's words again, 'The creative illusion which analysts call the transference' is just as necessary, usable and creative in psychotherapy as in analysis. In relation to brief psychotherapy perhaps the straightforward words 'to make' should be substituted for 'to create'. Making it possible for a patient to make something better of himself than he has heretofore happens through his making use of the symbolic nature of the transference. It is action of a particular sort made possible by a particular attitude of mind.

Detecting the presence of transference projections and of potential symbols and symbolic events seems to me to have to be done in a very similar way in both therapy and analysis and, of course, this way can only be one's personal way of working. With some patients it seems preferable to wait, rather than to press on, with others to take more active steps. The temptations in this work are to hasten rather than to hold back, to get anxious when the working-through process is skimped, as it often is, and to form opinions too quickly and therefore with the risk of forming them in a forceful rather than a receptive way.

References

FORDHAM, M. (1958). 'Analytical psychology and psychotherapy', in *The objective psyche*. London, Routledge & Kegan Paul.

GLOVER, E. (1960). 'Psychoanalysis and psychotherapy', *Brit. J. med. Psychol.*, **33**, 1.

JACKSON, M. (1963). 'Symbol formation and the delusional transference', *J. analyt. Psychol.*, **8**, 2.

JONES, E. (1948). 'The theory of symbolism', in *Papers on psychoanalysis*. London, Baillière, Tindall & Cox, 5th ed.

JUNG, C. G. (1921). *Psychological types* (trans. 1923). London, Routledge & Kegan Paul.

——(1929). 'Problems of modern psychotherapy', in *Coll. wks.*, **16**.

——(1945). 'Medicine and psychotherapy', in *Coll. wks.*, **16**.

——(1951). 'Fundamental questions of psychotherapy', in *Coll. wks.*, **16**.

MALAN, D. H. (1963). *A study of brief psychotherapy*. London, Tavistock.

MILNER, M. (1955). 'The role of illusion in symbol formation', in *New directions in psychoanalysis*. London, Tavistock.

PLAUT, A. (1966). 'Reflections about not being able to imagine', *J. analyt. Psychol.*, **11**, 2.

SZUREK, S. A. (1958). *The roots of psychoanalysis and psychotherapy*. Oxford, Blackwell.

The personality of the analyst in interpretation and therapy*

KENNETH LAMBERT

1973

Analysis and Psychotherapy

The Fifth International Congress of Analytical Psychology (1971), on 'Success and failure in analysis', raised important questions about the relationship between psychotherapy and analysis, together with the problem of assigning a precise meaning to the words *success* and *failure*.

In the group discussion that followed the opening paper on 'Failure in analysis' by Michael Fordham, two issues emerged. They were, first, the failure of analysis, which can be described exactly, and, secondly, the failure of therapy, which is less easily assessed. The analytic failure described in the paper was to enable the patient to respond to the analysis of a projective identification that was central to her personal relationships. Her block was judged unshiftable after many years' work, and the treatment, after good notice, was terminated. In other respects the patient's fulfilment in her life had improved considerably—as well as her general capabilities and success in her profession. This, however, could not with certainty be attributed to the analytical treatment, though to the onlooker it appeared as if successful psychotherapy had taken place.

The subsequent group discussion extended to speculation about the future growth of the patient, and also was troubled over the function-type of her analyst and whether an analyst with a different superior function might have done differently with the patient. This finally caused a group analyst present, Harold Kaye, to suggest that the group was grappling with the

* First published in the *Journal of analytical psychology*, **18**, 1, with the title 'Agape as a therapeutic factor in analysis'.

18

problem of wishing to deny the fact of failure. Despite this, some members thought that the termination of the analysis in the end represented good feeling on the part of the analyst, and even wondered whether the ending of the analysis under such circumstances was not therapeutic in its own way.

Personal Qualities in the Therapist

During the year following the Congress, the Analytic Group in London has continued to discuss the issues raised. Papers by Fordham, Strauss and Bosanquet, on the subject of what analysis is, dealt largely with the question of whether the term analysis should be confined to the process of the reduction of complex structures to their simple elements, or whether it should be applied to the whole process of psychotherapy including its analytical aspects.

Other papers seemed to centre on basic personal attitudes on the part of the analyst. For instance, Hubback, in a paper on envy and the shadow (1972), showed the test of the analyst's personality involved in dealing with the often overwhelming envy exhibited towards him by his patient. Plaut (1972) also demonstrated the analytic attitude employed by Bion (1970) whereby, in pursuit of O, the analyst deals with each session without desire, without memory and without understanding— the way of negative capability—a way designed to enable his patient to develop in his own way and in his own time. In this process, the analyst intervenes either to foster this development as it unfolds or to interpret at a point where a decisive change is perceived as imminent. This indicates the patience, humility and freedom from the temptation to prejudge the issue required of the analyst and the vigilance required by him lest he operate in a preconceived controlling way.

A further development may be seen in the January 1972 number of the *Journal of analytical psychology*. Here Hillman writes about failure in terms of failure in analysis, of analysis and as analysis. This is, no doubt, intended to startle, though analysis turns out to be both a success and a failure, while analysis as failure does not amount to more than that a good deal of analysis should be helping patients into an experience of their depression, diminishment, despairs, etc., rather than irritating them beyond limits by emphasizing the virtues of progressiveness, success, creativity—even individuation and integration misused into becoming virtues that can be aimed at.

Next, Williams deals with the plight of the patient overwhelmed by primary envy towards the analyst and having to destroy the helpful efforts of his analyst. In this paper the special qualities of response demanded of the analyst if he would succeed therapeutically are emphasized. Another paper, by myself, shows the therapeutic effect of the mastery by the analyst of the operation of the talion law within him activated in his complementary counter-transference, so that, through his renewed concordant counter-transference, he can make interpretations that are assimilable by his patient as a result of positive feelings activated by gratitude.

Yet another paper, by Moore, demonstrates the therapeutic effect of the analyst's work upon himself in connection with a patient who felt impinged upon by environmental changes in connection with the analyst's consulting room. What was important was the experiencing of a sequence of anxiety, defensive denial and repression, assimilation, fear and resentment and ambivalence prior to the repair and a return to a quiet state. This sequence took place quickly in the analyst, but lasted over several sessions in the patient, for whom the analyst-mother could wait, not too impatiently and without unduly hurrying the patient's participation in the process.

Now if we look at this considerable variety of therapeutic attitudes, we can see that analytic interpretations within the transference/counter-transference situation all play a fundamental rôle. Nevertheless, underneath all these transactions and the skills involved in them, another therapeutic factor seems to be implied. This appears to be both an ability on the part of the analyst to go through a certain process in himself and also a certain quality of the analyst's personality as a whole, which he seems to be able to mobilize on his patient's behalf. This quality of personality seems to be connected with concern, patience, a capacity to remain-in-being for his patient and is connected with aspects of what used to be called *agape* in the Biblical sense but further developed by analytical work upon it. (See below, *agape* and the therapeutic attitude.)

This kind of *agape* contains a combination of eros, humane feeling and respect, not in a god-almighty sense but both cognisant of the shadow and limited in aim and scope, and enough to meet the need of a few patients. This attitudinal sub-stratum appears to be deeper than the transference/ counter-transference or the analyst's skill or knowledge or personality type or function. A possible name for it would be the *agape*-factor, and it may be understood as a function of the self.

Now, if this be so, we may find that we are dealing with a process that is well described by a term that has been in use for many years in a general sense, namely, analytical psycho-therapy. This recognizes that, even though, among a number of therapeutic elements in our work, analysis is the most fundamental of them all, nevertheless success is dependent on other factors besides—many of which may be regarded as enabling analytical work to be accepted by the patient—or rejected, or modified or elaborated and thereby rendered more effective in often unforeseen ways.

Among recent work on this subject we might mention the researches of Truax and Carkhuff (1967) into the nature of the basic personal gifts out of which the therapist may apply his techniques and specialized knowledge and without which he is likely to fail. It was found that three qualities—genuine-ness, non-possessive warmth and accurate empathy—seemed to be essential to the successful therapist. Incidentally it was also found that patients most likely to benefit were those in which 1, a high degree of inner or 'felt' disturbance was combined with a low level of behavioural or overt disturbance; 2, a high degree of readiness and positive expectancy supported hope for personal improvement; and 3, deep and extensive self-explora-tion was engaged in.

In principle Truax and Carkhuff seem to be making a valid point, although their statements suggest a greater idealization of the 'good analyst' than most analysts would find acceptable. Perhaps the most significant point for those engaged in training analysts rests on the fact that Truax and Carkhuff believe that they have demonstrated that the qualities of genuineness, non-possessive warmth and accurate empathy can be improved by training.

These authors considered their findings to be valid for all types of contemporary psychotherapy, which comprise a broad spectrum indeed. At one end of it will be found the procedure of pure classical psychoanalysis. In the middle will be found the procedures of a large number of analysts and analytical psychotherapists. The nearer to the analytic end these therapists are, the more likely they are to judge all the methods used in their therapy by the extent to which they serve the process of analysis. At the other end will be those methods that are mainly concerned with cathartic emotional experiences as such, together with methods that resemble acting out in non-analytical group therapy. Included at this end as well are methods of behaviour therapy with minimal interpretation or verbalization.

The Non-Analytical Content in Psychoanalysis (Rycroft)

In reality, however, the extremes do not ever exist in such purity. For instance, Rycroft (1968a, p. 64) has pointed out that there is much more content and implication in the pure analytical work of the psychoanalyst than simply verbal analytical interpretations on a symbolic level. There are also the following factors, which can carry considerable significance for both patient and analyst:

1. There is a room with a door closed against interruptions, and quiet enough. There is a couch.
2. There is an analyst present who is a person responding to the patient.
3. This analyst has an attitude. It is ideally not neutral, not purely intellectual, not a feeling, but something that Rycroft, following MacDougal, calls a 'sentiment'. A sentiment is an organized enduring disposition of emotional tendencies, maintained more or less consistently, even though it may suffer passing disturbances due to fatigue, preoccupation, etc. Most important of all, perhaps, this sentiment of Rycroft's arises from the analyst's prior experience as a patient who has been the object of similar steady concern on the part of another, that is to say, his own analyst. This seems to be the basis for interest in, concern for and empathy with the patient—as a natural spontaneous activity—spontaneous, I would emphasize, and not contrived, not over-compensatory and not part of an idealized system of good actions and attitudes.

4. This analyst makes interpretations designed to promote analytic understanding in the patient, but the making of them is a sign that the analyst is interested enough, 1, to be present and alert; 2, to listen, to understand and to remember. Furthermore, the analyst, by interpreting, shows that the patient's feelings and attitudes are known and shared by others. They are not freakish, unique or incomprehensible. Thus, in the analyst there is no sense of shock and no need to make the patient conform to the analyst's preconceptions.

I quote Rycroft only to show that, in the opinion of a psychoanalyst, there is much more than purely analytical content in interpretations—however correct in content, effect and timing they may be. The additional content may perhaps be summed up as signs of a basically benign attitude in a whole person towards the patient, whether the patient consciously takes it as a sign or not.

All this does not mean that for many of us there might not be a need to criticize or modify Rycroft's statement. For instance, there are some patients for whom the signs of the analyst's implied concern are manifestly not enough—to the extent that a considerable problem arises in connection with feelings of deprivation in the patient. The opposite is also true. For some patients, the signs of concern seem unbearably far too much and threateningly persecutory. Questions arise as to whether signs of concern should be obvious or played in a very low key indeed. What really matters is the actual presence of the concerned analyst in a way that is analogous to the importance of the actual presence of the good enough mother, in Winnicott's sense, responding to or holding the distressed infant. The inner concern of the analyst does not necessarily require any very noticeable outward expression and leaves plenty of room for spontaneous transference to the analyst as screen if necessary.

Analysis in Psychotherapy

So much for the non-analytical aspects of psychoanalysis as described by Rycroft. If we look at the other end of the spectrum, we certainly find implied analytical attitudes even in behaviour therapy and in cathartic types of group psychotherapy. Indeed, transference and resistance have been explicitly recognized as difficulties in behaviour therapy by Rhodes and Feather (1972). Nevertheless, most analytically-orientated therapists would feel that here the analytical content is dealt with in a manner far too elementary and over-simplified to promote ego-development or individuation. A possible conclusion to be drawn from all this is that everything turns on a judgement about 1, how rigorous the analytic aspect of the treatment needs to be in order to meet the problems of any particular patient, and 2, the degree to which the conditions and procedures of the treatment can be set up and orientated in order to enable analytic work to take place.

Jung's Early Model of Psychotherapy

However, such a judgement is not always easy to make and most analysts have patients with whom the issues are not at all clear. Accordingly, I have thought it worthwhile to remind ourselves of Jung's contribution to this question, made as long ago as 1929, in his essay entitled 'Problems of modern psychotherapy'. Here, as is well known, he considers the work of psychotherapy under the headings of what he calls four stages, namely confession, elucidation, education and transformation. Today, most of us would not think in terms of stages, but rather of certain ingredients all intermingled and inter-related in every direction, and certainly not developing in a straight line from confession to transformation. All these processes may even be observed to be taking place concurrently in the same session. Thus confessions of the patient may have to await the transformation of the analyst and may depend upon elucidation and education as enabling events just as much as the other way round.

It is, however, the content distilled from these processes by Jung that it can be rewarding to re-examine.

CONFESSION

For Jung, confession is the cure for psychic isolation—both from oneself and others. Repression and psychic concealment represent greater 'sin' than that which is concealed. In large doses, absolute secrets are poison, though in smaller doses they can be medicament and the basis of individuation. Unconscious secrets are more injurious than conscious ones. Purely private secrets can be destructive, whereas secrets shared with one or several persons can be beneficial. Complexes are composed of non-shared secrets and develop a malign life of their own. Without benefit of cathartic confession, 'an impenetrable wall shuts a man off from the vital feeling that he is a man among other men' (p. 59). However familiar, what Jung says is, in reality, strong meat, and a therapist who puts himself at the disposal of another human being for this purpose is involved in providing one of the most fundamental services of all. It is so fundamental and the relief experienced by the patient is so dramatic that quite a number of people, including patients, feel that this is basically the whole story. I can think of a patient for whom cathartic confession, as a long-term often-repeated process, session after session, seems to be really the essence of the matter.

Interpretative elucidation comes very much as a runner up in his estimation of the worth of his treatment. Yet he needs elucidation on the subject of what it is he is feeling so guilty about, and also reconstructive interpretation of how he lives his past in the present in the transference/counter-transference situation and in the outside world. This work is, in fact, systematically done by me. Certainly transformation and change take place very slowly, but it remains also true that he leans very much on the side of catharsis, together with a need for validation, by which I mean that he needs from me some implied or explicit confirmation that his feelings, emotions and passions, although greedy and anal, are not uniquely bad or alarmingly different from those of the rest of humanity.

Jung pointed out that a problem arises in connection with this kind of psychotherapy owing to the fact that the release of suppressed emotion, recognized with the head and confirmed by the heart, is sometimes felt to be all that is needed. People who have had a vivid experience of that kind can feel that the process has an air of finality. Sometimes this may be the case but, Jung added, the cathartic confessional process does not work in those cases where a resistance to uncovering any unconscious guilt or emotion is so great that the patient sticks absolutely to his conscious version of his trouble or his secret. It also fails if the patient remains bound to his doctor or, on the other hand, remains out of real touch with the doctor and glued to an endless repeated catharsis of himself, without any reference to his doctor's insights and at the expense of a sound adaptation to life.

In the case of my patient, he was in danger on all three counts. There was a great resistance to becoming more deeply conscious of any aspect of the problems he posed. He tended to remain attached to me, and he tended to repeat his statements of his problem continuously, with very little reference to me as a person. It was as if I were to be cast for the archetypal rôle of the priest in the confessional. I was viewed impersonally enough to betray a reaction formation against his secret, intense but split-off interest in me as a person with an arse to be sniffed. Such a patient experiences real difficulty over analytic interpretations, for they often appear to him to be either insulting, persecutory or useless.

ELUCIDATION

Nevertheless, it is clear that my patient belonged to those that are covered by Jung's assertion that when catharsis is not enough, psychotherapists are bound to go on to elucidation, compared by him with Freud's 'interpretative method'. Jung's idea, it is worth recalling, was that those who cannot give themselves to catharsis stand in an identity relationship to parents and hence prematurely usurp the parents' authority, power, independence, etc.—presumably, though he does not say so, whether they are conformists or rebels. Hence, he held, the transference has to be interpreted somewhat minutely, a minuteness that he ascribed to Freud, so that the 'shadow side' comes out. While very critical of Freud for 'reductionism', Jung nevertheless described the results of elucidation through the method of interpretation in the following terms. They resulted in 1, greater modesty on the part of patients through recognition of inept childish self-indulgence, and 2, an ability to replace self-indulgence by a sense of responsibility. The man with this insight will turn his retrogressive longings for a child's paradise into the service of progressive work. He will then be able to enrich his normal adaptation to life by developing forbearance with his shortcomings and freedom from sentimentality and illusion.

This somewhat severe statement seems to miss the positive

and lively aspects of the childlike qualities of the human being and to concentrate on negative aspects like 'inept childish demands', 'childish self-indulgence' and 'retrogressive longings for a child's paradise'. Indeed we are bound to admit that Jung rather underplayed the fact that elucidation or analysis can release the creative forward movement that is also part of a healthy child's development, as well as part of the positive growing childlike qualities found in the adult.

EDUCATION

Whether this is so or not he moves on to the question of what he calls education. He feels that, though elucidation helps people with imagination and enterprise, it does not help those with little moral imagination, who cannot tolerate deflation, who can only doubt their new self-knowledge and so are left as intelligent but still incapable children, helplessly striving to gain the power to become successful social beings. Such patients, as we know, he felt could be helped by Adler, the great educator—beloved, as he says, of clergymen and teachers, in contradistinction to doctors and intellectuals, who fancy Freud and 'who are one and all bad nurses and educators' (ibid. p. 68). It is by this third aspect of psychotherapy, called education, that Jung reckons the psychotherapist may manage to bring his patient into normal adaptation to everyday reality.

TRANSFORMATION

Catharsis, elucidation and education then are linked as three processes that seem to Jung to be all on one side of a divide On the other side, a fourth process, which he obviously especially values, is called by him the stage of transformation. Under it a number of ideas are subsumed. They might be distinguished as follows:

1. To be 'normal' or 'adapted', though a necessary aim for the unsuccessful and unadapted, involves, for exceptionally able people, the danger of neurosis as a result of feeling cramped in a Procrustean bed of standard collective living.

2. The personalities of the doctor and patient are 'infinitely more important for the outcome of the treatment than what the doctor says and thinks' (p. 71).

3. For 'two personalities to meet is like mixing two different

chemical substances' (p. 71). Hence, if the doctor shields himself, he 'denies himself the use of a highly important organ of information' (p. 71) and here counter-transference, as an aspect of this, is already in 1929 being recognized by Jung.

4. An ethical demand is made of the doctor, namely, that he must 'be the man through whom you wish to influence others' (p. 73). In other words, 'the fact of being convinced and not the thing we are convinced of—that is what has always and at all times worked' (p. 73). The doctor cannot with hope of success demand of a patient anything that he has not handled in himself.

5. In a treatment involving transformation, there is a kind of interaction between patient and doctor whereby a process called subduing the demon of the disease may take place in the doctor—if he is the stronger and more stable personality. Otherwise the patient's illness may overcome the doctor to the traumatic disadvantage of the latter. The doctor is in the analysis, so that self-criticism and self-examination become essential as he needs to be able to be transformed himself.

These five points show plainly that Jung's concept of transformation refers to a rich experiential content, which may be stated in the following two sentences:

A therapist, working upon his own development in a self-critical and transformative way, may be able, through the admixture of his own personality with that of his patient, to bring about a subduing of the demon of the patient's disease so that the patient is transformed. Transformation refers to a radical personality change—to be contrasted with a less radical movement into normality or social adaptation.

Now when we look at this statement from our present vantage point we can see plenty to criticize:

1. There is no mention of the therapist's own experience of analytic psychotherapy.

2. There is an absence of any description of processes of projection and introjection in the analyst–patient relationship whereby, for instance, the analyst introjects something of the patient, compares it with his own experience and with reasonable good fortune can give it back to the patient in an assimilable form in an interpretation. This lack makes the transformation process in Jung's essay cut off from and devoid of the elucidatory or educative processes already mentioned.

3. The distinction between normality and transformation is so sharply made as to suggest that normality equals false conformity.

4. It leaves out the fact that in early development we can in fact find individuation, genuine growth and integration. In other words, the statement seems to be that of someone without an analyst and with memories of having to relate to a dubiously sound early environment, in both of which areas we now know Jung to have suffered deprivation.

5. The final criticism of the essay as it stands is that, although it implies the concepts of the self, individuation and integration, these ideas are not mentioned. Yet it seems as if the importance he places upon the personality of the analyst involves the latter in some realization of the processes in question.

Nevertheless, if we consider this essay of Jung's in terms of its essential content and disregard the notion that these four features represent stages of therapeutic development, we have what is surely a kind of seed-plot essay on analytic psychotherapy. What we know and practise today represents a development, refinement and elaboration of the essential points raised by Jung and we find confession, elucidation, education and transformation all working together, often at the same time within one session or over one phase of a treatment. Furthermore, we may say that the whole spectrum of psychotherapy may be surveyed in terms of the relative significance and meaning given by therapists to the four ingredients named by Jung. Thus this early work of Jung's keeps its importance, even in the light of his later studies of alchemical symbolism, interpreted in terms of the patient–analyst relationship, in the 'Psychology of the transference' published seventeen years later in 1946.

Personal Motivations in the Practice of Analytical Psychotherapy

So far then, we have been seeing how, from many points of view, again and again, emphasis has been laid upon the basic attitude of the therapist's personality—with Jung as perhaps the foremost in emphasizing this in his own way. It seems, therefore, valid to take a closer look at this attitude and its motivations as formulated by Rycroft and Racker.

RYCROFT AND THE ESTABLISHMENT OF AN ANALYTICAL SENTIMENT

We have already noticed that Rycroft describes what he calls the establishment in the analyst of a sentiment in MacDougal's sense. How does this organized enduring disposition of emotional tendencies get off the ground and how can it be maintained more or less consistently?

His reply is that, fundamentally, it arises from his own experience of being the object of similar concern on the part of his analyst. Furthermore, his inner drive to choose the analytic profession receives additional reinforcement by 1, the analytic setting, which meets his needs, protects from distraction and sets limits and boundaries to contact with his patients; by 2, the fact of his having a number of patients; by 3, his capacity to split in such a way as to enable him to enter into an imaginative involvement with each one of them (1968a, p. 73).

These considerations adduced by Rycroft appear to be of equal importance to Jungians and Freudians. Nevertheless, we are entitled to wonder whether Rycroft is not dealing with the analyst's 'sentiment' almost as if it arose solely out of himself, and not in part, anyway, out of an interplay that gradually develops between his patient and himself. If this is true, then we must suspect that he is writing with the situation in mind where a patient behaves for long periods in a hateful way and blocks every one of his analyst's responses and approaches, despite the most careful analysis of his negative behaviour. It is the painful situation where the patient feels utterly destroyed, devoured or sadistically penetrated by the very sentiment of concern that Rycroft speaks of.

The analyst, under these circumstances, may indeed be able to turn his complementary counter-transference feelings of hate into concordance (Racker, 1968) and empathy and respond to the whole matter as to a challenge. But he will not be able to rely on any help afforded him by the patient and he will need all the inner and outer assistance described by Rycroft. Even then, as we all know, there remains the possibility of partial or complete failure as described by Fordham (1971) and Hillman (1972). See also Bion's unshakeably envious patients with their totally negative therapeutic reaction attributed by him to the –K factor (1962, p. 96).

RACKER AND THE MASTERY OF THE TALIONIC RESPONSE

However, things are not generally as desperate as that, and it is worthwhile reminding ourselves of Racker's description of the dynamism of the process that starts with the patient's application for help and the activation of the analyst's predisposition to mobilize his feelings and skills for the analysis of this particular patient in a concordant way.

The response and counter-response situation may then be able to get going in the following way. The analyst's predisposed concordance may be met with the patient's beginnings of a positive transference, with a resultant deepening of the analyst's positive counter-transference. A safe enough situation is thus provided for the patient tentatively to bring out some negative transference. Then, through the operation of the talion law, complementary negative counter-transference in the analyst becomes activated. The critical point here is whether the analyst can nevertheless succeed in mastering his own revengeful talionic feelings and become able to interpret, in a concordant way, the patient's inner drama into which he, as the analyst, has been drawn. Then gratitude for such a non-talionic response may enable the patient's positive transference to allow him to benefit from further analytic interpretations (Racker, 1968).

I would suggest, therefore, that Racker adds to Rycroft's rather static-sounding concept of the analyst's 'sentiment' the understanding that an effective therapeutic attitude in the analyst arises out of the dynamic interplay between himself and his patient. His own experience of gratitude, felt in the various relationships arising between himself and his own analyst, supervisors, etc., provides some of the motivation for the practice of therapy. This also enables him to develop the skill to use concordantly and therapeutically both his empathic involvement with his patient and his experience of reverberation, in his own psyche-soma, to the impact of the patient's disorder or primitive love and violence towards him as object. The connection here with Jung is quite evident.

Agape and the Therapeutic Attitude

I should like to pass on now from Jung, Rycroft and Racker in order to refer to a notion well known in our cultural history and relate it to our problem—namely the experiences subsumed under the word *agape*, often translated as *love*—or *charity* as in the authorized version of St Paul's Epistle to the Corinthians (Sanday and Headam, 1908). *Agape* first came into the Greek translation of the Old Testament called the Septuagint. Still more was it used in the New Testament for love in a special sense. Prior to this, in classical Greek there was no word for the noun, but only the verb *agapao*, used somewhat indiscriminately with two other words *erao* and *phileo*. Both words meant to love, though sexual passion got more associated with *erao* (*eros*), while warm domestic affection, the ties between master and servant and, in Homer, between gods and men, were more associated with *phileo*.

Agapao was used in senses near to *phileo*, but, while warm and affectionate, expressed also the idea of esteem. In the Septuagint *agapao* became mostly used (268 as against 12 times for *phileo*) and it combined a wide range of the word *love*—family love, the love of Samson for Delilah, the love of Hosea for his adulterous wife—right on to the love of God for man and vice versa—not excluding severity, anger and hate (ibid, p. 374). This broad meaning survived in the New Testament, but later and more recently, in some Christian cultures, a rather wide distinction tended to be made between *eros* and *agape*, refining the latter to a more spiritualized non-erotic care for the eternal destiny of others arising from the action of God upon the soul— and not from the feelings and emotions of man. This later meaning carries deeper implications than can be found in St Paul's First Epistle to the Corinthians XIII 4–8. Here *agape* is used by St Paul in an idealized way involving denial of the shadow rather than integration of it; for envy, pride, self-seeking, angry response, the perception of evil in self and others, tendency to obscure the truth, lack of patience and endurance, etc., are all denied any valid place in the human psyche.

I think that one of the results of analytic endeavour over the last few decades may have been to use and modify the psychological content that the word *agape* in its developing history has referred to. It may be that the specific attitude that appears to be a requirement for an analyst to do useful therapeutic work is an expression of *agape* that is appropriate for today.

We can approach this by comparing Rycroft's and Racker's description of the analyst's basic attitude (see above) with the dictionary translation of *agape* which is 'love, generosity, kindly concern, devotedness' or of the verb *agapao* which is 'to love, value, esteem, feel or manifest generous concern for, be faithful towards, to delight in, to set store upon'. There is a certain closeness here though, from the Jungian point of view, it is clear that the shadow has been left out in both the older and the more recent senses of the word. We can now see that the word *agape* could be stretched to include experiencing and overcoming primitive or infantile impulses of hatred, anger, murderousness, sexual aggression, etc., towards the object, as well as deploying the generous impulses described in the dictionary translations.

Naturally everything depends upon what is done with the emotions thus entertained. James Hillman, in his lecture 'Schism as differing visions' (1971), refers to the tendency for animosity to develop in states of schism, and adds, 'We may after all stay together in hatred, just as we may separate in love. Psychology usually puts hatred with parting, love with union, but is this not too easy? It is easy to leave you in hatred, and easy to stay with you in love. But the reverse of these pairings is that psychological art we call "consciousness"' (p. 21).

I think that this is a way of stating something important for the quality of an analyst's *agape*—even if it still contains an element of idealization. What is required is an attitude that is benign enough because the malignant elements have been made conscious and partly overcome. Some work gets done for a few people who come the analyst's way and who can benefit deeply from this special attitude. In addition, it could be argued that the later rather over-spiritualized Christian view of *agape* already mentioned foreshadows something central for the therapist as well. This view is closely connected with the idea of love of fellow man (or fellow Christian) as child or creature of God. It is possible to translate the essence of this into the Jungian analyst's respect for his patient's potential self, containing yet transcending good and evil; cf. Jung's work in *Answer to Job* on the two sides of God and their incarnation in the two sides of the psyche of man, who is his creature and made in his image (Jung, 1952).

Having stated this, we may take soundings from the few papers by analytical psychotherapists that we have mentioned already. If we do so, aspects of *agape*, as I have described it, seem to be involved. In Fordham's case of failure, for instance, there was a very long sustained effort, plainly costly to himself, for the case exercised him enough to present aspects of it to colleagues on several occasions. In the cases of Hubback (1972) and Williams (1972), as well as in Bion's cases (1962), the response demanded of the analysts by their intensely destructive envious patients requires patience, control of anger and subtlety to a very high degree. Hillman's paper requires of the analyst the willingness to go along with the tendencies to depression, diminishment and self-destructive feelings of the patient, however painful they may be, and however tempted he may be to promote premature positiveness and growth. In Plaut's paper, the attitude of O requires a considerable quality of non-godalmightiness, respect for the unknown future develop-ment of the patient and a restraint of other aims for the sake of that development. As Plaut pointed out, following Bion (1970), if the main vertex* of the analyst's aims is elsewhere, say, the aim to make money, then the patient will not reach his real development. In Moore's paper (1972), the analyst not only had to solve the problem in herself of the emotions brought about by the change in the environment, but also restrain herself and wait for the patient's working of it out herself at her much slower pace. In my paper on transference/counter-transference (1972) the analyst has to struggle with the working of the talion law producing angry and other instinctual feelings in order to serve the development of the patient in a concordant way. For Jung, the analyst must risk change in his own per-sonality for the sake of his patient.

All these papers contain something of the *agape* factor involved in the therapist's work. The vertices involved and mentioned by Plaut are not, however, maintained by the analyst out of saintly or masochistic motivations, but rather for scientific reasons which may also be understood as an ex-pression of *agape*. Nor is the attitude of *agape* inconsistent with the gratifying sense of achievement experienced by the analyst who has done a successful work in genuinely promoting the true self of the patient. An amplification of this last point would be to consider quite another aspect of *agape*. It was the name

* 'Vertex' is Bion's term which he uses in preference to 'point of view'. See *Trans-formations*, London, Heinemann (1965), pp. 65, 91.

given to a feast. The Jews, the early Christians and many others at the beginning of our era held community meals and feasts. The name given to them by the Christians was the *agape*, and this no doubt had links with the Eucharist. In contemporary terms, the image of the feast often appears in patients' dreams with its oral and other instinctual associations. These sometimes point to experiences of feeding, growth and integration within the analytical relationship that may be enjoyed by patient and therapist in accordance with whatever level of development each has reached.

Facilitating Conditions in the Therapeutic Set-up

There is, however, a growing body of experience to suggest that, apart from the knowledge, the skill, the personal motivation and the *agape*-factor of the analyst, the therapeutic set-up, in order to be a facilitating one, demands certain other conditions. These may be established by mutual agreement between the analyst and the patient, and are helpful in the enabling of the patient to use interpretations to his benefit. They bring certain reality factors into the treatment and may be termed limitation, reliability, continuity and ritual.

LIMITATION

I think it is arguable that a certain delimitation of the *agape*-factor of the analyst is important. He needs to be able to mobilize his sentiment, his predisposition and his capacity for concern and openness within the limits of his human personal condition. He can do this for a relatively few people in any period of his life and if he stretches himself too far or dissipates such capacities for *agape* as he possesses, his sensitivity to his patients and their capacity to benefit from treatment can diminish. If this happens, a certain reality element enters into the situation, so that both patient and analyst may become covertly or overtly destructive for reality reasons rather than transference reasons. Other reality limitations to the analyst's *agape*-factor are connected with the individual analyst's needs, which vary widely and are connected with fees, optimal hours of work, suitable conditions of work, enough satisfaction of scientific curiosity, and a due respect given to the needs of his private life.

RELIABILITY

The analyst needs to be capable of mobilizing such capacities for reliability as he may possess, if the patient is to feel safe enough to regress and depend upon him. He needs to be able to trust that his therapist will, at the agreed time, be there to receive him and to attend to him. Otherwise, destructive rage based upon reality factors will bring about a shattering of the interpretations in the mind of the patient and in his capacity to make use of them.

Continuity

A further important piece of reality background to treatment is continuity—'a keeping up of steam', a steady continuous working with the patient that is as little interrupted as possible. This involves the well-known point about the holidays of the patient coinciding with those of the therapist as much as possible, and the point about securing that number of sessions that is optimal for the work of both analyst and patient. This last point is often argued in terms of estimating how much in the way of gaps a regressed patient can tolerate without spontaneously developing defences that become progressively more difficult to analyse. I personally feel this consideration to be true and vital for the patient's well-being. From the point of view of the analyst we may remind ourselves of a point made by Plaut, namely that frequent sessions assist the analyst to maintain the state of mind necessary for the open-minded, pursuit of Bion's O. There is another sense, too, in which it is helpful for the analyst as well as the patient. The point has been made by Meltzer in his paper 'Psychoanalysis as a human activity', published in his book *The psychoanalytical process* (1967). Meltzer is describing psychoanalysis as an act of virtuosity, a combination of artistic and athletic activity—with strenuosity, pace and a keeping up to form—a sustained effort depending upon regularity of analytic activities—not only with individual patients but also in terms of the organization of his practice. He reports the figure of the analyst, thus stretched, at certain phases of the analysis, as appearing in the dreams of his patients as 'the long-distance runner', a 'mountain climber' (p. 95). Sudden interruptions to this continuity, apart from holidays, whether inaugurated by patient or analyst, can temporarily knock the analyst off form or injure his sensitivity.

RITUAL

The last point I want to make about the background conditions needed for interpretative success rests upon certain aspects of 'ritual' found in the analytical process. Some years ago our attention was drawn to aspects of this by Plaut and I remember not taking too kindly to it as, at the time, I rather undervalued ritual as such. This was partly because rituals found in obsessional neurosis, and rituals conceived of by Jung as protective against direct religious experience, were not usually distinguished from rituals that are enabling, holding or supportive of real experience. Recently, too, Home (1972), the psychoanalyst, raised the question in a discussion as to whether enough has been made of the ritual aspect of analysis and as to whether the analyst in session may not suitably be thought of as in a way analogous to a priest presiding over a ritual, within which the patient and the analyst may feel safely contained and sustained, and where analysis, experimentation and synthesis may be set free. I find this suggestion close to my experience and a meaningful analogy that has the advantage of being rooted in the past. The constantly repeated ritual is, of course, the frequent regular sessions, the normal length of the sessions, the familiarity of the waiting-room and the regular progression from it to the consulting-room, the furniture of the consulting-room, the relative position of the patient and analyst, etc. Within this containing ritual, freedom of speech and feeling and movement on the couch are permitted. Regression, change and growth suffer minimal disturbance and are allowed maximal dynamism against a steady background. The patient can 'cut and come again', repeat, relive and repair within the familiar round of sessions, with time enough and minimal pressure from external sources. The analyst has been trained by a professional analytic society with a developing life, and his effectiveness depends upon the validity of his own personal experience and his ability to stand by it.

The obvious comparable activity is that of the priest, authorized by the church and believing in the ritual process over which he presides. Within the ritual, changes take place

37

according to the calendar and some spontaneity is allowed in the sermon. The difference is that there is more spontaneity involved within analytical psychotherapy, whose ritual is less rigid and closer to that of ordered family life.

The Nature of Interpretation

So far, then, we have looked at the main constituents of analytical psychotherapy with the help of Jung and in relation to the wider field of analytic psychotherapy. This has led us to consider the personal qualities of the analyst and those working conditions that are most enabling for the patient so that he can benefit from interpretations. The way is now open to conclude with a short description of the development within the history of analytic practice of the significance and aim of interpretation.

DERIVATIONS

Partridge in *Origins* demonstrates the derivation of the word 'interpretation' from the Latin *pretium* meaning 'price', with parallels in praise, precious, appreciate and depreciate (1958, p. 525). An interpretation refers to the work of a negotiator, intermediary or a commission agent. Presumably analysts are in some way all of these. They describe and negotiate between various parts of the patient's personality and in discussion with the patient assign them weight or value as between, for instance, his complexities and his simplicities, his ego and unconscious, his ego and self, etc., etc. This also applies to the patient's transference and other interpersonal relationships.

DEFINITIONS

There have, of course, been many definitions of 'interpretation' in analytical psychotherapy, and investigation shows that the subject is not quite simple. We may take a few samples. Bion (1970) describes interpretations as transformations which display the invariants when an experience felt and described in one way is described in another. As a painter's experience is transformed into a painting, so a psychoanalytical experience is transformed into a psychoanalytical description. Rycroft (1968b) defines interpretation as 'The process of elucidating and expounding the meaning of something abstruse, obscure, etc.', and psychoanalytic interpretations as 'statements made by the analyst to the patient in which he attributes to a dream, a symptom, or a chain of free associations'—surely we should add behaviour, fantasy, visions, painting, models, etc.—'some meaning over and above (under and below) that given to it by the patient' (p. 76). Fordham (1971), in relation to work with children, gives a simple definition, i.e. 'interpretation is one means of communication with a child with a view to bringing unconscious contents into consciousness and explaining the origin of his affects'. There is indeed something in common in all three definitions, but it is worthwhile looking into something of the history of the idea of interpretations, helped as we are now by the work done on the subject by Sandler, Dare and Holder (1971).

Development in the Idea of Interpretation

According to these authors, the early Freud (1893–5), in the mid-nineties, held that verbal interventions (not, by the way, called by him interpretations) were to be used only to facilitate the stream of associations and material. The idea was to release dammed-up affect leading to important traumatic events in the patient's past. That was all.

At the turn of the century, the word interpretation became used for the analyst's understanding of the latent content of dreams, namely their hidden sources and meaning. At that time it was considered that the analyst should didactically communicate the meaning to the patient (Freud, 1900).

From 1910, through into the twenties, Freud's attention shifted to the timing of the communication of interpretations to the patient. Now the analyst was to withhold his interpretation until the right moment, sometimes thought of as the point when resistances appeared (1926). In 1937 Freud began to differentiate between 'interpretations' and 'constructions' in analysis—reconstruction as we call it today. Construction was to lay before the patient a piece of early history—a preliminary labour designed to facilitate the emergence of memories of the past and their reflection in the present. Interpretations were to deal with particular and single elements. But, all during this time, it seems that the real debate that was going on was about the 'when', the 'what' and the 'form' of interpretations. Behind this can be discerned the shift in orientation from 'topographical' theory to 'structural' theory where the newly discovered dynamisms lead the analyst to consider the effect of what he has to say upon the patient. By 1945 we find Fenichel pushing the question of timing so far as to refer to interpretations as 'helping something unconscious to become conscious by naming it at the moment it is striving to break through'.

Since then, ever greater elaboration and expansion of the subject has taken place, and a good deal of differentiation has been worked out between interpretations proper and a wide range of other verbal interventions, which included instructions given for setting up the analytic situation; reconstructions; preparations for interpretation; questions or comments aimed at eliciting and elucidating material; confrontations and clarifications. Later there arose a general agreement to use the word *interpretation* for all interventions having the aim of making the patient aware of some aspect of his psychological functioning of which he had previously been unaware.

Under this heading come five types of interpretation:

1. Content interpretation, comprising
    (a) relating manifest surface material to childhood wishes and fantasies.
    (b) the translation of symbolic meaning in dreams and fantasies.
2. Defence interpretations.
3. Transference interpretations.
4. Direct interpretations, i.e. those made 'as an immediate response to the patient's material without waiting for further associations or clarifications' (Sandler, Dare and Holder, 1971).
5. 'Mutative' interpretations. These were described first by James Strachey (1934), who thought that crucial change could only be brought about in a patient by interpretations made in direct connection with the here-and-now transference situation. Strachey's views have built up considerable prestige for the mutative value of transference interpretations and this also strongly influenced the Society of Analytical Psychology.

Interpretation and the Personality of the Analyst

A further development in the discriminatory work upon interpretation has been elaborated by Bion (1962) with his differentiation of the analyst's interventions into six types of event. The first is a 'definitory hypothesis', which is conveyed to the patient by some such sentence as 'I think that you are showing the signs of suffering from an underlying depression'—or something more direct. Secondly, there is 'notation', where the material is compared with similiar material brought up in past sessions. Thirdly, there is 'attention', when, out of a kind of reverie, the analyst finds the central point that gives coherence to a mass of chaotic material conveyed in a session. Fourthly, in 'enquiry' the analyst makes a 'probing' interpretation in order to release further material.

So far, then, these, four events are all interventions that can be seen as enabling or conducive to interpretation. The other two interventions are expressive of something central to the personality of the analyst. One, understandable as potentially benign, is actually called 'action' by Bion and, like Strachey's 'mutative' interpretation, is designed to operate upon the patient's problems of development in some decisive way. Out of his transference/counter-transference involvement the analyst decides on his own responsibility to make an interpretation intended to be a meaningful and decisive communication from one person to another.

The other intervention may be regarded as arising from a more or less malign happening in the analyst. Bion calls it a 'psi' phenomenon and it represents an intervention by the analyst designed to relieve anxiety in himself based, as is now known, upon unanalysed neurotic counter-transference, or upon feeling lost or bewildered about the progress of the patient, or upon some desire for the 'success' of the treatment. Unless corrected and repaired it is likely that 'psi' through the analyst may, by serious omission or distortion, operate, destructively upon the patient's developing psyche, for 'psi' interventions are really evacuants rather than meaningful communications.

These two interventions, as described by Bion, are decisive impacts made by the analyst's personality upon the patient. In the first case, the analyst is in a position to operate meaningfully out of his *agape*-originated involvement in responsible action for the benefit of his patient. In the other case, the analyst's *agape* has failed in so far as his concern is not for his patient but rather for the relief of his own anxiety and the promotion of his own peace of mind.

Part-Object Psychology

That the personality of the analyst is involved in his interpretations raises the whole question of part-object psychology. This well-known concept of Klein's has led us to understand how, for the infant, the breast, the breast-penis and the penis and, later, other parts of the body, represent, in a central way, the mother and, later, the father in his perception and experience of them. Transactions between the infant and the mother/father are readily understandable when they are seen as varying ways of relating to these part-objects prior to the infant's becoming able to perceive mother and father as whole persons. Many patients relate to themselves and to others as if to the part-objects of their infancy, and this comes out in their ways of dealing with their analysts as if their interpretations were part-objects. Racker (1968) has, among others, demonstrated the patient's use of the analyst's interpretations as if they were a breast or penis or breast-penis. Violent attacks, rejections, loving regard, sucking, biting, pulling, devouring— all these may be understood and felt by the analyst as directed upon his interpretation. The patient's response is not understandable as a response to the meaning conveyed by the interpretation, for the latter has become something else, i.e. the breast, etc. This point has also been made by Fordham (1962) in his description of ways in which patients deal with the interpretations. 'For instance, the analyst's interventions can be ignored, spoiled and distorted, their meaning twisted and made unreal; they can be muddled up, chewed, hollowed out to become empty, spat out, pushed back into him and made into persecutors. On the other hand they can be admired, loved, tasted, savoured and ingested to be built into the patient's self with profit and concretely paid for with gratitude. None of these consequences need have bearing on the accuracy or relevance of interventions themselves, though they often have much to do with how they are expressed.' Again, we see the interpretation being treated as essentially one part of the analyst by the patient, though in time the patient may become able to treat the interpretation not only as a part-object but also even more as an interpersonal communication.

The Timing of Interpretation

A further concomitant of the personal involvement of the analyst in his interpretative action in response to his patient can be an increase in sensitivity in the timing of transference interpretations. Racker (1968), for instance, has shown a way in which the occasions when complementary or concordant counter-transference feelings in the analyst get activated may be taken as indicating the time for beginning transference-interpretations. Of course, such a sensitivity to the problem of timing not only increases with practice during the lifetime of an analyst, but also develops similarly in the course of each particular analysis as patient and therapist get to know each other.

Finally, it would be inappropriate not to mention here the affirmation made by the psychoanalyst Balint (1968) that the particular language and frame of reference of a psychoanalyst must inevitably determine the way a patient comes to understand himself. This agrees with Jung's emphasis upon the importance of the personality and real attitudes of the analyst for the outcome of the treatment. In other words, however much the analyst attempts into success to speak the language of the patient, to empathize into his situation, etc., his own personality remains an essential factor.

References

BALINT, M. (1968). *The basic fault.* London, Tavistock.

BION, W. R. (1962). *Learning from experience.* London, Heinemann.

——(1970). *Attention and interpretation.* London, Tavistock.

FENICHEL, O. (1945). *The psychoanalytic theory of neurosis.* London, Routledge & Kegan Paul.

FORDHAM, M. (1962). *Uses and abuses of interpretation in the dialectical relationship* (not yet published).

——(1971). *Failure in analysis* (not yet published).

——(1971). *Interpretations* (not yet published).

FREUD, S. (1893–5). *Studies on hysteria.* Standard edition, 2. London, Hogarth.

FREUD, S. (1900). *The interpretation of dreams.* Standard edition, 4–5, London, Hogarth.
——(1926). *The question of lay analysis.* Standard edition, 20, London, Hogarth.
——(1937). *Constructions in analysis.* Standard edition, 23, London, Hogarth.
HILLMAN, J. (1971). 'Schism as differing visions'. London. Guild of Pastoral Psychology, Pamphlet No. 162.
——(1972). 'Three ways of failure and analysis'. *J. analyt. Psychol.,* 17, 1.
HOME, H. J. H. (1972). Private communication.
HUBBACK, J. (1972). 'Envy and the shadow'. *J. analyt. Psychol.,* 17, 2.
JUNG, C. G. (1929). 'Problems of modern psychotherapy'. *Coll. wks.,* 16.
——(1946). 'Psychology of the transference'. *Coll. wks.,* 16.
——(1952). 'Answer to Job'. *Coll. wks.,* 11.
LAMBERT, K. (1972). 'Transference/counter-transference: talion law and gratitude'. *J. analyt. Psychol.,* 17, 1.*
MELTZER, D. (1967). *The psycho-analytical process.* London, Heinemann.
MOORE, N. (1972). 'Counter-transference, anxiety and change'. *J. analyt. Psychol.,* 17, 1.
PARTRIDGE, E. (1958). *Origins.* London, Routledge & Kegan Paul.
PLAUT, A. (1972). Unpublished.
RACKER, H. (1968). *Transference and counter-transference.* London, Hogarth.
RHODES, J. M. & FEATHER, B. W. (1972). 'Transference and resistance observed in behaviour therapy'. *Br. J. med. Psychol.,* 45, 99.
RYCROFT, C. (1968a). *Imagination and reality.* London, Hogarth.
——(1968b). *A critical dictionary of psycho-analysis.* London, Nelson.
SANDAY, W. & HEADAM, A. C. (1908). *A critical and exegetical commentary on the epistle to the Romans.* Edinburgh, T. & T. Clark.
SANDLER, S., DARE, C. & HOLDER, A. (1971). *Basic psychoanalytic concepts.* X. Interpretations and other interventions. *Br. J. Psychiat.,* 118, 542.
STRACHEY, J. (1934). 'The nature of the therapeutic action of psycho-analysis'. *Int. J. Psycho-Anal.,* 15, 1.
TRUAX, C. G. & CARKHUFF, R. R. (1967). *Towards effective counselling and psychotherapy.* Chicago, Aldine.
WILLIAMS, M. (1972). 'Success and failure in analysis: primary envy and the fate of the good'. *J. analyt. Psychol.,* 17, 1.

Flexibility in analytic technique*

LOUIS ZINKIN

1969

Introduction

Analytical psychologists as a group appear to concern themselves less with problems of technique than perhaps any other
comparable group of therapists. Most of the published work
follows Jung's own writings in concentrating on psychological
content rather than on method, and yet this very content, the
data on which we depend to enlarge our knowledge, may well
depend on the method used to collect it. If, for example, we
are discussing dream material, it may be relevant to consider
such questions as 'Was the dream related spontaneously by the
patient or had the analyst asked the patient to tell his dreams
(as Jung frequently did)?'; 'What was the context of the dream
in terms of the on-going analytical process—had the associations arisen spontaneously in the patient or had the analyst
picked out dream-elements and asked him to associate to
them?'; 'Do dreams in general play a major or minor part in
what the patient tells the analyst?'; and so on.

The more these considerations are ignored, the more easily
we shall arrive at the collective, universal symbolism of the
dream, but we shall at the same time lose the significance of
this symbolism for the dreamer. It is this latter aspect that has
been relatively neglected in the literature, but it is this with
which we are primarily concerned in our actual work with
patients.

In this day-to-day work of analysis, the analyst lives in a
state of perpetual conflict between his wish to react spontaneously 'as a person' to the patient and the need to put his
special analytical skills at the patient's service. Thus, as well as
'responding' to the patient, he is constantly reflecting on his

* First published in the *Journal of analytical psychology*, 14, 2.

contribution to the analytic dialogue—whether to comment, remain silent, make an interpretation or leave it till later, how much to say, how to phrase it, and so on. A very experienced analyst working well may be barely conscious of this process of reflection. It tends to become conscious when difficulties occur in the analysis and, in particular, in the early stages of treatment. Whether conscious or not, it constitutes the 'technique' of the analyst (other than arranging details of the setting—such as use of couch or chair and frequency of sessions).

To some extent we need to consider not only the analyst's contributions to the dialogue but also the patient's. Although, in theory, the patient has freedom to talk in any way he pleases, the analyst, in practice, puts all sorts of pressures on him, encouraging some kinds of talk and discouraging others. This pressure may be overt, as when asking him to associate or interpreting a stream of defensive chatter, or covert, i.e., the patient will respond to the degree of interest shown by the analyst in the various topics he may bring up.

Thus the analyst is actively engaged, together with the patient, in setting up an interaction that will be of therapeutic value to the patient. The analyst is, however loosely, structuring the analytic situation.

The analyst's problem is that as soon as he conceives of analysis as a structured process, he has a responsibility to his patient to structure it according to his needs. These needs vary, not only from patient to patient; they can vary from moment to moment with the same patient. How far can the analyst make the necessary readjustments without sacrificing his 'analytic' method? If we consider the familiar chess analogy, each move we make is a response to each move the patient makes, within the rules of the game. But this is not all. If we are to use our analytic skills in the widest possible range of patients, should we not be ready to change the rules, or even, perhaps, change the game for the sake of our patients? This implies not only the ability to recognize the patient's moves, but also a readiness to appreciate that the patient's notions of the game may be different from ours. If so, we are faced with a choice: should we play his game, or induce him to play ours, or can we find some compromise?

All this implies a framework or model of interaction, and if the analyst is to be flexible in his approach to different sorts of patients he needs to be conscious of some kind of framework. He is less likely to be anxious about changes in technique if he knows the nature and purpose of the change within a larger context.

In this paper I wish to discuss the kind of model that I believe is implicit in the approach of analytical psychologists as a group. To do this, I have chosen to consider it in relation to psychoanalysis because, historically, Jung's position was a development from, as well as a reaction against, Freud's. It should be borne in mind that the techniques in both schools have developed considerably since the historical split and have become much more similar and in my view are now essentially the same, with differences only in emphasis.

Analytical Psychology and Psychoanalysis

In some important respects Freud's and Jung's approaches depended on different implied images of the analytical inter-action. Freud, as is well known, developed his specific technique out of hypnosis, and psychoanalysis proper can be said to have begun when he formulated the 'basic rule' that he derived from his discovery of the value of free association. This discovery was a crucial one. Ernest Jones (1953, p. 241), in his biography, says 'The devising of this method was one of the two great deeds of Freud's scientific life'. The basic rule, of course, was for the patient to say anything that came into his head. Freud, in his paper of 1913, 'On beginning the treatment', recommends that this be explained to the patient at the start, and he quotes an example of what might be said. This explanation to the patient of what he is to do runs into nearly three hundred words.

Moreover, he recommends that the patient should be reminded of the rule when he departs from it. I doubt if many psychoanalysts today would make such an explicit statement to the patient, but it is important to bear in mind that this model of the patient free-associating is central to psycho-analytic thinking. The patient must 'eliminate conceptual goals' (Fenichel, 1946, p. 24) and produces a chain of associa-tions that provides the 'material' that the analyst interprets. If the patient was silent, Freud saw this as resistance and, if the patient protested that he had no thoughts, Freud would

47

tell him this was quite impossible. So it was at least hoped that the patient would talk all the time. The rôle of the analyst, while the patient is carrying on this monologue, is to listen with evenly hovering attention, to conceal his own personality, and to 'intervene' with interpretations from time to time. Thus the analyst's rôle was very clearly differentiated from that of the patient.

Psychoanalysts following Freud have, in spite of modifications in technique, clung to these two basic concepts: the validity of free association and the clear differentiation of rôle in analyst and analysand.

Now both these concepts have been repeatedly questioned by Jung. Although he recommended the reductive method with certain patients, in the face of his criticisms it is difficult to imagine him ever using it. Considering the magnitude of Freud's theoretical insights, which he obtained with his method, it may be said that it required a great deal of courage for Jung to reject it. That he did so stems, I believe, from a fundamentally different value placed on human interaction, which he symbolized in the metaphor of alchemical reaction and developed as a dialectical procedure.

In a recent paper, Michael Fordham (1969) attempts to synthesize the ideas of 'technique' and human 'alchemical' interaction in a way that makes it clear we are dealing with a pair of opposites. Freud's method, as he described it, appears, at first sight, to be a quite inhuman one. The patient talks, the analyst comments, but at no point does either really appear to address the other. The patient is talking and the analyst talks *about* this talk. In Buber's terms it tends to be more of an 'I–it' than an 'I–thou' relationship.

In contrast, Jung's dialectical procedure is essentially conceived as a dialogue in which two people of equal status address one another spontaneously. The contrast may be regarded as a conflict between two different concepts of psychotherapy based on the Logos and Eros opposition, each of which has its own language. One emphasizes analysis as a science, the other as an art; one values 'technique', the other values spontaneity; one values 'making the unconscious conscious' or insight, the other 'corrective emotional experience'; one values thinking, categorizing, drawing distinctions, reflection, the other feeling, relationship, growth and transformation.

(In my view Freud's and Jung's approaches produce paradoxical results. It was Freud's methods that led to greater understanding of human relationship and Jung's that led to greater knowledge of the 'objective psyche', of autonomous psychic processes. Somehow he begins by valuing the personal and ends by valuing the collective. Perhaps each had to compensate in his life's work for a one-sided standpoint.)

Free Association

I should now like to consider the rôle of free association in the analytic process. This is a complex topic and I cannot deal with it exhaustively here. It has been well reviewed from an analytic viewpoint by Zilboorg (1952) and by Leopold Bellak (1961). Bellak's paper, particularly, allows for the developments in psychoanalytic theory since Freud first propounded the idea. He regards the concept as tied to the early topological model and points out that 'It assumes freedom from any but intrapsychic determinants. We now know that any number of particularly pre-consciously perceived data and mental sets have clinically an organizing effect'. He considers that the analyst 'conveys different rules for associating' at different stages of the analytic process and that 'controlled association and mental sets of act psychology play a major rôle'. However, he does not fundamentally question whether it occurs at all.

Bellak's conclusions are surprisingly similar to Jung's. He also did not doubt that free association occurs, but he did doubt the value of following long chains of associations which, he believed, always lead to the same complexes, which are already known. He devised a specific method of controlled association in his technique of dream analysis. The dream is here allowed to act as the organizing principle and the patient is not allowed to wander too far from it. Rather he is constantly brought back to various aspects of the dream itself. In my experience, quite apart from dream analysis, a similar process takes place naturally in analysis, whatever the patient talks about. Items of talk can be seen as radiating from a central core, which is the complex, and this complex provides the 'set'. The various items of talk can be seen to have links with each other, but these links are determined by, and subservient to, their common relationship to the central complex.

49

This central complex may be seen as an archetypal theme that can be looked at either from its imagery or from its instinctive side, but I find it most useful to consider it in terms of the relationship between the patient and myself. For example, in one session a patient began by commenting on the brightness of the sky and said he felt this as something hostile. He went on to tell me how he had seen his girl-friend during the weekend but felt nothing for her. He had tried to summon up some love for her but could not.

After a short silence, he complained of the cold and wished that the window could be closed. He then talked about his work and how tedious it was. He described a committee he had been on that was a waste of time. Everybody on it aired their grouses and their need for money, but it made no difference because the amount of money available was so limited and because its allocation was already decided. He then had an image of pushing his fist through the glass of the window. This he thought of as somehow satisfying but quite painless. He then mentioned that he was going to see his parents the following weekend. He supposed that nothing would really happen during this meeting—it would all just be polite and formal.

All these statements were made in the same precise and expressionless voice. There was no affect expressed in his verbal communications. His acute anxiety could be seen only in the tense rigidity of his body, and he once or twice clenched his fist. In this session, it seemed to me, he was trying to make a boundary in which everything good would be contained and everything bad kept outside—where, however, it threatened him. He wished to have a passive homosexual relationship with me (which is a displacement of passive fusion wishes with the mother) but feared (and at a deeper level desired) an active, exciting relationship expressed as aggressive, penetrating intercourse. (Again a displacement of fantasies of an attacking, penetrating nipple.)

I was able to relate all the items of his talk to this framework and I could base all my interventions on various aspects of it. That I could do this partly depended on my previous knowledge of him, his infantile history and my experience of similar symbolic images that he had produced in the past. It was not a case of following a line of associations until I arrived at a complex. This very schizoid patient was talking like a character in a play by Beckett. He was not, unfortunately, leading me anywhere. He was going round in circles.

I should like to emphasize here, for reasons that will later be apparent, that Jung's way of looking at chains of associations was based on a circular image rather than on the linear image of Freud.

Rôles of Analyst and Analysand

Jung's emphasis on the equal status of analyst and analysand (symbolized by their sitting facing each other) has somewhat obscured the fact that each participant has an essentially different rôle. The increasing use of the couch by analytical psychologists in Great Britain has perhaps reflected a realization that the analyst and patient can have quite different rôles without the status or individuality of the participants being in question. The complementary relationship between patient and analyst has been well discussed by Shands (1960) largely in terms of communication theory. In this book he describes the relationship as essentially 'asymmetrical and non-reciprocal'. The patient has to allow himself to be the object of observation. His function is to show himself, to express himself, to assume different rôles, to explore all the avenues of communication that are open to him, all the possible modes of relationship with the analyst. The analyst in turn provides him with a framework in which this can happen. The patient has to learn a highly complex *skill* and the essence of this skill is that its performance depends on its unselfconsciousness. The more the patient looks at, judges, controls and organizes what he does, the less he can actually do it. Therefore the analyst must be left to do this job.

To put it another way, the patient provides raw data and the analyst organizes them. He reflects back to the patient what is going on in an organized form. He is able to perform this function for the patient precisely because he *is* an observer. He is able to go backwards and forwards and around the material, relating it to other points of reference, both in time and space. At the point at which the analyst makes an interpretation, he is addressing the hitherto suspended part of the patient, that part (of the ego) that can also reflect, judge and organize. The patient can then compare his own modes of organization with the analyst's. Ultimately, as the process goes on, the gap closes, and the patient is able to take over more of the analyst's function. Thus the relationship that began as asymmetrical and non-reciprocal tends to become symmetrical and reciprocal.

Phases of Analysis

Now in practice, of course, the patient almost never begins with this concept of the analytic process. He not only needs to learn it, he needs to learn that he needs to learn it. I think there are, essentially, three phases in every analysis. The first is one in which analyst and patient are trying to establish a working relationship that is mutually satisfactory. In this phase, both parties have to discover ways of communicating with each other. The second is a phase in which this is established and all the work is done on the basis of the working relationship. The third phase (which I shall not deal with further in this paper) is concerned with the resolution leading to ending the relationship and terminating the analysis.

In my experience the first phase may be very short or it may dominate the analysis for months or years. The division is actually rather an artificial one, because phase one and phase two overlap and merge into one another. But I do experience a feeling with some patients of moving from one to the other. At this point the analysis has a more comfortable feeling. Communications can now take place in a sort of shorthand and lengthy explanations be avoided. I am allowed at this stage to have my own natural style. Of course my interpretations may be denied, contradicted, ignored and so on, but basically my rôle in making them is accepted.

Sometimes, as I have indicated, patients may be stuck in phase one. I suppose we all have our quota of patients who belong to this category. We think of them as 'impossible patients' or perhaps, more charitably, as those not suitable for orthodox analysis. In others, there are constant switches between the two phases. There are good, productive periods and periods in which we have to work actively in re-establishing the analytic rôle. This fluctuation can take place even in the same session and it is perhaps better to think in terms of phase one and phase two states than of two distinct classes of patients.

An interesting example of the kind of switch I mean occurs in Fordham's recent paper (1969). He describes a case where, after he had made an interpretation about the patient's infantile sexual fantasies concerning her little boy's wish to look at her genitals, she retorted 'It's you who want to look'. Now this could have been taken as an illusory transference perception which could have been analysed in the usual way. But the analyst looked at it differently because he used to wonder if the patient was right, and at this point their rôles become reversed. The patient becomes the analyst who can make interpretations about the motivation of the other person, and this is a shared experience. In this case, of course, the normal rôles were quickly resumed, however. This was helped by the fact that the patient's 'interpretation' was insufficiently correct—as is usually the case when the analyst says little to the patient about himself.

Conditions Necessary for a Phase Two Situation

The transition from phase one to phase two can take place only if a certain degree of personality development has been reached. This involves:

1. A reasonably intact boundary—a concept of 'me' and 'you' as separate persons. One patient spent a session conclusively and triumphantly proving to me that I had a certain feeling towards him when I did a certain thing. (This was my announcement that I would charge him for sessions cancelled by him.) He saw this as a hostile act of revenge for something he had done to me (he had threatened to pay me less than my full fee because I had cut his session short by five minutes). He produced a great deal of evidence to support his belief and it was important to realize that he could not conceive that I had any independent way, other than my consideration of these arguments, of knowing what my own feeling was.

2. The ability to conceive analysis as an 'as if' situation. In some respects, analysis is analogous to a drama, where actors and audience both know that the action is not really happening, or, in a similar way, to children's play. This 'as if' ability enables patients to tolerate and express very powerful transference emotions within the analytic situation and enables the

analyst to point out that the patient sees him as 'such and such' in the knowledge that both know he is 'not really like that'.

In one session a patient talked of her analysis as 'a load of rubbish' and said she would not come any more. She was subsequently horrified to find that I could even begin to take this seriously as a statement about her analysis. Of course she did not mean it. That aggressive anal fantasies could really lead to final separation was, in fact, terrifying to her. She was only playing and I had to be aware of this. With this particular patient her central problem, as it happens, is that in fact she can never be sure which language she is speaking. Is it 'pretending' or is it 'for real'?

3. The art of being a patient, as I suggested earlier, consists of being able voluntarily to give up parts of the self to the analyst, particularly those parts involved in evaluating, organizing, comparing and reflecting. It is essential that this be done without loss to the personality. That is to say, the processes involved should not, to use Kleinian terminology, be splitting and projective identification. The patient should be able to take back these functions—they are temporarily lent to the analyst rather than lost to him.

As a corollary to this, it may be said that if a patient cannot allow himself to be a patient he likewise cannot allow the analyst to be an analyst: e.g., a patient has said to me in response to an interpretation, 'That's not true! I don't think that you believe it either. You're just saying it to provoke me'. This kind of statement cannot be corrected by the analyst as long as he is perceived as not believing what he says. In other words, analysis cannot proceed unless it is believed that the analyst, at the very least, does not deliberately make false statements.

What I am endeavouring to show is that the kind of analysis envisaged by Freud can take place only if a number of conditions are met, and that it requires a particular developmental stage to be reached by the patient. Unless this has been achieved, interpretations cannot be accepted, not simply because the patient sees them as incorrect, through a resistance to forbidden unconscious contents, but because he does not perceive the analyst as a separate person, with an independent judgement, who is in a position to make interpretations at all. I suspect that this state of affairs obtains at times in every analysis. Does analysis now become impossible? I think not, because we have available a totally different model of the analytic process in which meaningful communications can still be made to the patient. This is the model of the dialectical procedure, which does not replace the Freudian model but which is combined with it and complementary to it.

Conceptual Models: The Circle, the Line and the Spiral

In Shands's book, which I quoted earlier, he points out that 'in physics, two alternative pictures of processes have been used. One describes the universe in terms of cyclic movement; heavenly bodies could be seen travelling through their paths and ever returning to the point from which they started. The second basic pattern is the running down of the universe; the whole is seen as gradually moving in obedience to "Time's arrow" towards a "heat death" and the eventual victory of the entropic process in disorder' (Shands, 1960, p. 121).

Shands illustrates how these two different types of explanation may be relevant in describing physiological processes. They can be described as a causally determined chain of events (linear) or in terms of a circular process, e.g., 'What makes the heart beat?—Because it was designed to do so'. Thus there is a circular model and a linear model. He then, very interestingly, shows how these points of view may be combined into a spiral, i.e., a circular motion through time. He contrasts uncontrolled spiral processes that lead to disorder, owing to a preponderance of one side of the circle, with the controlled spiral, in which the termination of the spiral can be described as a positively sought goal. In his book he gives many examples, in terms of physics and physiology and embryology, of the controlled spiral.

The spiral, of course, was well-known to Jung as an archetypal image relating to growth and individuation. In his 'Introduction to the religious and psychological problems of alchemy' he says: 'The way to the goal seems chaotic and interminable at first, and only gradually do the signs increase that it is leading anywhere. The way is not straight but appears to go round in circles. More accurate knowledge has proved it to go in spirals: the dream-motifs always return after certain intervals to definite forms, whose characteristic it is to define a centre' (Jung, 1944, p. 28). He has drawn attention to spiral images that depict this process, which is the *circumambulatio* combined with movement towards a centre, e.g., the coils of the Kundalini serpent or the snake of the caduceus of Aesculapius.

Later he says: 'We can hardly help feeling that the unconscious process moves spiral-wise round a centre, gradually getting closer, while the characteristics of the centre grow more and more distinct' (Jung, 1944, p. 201).

Now it seems to me that, although Jung understood both types of explanation, linear and circular, when describing psychological processes his special contribution was of the second sort. Thus he saw the psyche in terms of self-regulated natural growth and rhythms, and of compensatory processes going on as an attempt to achieve balance and wholeness. These concepts belong to the Eros or lunar as opposed to the Logos or solar worlds, which I contrasted in comparing Freud's and Jung's approaches to the analytical process. The cyclical, rhythmic model underlies, for example, Fordham's integration–deintegration concept in so far as it refers to a natural alternation of states within the psyche.

This model, so valuable in describing the psyche, can also be used to describe the total interaction between two people, or to a group, as Hobson (1964) has shown. Provided that the analyst can secure a clear-cut boundary that will contain the interaction, he can allow himself to respond to the patient's needs in such a way that conflicts are constellated between them and only at a later stage internalized by the patient as a separate individual. The analyst makes it clear that he is in opposition to the patient and this opposition will act as a compensatory force to whatever the patient is expressing. This idea brings us much nearer to Jung's 'alchemical interaction'.

So I believe that this model can come to our rescue whenever we are deprived of our so-called 'orthodox' analytic rôle, which includes making interpretations that give the patient insight, making the unconscious conscious. If we cannot do this, what techniques remain open to us? In some cases verbal communication cannot be used at all and the use of tokens such as glasses of milk, or holding the patient's hand, may be needed, as Frieda Fordham has described (1964). There is, however, a large intermediate area where verbal or at least vocal modes of communication can be used that are not interpretations in the sense I have defined. It is preferable to make use of these wherever possible because the transition to the more 'orthodox' analytic procedure is more easily accomplished.

I was led into thinking about this compensatory activity of the analyst by a patient who produced in me a countertransference that bothered me a good deal. This was a woman who, after a few sessions, declared her love for me while expressing unmistakable hatred and contempt for every other male figure that she talked about. These men, in turn, she described as all rejecting her while pretending to offer her help. When she described her loving feelings towards me, she used a particularly honeyed tone which nauseated me and I found myself responding to her in a particularly cold and detached way. She bombarded me with letters and love poems and would frequently telephone me between sessions, saying she was desperate.

What bothered me was that I was quite unmoved by her plight and objectively I could see that her situation was a pitiable one. In my detached voice, which I could not alter, I made repeated interpretations to her of her need to idealize me because of her fears that I would let her down, as all other men had, particularly her father. Then I began to realize that I lacked sympathy because her distress, together with her avowed love of me, was not genuine. She did not feel them herself. She would talk as though she had overwhelming sexual feelings for me, which she could barely control, but there were no bodily signs that she was sexually excited, or even tense, in my presence. The only affect between us that was genuine was my cold hostility to hers and this really belonged to her.

What I did then was to tell her that her loving feelings were not real, that she had a fantasy of loving me rather than a real experience of doing so. This produced only a token denial with some pseudo-despair. Then she appeared to accept my statement. This somehow 'cleared the air' for me and I now felt more my usual analytic self and my voice went back to normal, so to speak. In the next session there was evidence that she had experienced real feelings of hatred towards me since I had last seen her.

Now I was not really sure I did the right thing here. Perhaps I should have contained my hating feelings and allowed her 'love' to continue? Perhaps I had interpreted out of a need to relieve my own anxiety and restore my own image of myself as a sympathetic analyst.

In the past there had been numerous similar situations. There would be a father-figure whom she would idealize, but who would eventually reject her as she made unrealistic demands on him. This would always represent a triumph for her, as in proving the badness of the other person she preserved her own good image.

On reflecting further about her professed love for me, I began to consider that I had been wrong in regarding it as false. The feeling was genuine, but was not as she described it. She had had a great problem in lying on the couch without looking at me. She felt distressed at being cut off from me, and when she turned over she gazed at me with an expression of utter bliss and reported that 'now all the tension has gone'. On such occasions my own affect was not a loving one. Perhaps I should have felt sympathetic or pleased, but somehow I did not. Unwillingly, I recognized a feeling of hatred in me that had been evoked by her (projective identification). It was as though she treated me as a blank screen on which she hallucinated 'a good breast'. In other words, this is an extremely primitive kind of love that contains no hate. The hate is projected into an object that then persecutes her. I think that, had I successfully continued to act as the professionally neutral analyst, she might well have wrecked the analysis as surely as she had other similar relationships in the past. She needed to hate me and she needed me to hate her before she could do so.

This way of thinking about a patient depends on a closed system model, i.e., there is some hating going on. Is it hers or mine, or how is it distributed?

I have said that before I disputed the genuineness of her feeling, my voice was cold and hostile. I think she aroused in me a cold, detached, intellectual response that compensated for her own uncritical, sentimental effusiveness. On thinking about my other patients, I find I quite often react in this compensatory way; e.g., to a patient given to abstract theorizing, where everything is precise and unambiguous, I would respond by speaking with a good deal of feeling in my voice, tending to talk in vague hints, suggesting my meaning rather than clearly articulating it. Thus an interaction goes on all the time, which is quite separate from the content of any interpretation I may make.

Here again we have the alchemical interaction, the circular (analyst as participant) rather than the linear (or analyst as observer) model. The patient's internal conflict is constellated between her and me, where it is contained. I reflect back to her something of herself. It is retained within a closed system, rather than lost in an open system as similar projections would be when acted out in the outside world. I am not suggesting that this kind of interaction is sufficient to give the patient any usable insight or to make progress. All it does is provide the conditions that will make insight and progress possible. This will depend on the application of the linear model later, when what has happened between us and been observed by me can be explained to her and used by her. Indeed making progress is essentially a linear (or solar) concept. Progress is often not the principal need of the patient and the idea that it is can be a persecutory one both to patient and analyst.

Once it is accepted that the analyst has functions other than making interpretations of the material provided by the patient, enormous technical problems arise. At times I have found myself arguing with a patient, answering questions directly, giving advice, supporting the patient and expressing my feelings openly. I think I can justify these unorthodox procedures by explaining that in each case, had I not done so, my patient would have been not frustrated only, but deprived.

Among those who have specialized in the treatment of psychotic patients there is a good deal of variation in the degree to which it is considered desirable for the patient's infantile needs to be directly gratified by the therapist. Most, however, would accept that up to a point it is essential.

Searles (1961), for example, considers that with a schizophrenic patient the analyst needs to enter into a symbiotic relationship with the patient. This has two phases: one of ambivalent symbiosis and one of pre-ambivalent or full symbiosis. His description of the ambivalent phase, in which he experiences a state of entanglement with the patient, is remarkably like Jung's description of the alchemical interaction. It is only after a further phase, which he calls the phase of resolution of the symbiosis, that he regards ordinary analysis of the transference as possible.

In practice the division of patients into neurotic and psychotic, so important in psychiatric diagnosis, becomes a deceptive over-simplification in the analytic situation, where psychotic mechanisms can always be seen. My impression is that what Searles calls ordinary 'analysis of the transference' is always extremely difficult both to achieve and to maintain, because the very conditions that we set up to foster the development of transference–illusion also encourage regression to the point where *delusional* transference occurs, particularly in patients with a weak ego-structure. Often this is consequent on regression to primitive levels where ego-boundaries are lost and symbiosis occurs—even if only temporarily in the analytic hour. It is in this situation that the analyst needs to let himself be 'involved' with the patient. Entering into the relationship in this way is full of dangers to the analyst, as Jung clearly saw. The analyst's ego must remain in control.

I cannot claim to have solved all the problems involved—only to have conceptualized some general principles. Shands says:

> Spiral processes require controls and if uncontrolled tend to fall into disorder owing to a preponderance of one side of the circle.
>
> In visual terms one can say that the spiral process has a natural tendency to assume a funnel shape, with a progressively increasing or decreasing excursion. When controlled, this funnel shape is changed to a tubular shape; with increasing competence, the tubular shape can be said to have a decreasing diameter (Shands 1960, p. 122).

Applying this principle, I would say that the control of the spiral is the responsibility of the analyst. He must maintain a balance between distance and closeness to the patient, between separation and entanglement, between emotional response and detached interpretation. He should do what is necessary to maintain this balance, but only what is necessary. It is in deciding the precise point of balance from moment to moment that flexibility of technique consists.

References

BELLAK, L. (1961). 'Free association: conceptual and clinical aspects', *Int. J. Psycho-Anal.*, 42.

FENICHEL, O. (1946). *The psychoanalytic theory of neurosis.* London, Routledge & Kegan Paul.

FORDHAM, F. (1964). 'The care of regressed patients and the child archetype', *J. analyt. Psychol.*, **9**, 1.

FORDHAM, M. (1969). 'Technique and counter-transference', *J. analyt. Psychol.*, **14**, 2.*

FREUD, S. (1913). 'On beginning the treatment', *S.E.*, **12**, 121.

HOBSON, R. F. (1964). 'Group diagnosis and analytical psychology', *J. analyt. Psychol.*, **9**, 1.

JONES, E. (1953). *The life and work of Sigmund Freud*, Vol. 1, New York, Basic Books.

JUNG, C. G. (1944). 'Psychology and alchemy', in *Coll. wks.*, **12**.

SEARLES, H. (1961). 'Phases of patient-therapist interaction in the psychotherapy of chronic schizophrenia', *Collected Papers*, New York, International University Press.

SHANDS, H. C. (1960). *Thinking and psychotherapy*, Cambridge, Mass., Harvard University Press.

ZILBOORG, G. (1952). 'Some sidelights on free associations', *Int. J. Psycho-Anal.*, **33**.

Some notes on the process of reconstruction*

KENNETH LAMBERT

1970

Introduction

Analytical psychologists in London have in recent years increased their interest in reconstruction as an effective tool in reductive analysis. Frieda Fordham (1964) and Michael Fordham (1966) have made a number of theoretical and clinical references to its use in the treatment of regressed and other patients. In the London Society of Analytical Psychology it has been discussed in recent meetings between the training analysts and the Professional Committee, and in 1967 it became a main topic in the series of first year training seminars.

Nevertheless, the use of the word is infrequent and it needs searching for in the literature. Freud used the word *construction*, and sometimes *reconstruction*, in his essay on the Rat Man (1909), and specifically *reconstruction* in a late essay on technique (1937). Here Freud compares the analyst's work with that of the archaeologist in terms of their resemblance, since

> both have an undisputed right to reconstruct by means of supplementing and combining the surviving remains. Both of them, moreover, are subject to many of the same difficulties and sources of error. The analyst works under more favourable conditions than the archaeologist since he has at his disposal material which can have no counterpart in excavations, such as the repetition of reactions dating from infancy and all that emerges in connexion with these repetitions through the transference (1937, p. 259).

It is also in connection with these passages that Klein affirms 'the right—indeed the necessity—to reconstruct from the

* First published in the *Journal of analytical psychology*, 15, 1.

62

material presented to us by our patients' detail and data about earlier stages' (1957, p. 1).

Rubinfine (1967) elaborates on the use of the couch in promoting feeling states in the patient that facilitate the work of reconstruction, and discusses a theory of memory that throws light on the way in which a patient's unconscious memories of his pre-verbal and other experiences form patterned modes of experiencing that over-determine his experiences of the present and under which they are subsumed. At the same time he demonstrates a case where an actual historical highly loaded traumatic event and a specific response to it were reactivated and lived out inside and outside the transference. Novey (1964), in assessing the importance of the actual historical event in the therapy, states that historical reconstruction is an intrinsic part of the process of therapy. 'An attempt is made to see the patient and have him see himself in some continuing context in which his present modes of experiencing and of dealing with himself and others are a logical outgrowth' (p. 279).

Klauber (1968) discusses reconstruction in the course of a study of the relation of psychoanalysis to both scientific and historical method. In contrast to the usual method of science, psychoanalytical method

> instead of finding unitary explanations for unitary events, must find multiple explanations for unitary events . . . the sense of conviction which can be derived from such explanations is therefore due, not to the elucidation of a single law, but to the judgement that a complex assessment of the inter-relationship of psychological motives and external pressures has been satisfactorily achieved. This is a judgement of process, rooted in the immediate or distant past of the individual and as such a judgement of historical type (p. 83).

Influenced by Croce and, above all, Collingwood with his definition of the historical process as one 'in which the past, so far as it is historically known, survives in the present', and his better-known phrase, 'all history is contemporary history', Klauber attempts to assess accurately how this operates in the analytical session and warns against over-simplified expressions such as 'repetition in the transference'. He emphasizes that such a phrase is clearly a metaphor that does not describe accurately the transference transaction in which the patient experiences a relationship with his analyst in a way more suited to a relationship occurring in the past than to the realities of the present. Klauber writes that this is because 're-cathected by the desire for introspection and understanding in order to overcome frustration, the repressed memories now strive towards recall within the psychoanalytic session' (p. 86).

It is unclear whether Jung thought specifically in terms of the kind of reconstruction that will be discussed in this paper, i.e., as an essential tool in the analysis of individuals that can lead to synthesis and the emergence of the self. A private communication by Michael Fordham has made me indebted to him for the realization that Jung in his description of the emergence of the self as a cultural phenomenon in history did in fact use reconstruction in an unforgettable and brilliantly creative way. *Answer to Job* (1952), *Aion* (1951) and *Mysterium coniunctionis* (1955–56) represent a reconstruction of developmental processes in the history of the Western European consciousness. This work has thrown light upon the problems of contemporary people seen in the large, uncovers how these problems have come to take the form they have, and opens out a line of development leading to the increased possibility of, and experimentation in, synthesis and the integration of personality. Likewise, Jung's studies in *Psychology and alchemy* (1944) and *The psychology of the transference* (1946) indicate the gradual emergence into the European consciousness of a basal chthonic element denied in the earlier phases of its development (cf. Lambert, 1962, pp. 195–6).

Despite all this, Jung tended to criticize reductive analysis with its reconstructive implications as 'nothing but' analysis. This is shown in his well-known words, 'the continual reduction of all projections to their origins . . . never produces an adapted attitude to life, for it constantly destroys the patient's every attempt to build up a normal human relationship by resolving it back to its elements' (Jung, 1921–28, p. 135), and he follows up this passage by listing some of the negative potentialities of reductive work. But it seems likely that these should be understood as a consequence of either misuse of the method by the analyst or a defensive manœuvre on the part of the patient. On the contrary, experience suggests that reductive analysis with reconstruction within the transference can both remove blocks to a patient's creative functioning in personal relationships, etc., in the present and also promote synthetic development and growth. This indeed is largely affirmed by Jung in the same essay when he writes: 'As a result of reductive analysis, the patient is deprived of his faulty adaptation, and led back to his beginnings'. He further adds that this process should enable the patient to 'turn to the doctor . . . as an object of purely human relationship in which each individual is guaranteed his proper place. Naturally this is impossible until all the projections have been consciously recognized; consequently they must be subjected to a reductive analysis before all else, provided of course that the legitimacy and importance of the underlying claim to personal relationship is constantly borne in mind' (*ibid.*).

These passages seem to suggest an implicit acceptance on Jung's part of reconstruction in the analysis of the individual in addition to his outstanding use of it on the cultural plane during the later part of his life.

The foregoing quotations from the literature certainly suggest how fundamental reconstruction is felt to be, and the relative paucity of the references to it may well be explained in terms of a point recently made to me in a private communication by Michael Fordham that it is so much of the stuff of analysis that analysts take it for granted. If this is true, it follows that to write a paper of notes on reconstruction may involve some distortion by highlighting the subject out of context. It is, however, this point that makes the form of 'notes' a suitable one, and I shall use this form to touch on a number of points somewhat piecemeal and to draw a conclusion from them.

Some Essential Points in the Reconstructive Process

The *first* point is that reconstruction is taking place when an analyst finds himself communicating in response to his patient in the following kind of way. He identifies and describes a piece of the patient's behaviour inside and/or outside the transference situation. Remembering the patient's information about his early life and remembering his transference behaviour in previous sessions, he connects the behaviour with the patient's early life in terms of (1) the behaviour of his personal environment, and (2) the kind of response made by the patient.

Reconstructing the situation as it was, he shows how the patient's response at that time was probably inevitable and perhaps how that of the environment was as well. He then shows how the patient is responding exactly as if the situation of the past is the situation of today, despite the fact that it is not so and that actually the patient as an adult is not in the same vulnerable and relatively helpless position as he was at the beginning of his life. Thus the patient's present behaviour is no longer necessarily the only possible or the best adapted behaviour in the altered situation of today.

My *second* point is that reconstruction is that part of the analyst's work where he functions as an historian. Nevertheless, as Freud pointed out, in the same way that the analyst is in a more favourable position than the archaeologist, it is also clear that he is in a more favourable position than the historian. The historian has records, documents, accounts of the impact of events upon the minds of the people of the time, assessments of the long and short-term effects of events on later periods and even on contemporary life. He also studies historical development. But he has not much possibility of eliciting a response from the people involved in his historical studies, let alone any opportunities for analytical listening.

The analyst, however, is dealing, generally speaking, with the past alive at the present moment and determining the experience and behaviour of his patients as individuals in a way that is little changed, save that it is expressed in more adult-sounding terms. He has a vast quantity of material at his disposal to work upon—summarizable as:

1. Transference phenomena and memories of the recent and more distant past on the part of the patient, together with information obtained by the patient from his family and friends and passed on to the analyst;

2. His own counter-transference responses to the situation of the patient, which arise out of his capacity to introject it and work upon it in the light of his own analysis and memories, together with his general experience of the world. It is thus in this function as historian-analyst that the analyst may enable his patient to get the hang of his history and sometimes even to understand it completely anew and to get a quite different

feeling about the significance of single brute facts and the often repeated patterns of a neurotic life-history;

3. His observations of the responses of his patient to his interpretative and other work. Thus his work is subject to a check from a living person to a much greater extent than a historian's work can possibly be.

My *third* point is that reconstruction is practically forced upon the analyst when the patient's experience and behaviour are unadapted and delusionary and out of the true, and his emotions and affects disproportionate to the events he supposes himself to be reacting to. Reconstructive efforts are based upon the hypothesis that the patient is so saturated by unsatisfactory experiences in the past, though almost entirely unconscious of them, as to be unable to react creatively to the present real situation out of his present position, talents, age, etc. The urgent need here is for the patient to become more conscious of these influences.

For example, a patient, after nine months of analysis, began to realize that his real feelings about his work group, his own family, i.e., himself, wife and children, and his feelings about the relationship between myself and him and his wife and family were to him surprisingly unadapted to the present reality of the situation.

About his work he felt that the organization he worked in was futile; that he was a stranger, not fitting into it and feeling lost, and yet feeling that he had some special responsibility in it which he could not discover; and that his boss was non-involved and ineffective and yet possessed a strange power that he thought was mysterious and which he felt envy for. About his wife and children and himself he felt that they were shabby, undistinguished and nothing to be proud of, while at any rate he sometimes felt a stranger in his own home. About me, he felt that I made him depressed and angry and yet I had a power of insight and could be helpful, but that there was an alliance or even a love feeling between myself and his wife, whom I had never met. This made him jealous, and hostile towards his wife.

The facts of his history were that his father was old, patriarchal-looking and an invalid and his mother young and attractive, though, when he was angry with her, he thought she looked 'tarty'. Furthermore, he felt not at home in this family situation and saw very little of a sister at boarding school, five years older, whose company he greatly enjoyed. 'At the same time he too was at boarding school during his adolescence. Nevertheless, his mother seemed to expect him to take on responsibilities owing to the invalidism of his very old father, though what they were seemed unclear, and how he could fulfil them beyond his strength or comprehension. Also, although his oedipal feelings about his mother were further activated by these expectations of hers, yet, in the final analysis, his old father's word was law.

This childhood, therefore, was unhappy and confused. He felt the family unsatisfactory and he was more aware of shame about it than pride in it. He discovered in his analysis, through reconstruction in the transference, how deeply this old-established family pattern was still being lived and felt, thus hampering his work and his family life while profoundly affecting his transference relationship to me. His situation was very similar to that of modern people as described by Marshal McLuhan, who writes: 'When faced with a totally new situation we tend always to attach ourselves to the objects, to the flavour of the most recent past. We look at the present through a rear-view mirror. We march backwards into the future . . . we approach the new with the psychological conditioning and sensory responses of the old' (1967, pp. 74, 75, 92).

My *fourth* point is concerned with the scope of reconstruction. I would like to support the view that it is most effective when it can be managed in a twofold way. On the one hand, it includes a study of the environment of the patient as infant and child in terms of whether it is a more or less facilitating one—to use Winnicott's phrase. Certain historical events as well as certain often repeated patterns of events can be looked at in this light.

On the other hand, reconstruction includes a study of the actual specific ways in which the patient began to react according to an habitual and set pattern. By implication there can also be seen what ways of reacting and what potentialities were never released and remained primitive and undeveloped. Reconstruction facilitates the analyst's and the patient's understanding of the type of relationship that developed between him and the personal matrix of his early years and in particular how his mother dealt with his inner world, his omnipotence, omniscience, aggressions and his basal needs. This includes the crucial question of whether the environment supported and confirmed his worst inner persecutory fears and anxieties in such a way that the child became unduly defensive and delusionary, with a resultant crippling of psychic potentiality, or whether it facilitated a progressive development of the capacity for reality-testing and deployment of the slowly maturing personality.

My *fifth* point is that reconstruction is one of the elements that comes into the moment when, enough evidence having been assembled, the analyst settles for what Bion (1963 has called an interpretative 'action', i.e., an interpretation emerging as the cumulative point in what may have been a series of remarks including definitory hypotheses, probing comments, summings up of the gist of the patient's communications, calling his attention to points he has made in the past, etc. This interpretative 'action' is performed by the analyst in full responsibility and designed to operate on the patient's problems of development. The analyst's emotion and the transference situation will be in it and, in most cases, an important piece of reconstruction.

A *sixth* point naturally follows on the last and it is about how, in fact, reconstruction promotes therapy and under what conditions. The determinative point here is that reconstruction arises in connection with infantile and young child levels of the patient's personality where the essential element is the high degree of dependence involved. Reconstruction aims to link the patient with his more or less disturbed childhood, but from the point of view of therapy it is secondary—it is a tool in the hands of the analyst. The patient will be unable to link with his early experiences unless the analyst is consistent, continuous, reliable and sufficiently available in terms of sessions to be a good enough holding analyst. Reconstruction is offered as part of the process whereby a patient may, if need be, experience his early self in a more real and satisfactory way. It is not that the analyst becomes the mother of an infant and young child for a second time in the patient's life: this is clearly impossible. But the analyst can provide an accepting, non-moralizing, understanding and interpretative personal caring for a patient in a way that is suitable to his situation as an adult.

Granted this good enough holding analyst (Winnicott, 1965,

p. 240), then his reconstructive efforts supply guiding lines for the patient in the transference situation for understanding why he experiences life and behaves in the way that he does. It clears the way for experimenting with allowing himself to feel and experience life afresh, as he really can, out of the elements of his true self, first in the transference situation and then in the outside world. It is also through reconstruction that the nature of his over-determined and negative defensive systems can become real to him. Finally, continuous, steady and persistent reconstructive interpretations within the transference develop the capacity of the patient to experience and create certain radical differentiations that are a part of health, i.e., those between past and present, inner and outer experience and self and not-self, i.e., the other person.

Above all, perhaps, the work will foster the capacity of the patient to make object relationships. The analyst provides a substitute in suitable terms for the holding mother who gradually enables the young child to personalize, to make his sexual and aggressive impulses his own, i.e., ego-syntonic, instead of developing heavy defences against the fear of being swept away by blind autonomous impulse. In this way the patient is gradually released from the old maladapted ways of response, and a new way of deploying his real personality in personal relationships becomes progressively possible.

The seventh point is about the consequence that reconstruction as a part of reductive analysis does, in fact, serve synthesis as described by Jung in his famous statement: 'The synthetic view asserts that certain parts of the personality which are capable of development are in an infantile state as though in the womb' (Jung, 1935, p. 9). In other words, 'the synthetic view' does not necessarily imply that 'analysis' no longer operates and steps aside in favour of something called 'synthesis'. The patient, released from excessive anxiety and crippling defensiveness through reconstruction within the transference, begins to experience new feelings and potentialities (i.e., no longer quite still 'in the womb'), and these in turn require analysis within the transference. In a way, this activity is comparable with that of the mother who knows how to go along with the developing powers of the infant and toddler, enabling him to experiment with them in reasonable security and with firm enough holding.

It is fair to say that a renewed link with infancy and child-hood through the modification of defences, together with allowing into realization of newly-discovered and deployable capacities, represents a movement towards synthesis and integration in a patient's personality that develops spontan-eously alongside the reconstructive and reductive analysis in the transference. Jung's distinction between 'reductive' and 'synthetic' interpretations seems to be based on practical considerations rather than theoretical ones. He writes: 'Both interpretations can be shown to be correct. We might almost say that they amount to the same thing. But it makes an enormous difference in practice whether we interpret some-thing regressively or progressively' (*ibid.*, p. 9). We may wonder whether the word 'regressively' is being used pejoratively, and in a specialized sense, in view of the fact that reductive analysis, done with care, normally leads towards synthetic development and in that sense is progressive.

The *eighth* point may be regarded as an elaboration of the last two points and it is that reconstruction enables the patient to become aware of his 'tail' or, in other words, the historical development of his life and personality as a whole. This enables him to obtain (1) a better feeling for both the positive and negative elements in his early personal matrix, (2) an understanding of where his development went awry as well as according to the true, and (3) a sense of undeveloped possibi-lities. This sense of both his history and his potential provides part of the security out of which the synthesizing and pro-gressive processes of the individual develop, at first within the transference relationship and, later on, after the analytical treatment has been terminated. In the individual, this process is parallel to that which Jung opened the way to understanding on the level of cultural studies.

A final two points, *nine* and *ten*, arise on the subjects of (a) the results of the neglect of reconstruction in transference analysis and (b) objections sometimes raised to the use of reconstruction, as well as indications where reconstructive analysis may be considered inadvisable or premature.

With regard to the *ninth* point there is some evidence to suggest that in cases where the transference relationship turns out to be heavily saturated by infantile and early childhood content, interpretation of the patient's transference in the here and now, and without any reference to reconstructive insights, can lead to an enhancement of guilty and demoralized feelings in the patient. He can feel that the interpretation simply confirms his worst fears, namely, his complete inadequacy in a personal relationship with his analyst.

Without reconstruction, there can be no lightening of the situation by the understanding that it is the child in him that he is experiencing in relationship to his analyst or, again, by any insight into the dynamics that lead him into traumatized, confused and shattered experiences with his primary maternal object and the rest of the family, etc. In a demoralized way, he identifies with the most unsatisfactory elements in his nature and can lapse into despair or some of the classical defences against it. He loses his bearings through losing the distinction between the present and the past, between the infantile end of his spectrum and the adult, and between the impulse and the action.

Objections to reconstruction within the transference, i.e., point *ten*, sometimes take the form of fears that the analyst might use reconstruction as a defence against negative transference. This danger is obviously lessened if enough time is given for negative feelings to become conscious prior to interpretation. Another fear is that the patient might use reconstruction as a defence against accepting responsibility for his emotions and behaviour. This, however, is but one of several ways of avoiding the question of responsibility, and the analyst should be alert to the danger, which is dealt with by adequate transference interpretations.

A third difficulty is sometimes felt by analysts particularly when they are dealing with young patients at the student adolescent level. Reconstructive interpretations may then be used by the patient, actually as a part of his negative feelings towards his analyst, to attack his parents and hence alienate them from the analysis that they are supporting. In a case that I was supervising, the trainee analyst rightly hesitated for a long time before venturing on any reconstructive transference interpretations because of the considerations mentioned above. She contented herself with straight interpersonal transference interpretations without reference to infancy, childhood, the patient's history or any reconstructive aspects. This was also because it was a matter of touch and go as to whether the analysis would hold.

The patient, while clearly more dependent upon the analyst than she would admit, nevertheless showed signs of considerable demoralization. She temporarily suspended analysis for some weeks, during which she gained some encouraging experience as a student-teacher. When she returned it was not long before, in response to a hint from her, the analyst was able to bring in the beginnings of reconstructive interpretation in a way that was an advantage to the patient and unlikely to be used by her to jeopardize the analysis by attacking and alienating her parents with the understanding gained through reconstruction.

Reconstruction in a Case History

I shall now describe a case that involved a good deal of re-constructive work and where the patient made progress as a result, although an organic disease came in to cut short the analytic work.

My patient presented herself in her late forties as a gentle, quiet musician who had been an only child and, unmarried, had looked after her parents, ageing and sick, for a good deal of her life, side by side with making a number of bids for independence and making a living teaching music at home or in school. Her parents had both died and, though consequently she was now a free agent, she felt lacking in drive, tightly held in, dreamy and timeless. On the recommendation of friends she proposed herself for analysis.

After a diagnostic interview with a psychiatric colleague, whose opinion was that she was suitable for analysis, she began to function towards me as an agreeable daughter demanding little and enjoying my company, in fact repeating her procedure with her father. This was quietly pleasurable but it left me with a sense of not doing my work, which gave way to a sense of a turbulent if not nightmarish background as her history un-folded.

Her parents were artistic craftsmen working as a team. Her mother was a small, taut, bird-like woman, industrious and anxious about money. Though she was bossy, critical, dis-couraging and unaffectionate most of the time, she was associated with some good memories in my patient's mind of being taken by her on nature walks, identifying flowers, trees and especially birds. As she grew older, she deteriorated,

73

becoming increasingly anxious, terrified of being abandoned, anorexic, diabetic, physically more and more rigid and finally in deep depression, unable to accept any help. My patient nursed her through senile dementia to the end.

My patient's father was much older than her mother though he survived her by five years. Tall and asthenic, he was gentle, kindly, artistic and humorous but no match for his tough little wife. Good-natured, a singer of songs and a teller of stories, he could comfort my patient but could not intervene with the mother and even half-heartedly once or twice beat his daughter on mother's orders.

The sexual life of the parents was described to her by both parents separately. They agreed that it was practically non-existent save for a short period before her conception. Her mother disliked it but her father was always said to be game for more. After her mother's death, my patient jealously noticed that the old father rather enjoyed a bit of flirtation with the women who helped to nurse him.

To sum up, the differences between these two people were well revealed in the designs they painted in their craftsmanship. The mother's lines were bold, thick, violent and crude as compared with the father's feathery, light and delicate tracery.

My patient's childhood was described by her as painful. She developed a dreamy, withdrawn and obstinate character structure. Very sensitive and scared of other children, she was nevertheless sent to boarding school at the age of seven by her mother, who was busy with her life of craftsmanship. Her active mother tended to despair of her but continually impinged upon her in a painful way, constantly criticizing her and urging her to do something and not stand around dreaming.

Moreover, double-bind situations constantly arose between them mainly connected with the problem that whatever the child tried to do the mother would interrupt, commanding her to stop it and do something useful for her (the mother) instead. Frequently also, the mother, to discredit the father, who showed little interest in business, would bewail the shortage of money, although the pair had good artistic connections. As a result the confused and discouraged child, withdrawn and overtly striving to be obedient and to please, became quietly defiant and obstinate and skilled in the art of deception.

As she was a failure at school academically and otherwise,

and as she had some musical gifts, her mother decided that she was to become a great string instrumentalist. She was withdrawn from school at 15 and given over to a teacher who reckoned to produce soloists. Although competent enough, she could not rise to the heights required by her mother and was filled with depression, self-blame and misery. Soon afterwards, she persuaded her parents to let her go abroad to learn a wind instrument and there she was put to a recommended teacher, T. She found him fascinating, an opener-up of life and a first love object.

On her return she found her mother furious and unsympathetic. She was forbidden to see him again, and a short time later became seriously ill.

She spent depressed years caught in England by the war and, apart from meeting her mother's demands, teaching and playing music. After the war she renewed contact with T. and remained a faithful friend. She became a little freer and for a time insisted on having her own flat, after having survived an ugly and distressing scene on her mother's part about the move. Nevertheless, she was still fundamentally at her mother's beck and call—out of weakness and guilt—until she died. After her death her mother remained very much a living memory. Thus, not long after the parents died she was diagnosed diabetic, as her mother had been. Furthermore, for a number of years, she alternated between playing the stringed instrument which her mother had favoured and playing the wind instrument taught by T. Often she imagined she heard her mother's voice criticizing her.

It will be clear from these glimpses into her history that this patient had been in deep distress all her life and had been engaged in a veritable struggle for life and was not at all the quiet, amiable spinster that she almost felt was the whole truth about herself. The distress showed the following characteristics.

First of all, though she felt a continuous longing for a peace that could only flow from satisfactory fusionary experiences, yet the actual continuing experience of her early days was of harsh impingement. She experienced constant pressure upon her from her mother. Long after her mother's death she expected to hear sentences like, 'Don't stand around dreaming, do something. Can't you think of something useful to do?

Don't stand there looking so ridiculous. You are a lazy, stubborn girl. You will come to no good. These friends of yours are useless. You are wasting your time', etc. If my patient flew into a temper it got her nowhere because it was followed by a long, deadly silence on her mother's part. This painful experience added to her confusion and guilt so that there was no chance of her being able to assess her mother's words on a realistic basis.

A second feeling was of double-bind from her mother, for quite often the emotional situation degenerated into one expressed by such sentences as, 'Oh, do stop chattering away like that', followed later by complaints like, 'You never tell me anything.' Or again, 'You don't seem to want to do anything', followed later with, 'No, you can't play with that', (i.e., clay), 'you would make a mess'. She could sometimes see that she herself had a part to play in this painful double-bind situation, if not so much perhaps as had her mother.

A third feeling was of paralyzed withdrawal based upon speechless rage of which she was scarcely aware. Fear of the potential collision with reality, that was a corollary of the first two feelings, caused her quite often when angry to disconnect from the experience of space and time. Naturally this increased the guilt, anxiety and confusion she experienced in relation to many of the ordinary processes of life. The paralysis extended to moods when she could not do simple arithmetic as an adult. When she was a small child her teacher tried many methods of convincing her that one and one made two. She never succeeded because my patient's fusionary wish and conviction were that one and one made one.

It was the same with money if under stress. She would panic over paying bills or claiming rents. Dates, names, fixed appointments and diaries often daunted her in a way that made angry withdrawal the obvious explanation. Concentration when reading and playing music often deteriorated. But the most painful aspect of her withdrawal was her experience of shyness and total inability to ask for or fight for anything or to stand up to anybody. She was in fact well-liked for the kindly nature and inability to think badly of anybody that she presented to society; but she never believed that she had any friends and felt lonely and really so bad inside as to feel she had no right to exist, feel, have preferences or form judgements.

A constant barrage of self-criticism of a destructive type betrayed the presence of the internalized rage against the internalized critical mother.

Naturally enough, I made comments upon the amount of anger and rage and dogged obstinate resistance thus revealed and also her great anxiety about these impulses and feelings. I added that the violent ways and sharp tongue of her mother had made her feel so victimized that it masked and made it impossible for her to realize or experience her own anger and violent impulses. As time went on the anger that was in her became less totally foreign to her and she became interested and really pleased that she was not in reality a little mouse or a shy violet but a rather vigorous and angry woman. The idea pleased her, but the reality often eluded her and her anger was still mainly held inside, often inaccessible, and often in the transference felt to be mine against her. But at least she was longing to be able to stand up to someone and have it out with them.

A fourth set of painful experiences was in connection with her body. As would be expected in a patient with her kind of history, all her bodily processes were subject to over-control and anxious tension. On the question of feeding, the main impression I got was of stuffing to time-table. Her mother definitely 'knew best' when and what to give. The food was plain, unplentiful and to my patient unappetizing. After her mother died my patient developed compensatory impulses to learn and to do good cooking successfully. She was involved in a fair amount of compulsive nibbling between meals at the time when she entered analysis. Feeding anyway was made complicated by her diabetic condition and for a time, while closer to her childhood, her cooking degenerated and she was not eating much.

She had considerable anal difficulties and had no doubts at all about having undergone a rigorous toilet training. She had memories of a lot of sitting about on pots and a life-long experience of constipation. Very soon after starting analysis, she ceased to be constipated and, if anything, was loose. Interestingly enough, she said, 'I thought that was what always happened in analysis.' Piles, which she had always suffered from, had also been alleviated during her analysis. Her mother had been operated upon for this but my patient had refused.

In the matter of sleeping, as well, she felt that she had suffered from fixed early-to-bed routines connected with getting her out of the way of her busy mother. She had also been required by her mother to retire to bed in the afternoons, something she had been very angry and rebellious about. Indeed, this produced difficulties in using the couch in analysis for quite a long time. In adult life her sleeping tended to be a heavy dreamless sleep in which she aimed to get away from it all. It was combined with unwillingness to get up in the morning and a very slow coming to full consciousness when she had done so.

Sexual and affectional expression was very limited, starting with the ban on it in the home. Mother had no time for physical affectional expression. Towards father there were occasional loving feelings, but little contact, although there was some evidence from which oedipal feelings could be inferred. They came out much more with T., the music teacher. The blocked feeling for mother came out with a series of loved mother women, mainly without physical expression. Her displaced oral sexuality got expressed when playing a wind instrument which both T. and her father played—a trembling of the lip occurred for a long time, though this cleared up after interpretation. In her childhood there had been a considerable delay in crawling and walking and later a lot of generalized physical tension which she had learnt to modify by relaxation and postural therapy. Also a severe inhibition on making physical contact with others lasted through the earlier part of her life.

I have described enough to make it clear that underneath the reasonable, pleasant, compliant surface personality the situation was quite another. The reasonable self was maintained by a barrage of self-criticism from the introjected mother and by the model of her father. But her real self was in a permanent angry sulk and in a kind of seizure in all her spontaneous physical experiences—a paralyzed withdrawn negativism, a basal refusal and defiance of a sort that was extremely painful to her. Her work on the couch enabled her to get down to this next level. It lasted a long time and was characterized by blocking on free associations, useless repeated self-criticism and self-denigration, half-responding to interpretations and then destroying their potent effects by making nonsense of them, and messing up dates, times and appointments. She would, in

fact, be defiant while expressing friendliness and co-operative-
ness and occasionally gratitude, but there was the implication
stated in undertones that I was a tyrant or talking nonsense.

In my own counter-transference feelings of exasperation,
impatience and desperation, I could both feel how her mother
must have felt, deadlocked as she was in this situation, and
also sense my patient's distress over it all, for she was at the
time beginning to be able to cry or weep quietly after years of
tearlessness. At the same time I felt that what was important
for me was to accept all this negativeness and simply make
transference reconstructive interpretations. I had to refuse to
collude with her and the mother inside her, as I would have
been doing had I attempted to support any feeling that she
ought to be positive and co-operative. She clearly had a need
to be negativistic and to have acceptance of this embodied in
me. This was because her mother had been quite unable to
appreciate or understand the lack and inaccessibility of positive
interest on her daughter's part—although she herself lapsed
almost completely into the same state during the last years of
her life.

I shall now attempt to illustrate from sessions some pieces of
reconstructive interpretation within the transference.

On one occasion my patient was due to arrive for her session
at 11.20 a.m. She arrived dead on time. On the way up she
managed to get stuck momentarily in the lift, but after a short
panic got out of it and came into my room flustered and
panting. She had been running all the way to me from the bus.
She was now in great fear and panic, being sure and telling
me that I was going to be very angry with her for being so
late. I could not understand this until she told me that she had
convinced herself that her watch said twelve noon, i.e., she
would have been 40 minutes late.

On the couch she said that perhaps she was so disturbed
because of memories aroused during the previous session when
she had described visiting the place where she had lived with
her parents and an aunt for a few years from about the age of
eight. It appeared that it was especially during those years that
her mother became harshly critical of her. She said: 'Mother
was so angry with me if I was not one hundred per cent
efficient'. I interpreted that the memories were so strong that
she had been feeling that I was really her mother and that

coming to me was so like coming home and being scolded by mother that she had manipulated the time in her mind, panicked in the lift and really expected me to scold her angrily.

She then lay silent and at length said, 'I've gone silent and dried up again.' I said, 'You are feeling angry with me for being this scolding mother and now you are repeating with me the silent way in which you both held it all in and expressed it.'

She said, 'This incident throws light on how I make myself inefficient.' I agreed and then she added, 'Yes, I did it most in my teens—which was the most difficult time. Mother was always expecting me to mess up times and sometimes it felt like her messing up my times.' Responding to the last sentence I reminded her how difficult it had been for her to plan ahead because mother was always interfering and how it had sometimes felt that I was doing the same thing, especially over holidays. This referred to the fact that she would sometimes get the times of my holidays wrong when given good notice of them and make arrangements to have her own holidays during the wrong dates. She was silent and then said, 'I hate it when you talk about these things.' I replied, 'Yes, you naturally feel just as persecuted as you did when mother accused you of messing times and dates up and you hated it.' She then said, 'I tried also to mess up my times for getting to school, so mother got angry and sent me to another school. I suppose she was getting tired of trying to find out what she ought to do.' I replied, 'And you really expect me to get desperate as if I were your mother' and I reminded her how often she had said to me, 'How can you put up with me?' She said, 'I am surprised to hear you say that.' She had either erased it temporarily from her memory, perhaps because of its painful implication, or she had misheard me and reversed the meaning so that she thought I was asking how she could put up with me. Anyway, she then said that she did remember saying the sentence to me often.

After a silence she free-associated and said, 'Going to X'—the place already mentioned—'reminds me of being alone at home with my mother and my aunt. It's the first war and Daddy is out looking for bombs and the curtains are drawn and all is black. I was frightened and I think he couldn't stand it either because later he went abroad to aid refugees, i.e., to where T. lived. There he made a friend of an aristocratic lady and stayed with her. Later, when I was learning music, this lady suggested that I should study there. So I went and met T. there.' Referring to being alone with mother and the aunt and the drawn curtains, I said, 'Maybe you felt he had abandoned you to your mother and aunt.' My patient said, 'I remember that I got very guilty and upset about going out with the teacher T. when I was supposed to be practising.' I pointed out that she had not told me before of this connection between her father and T.

I then linked up oedipal feelings about being alone with T. and alone with father and I added: 'Sometimes you feel you are alone with me as with father; then you become afraid of mother's jealous anger, though sometimes you feel the opposite and then you are alone with me as mother, get frightened and long to get away to Dad'. I also reminded her that when she had first spoken of the place X she could not remember the name and called it 'that place near where you live', and so it further connected both her father and T. and myself. Interestingly enough, she had blocked out all memory of this, as if I were absent in the same way as her father had been at that time when he went to the war, to say nothing of his tendency to be psychologically an absentee father anyway.

As various parts of this material had been worked through in sessions previous to this, and as it seemed possible to do so, I summed the session up in terms of the transference and reconstruction, and said, 'Today you were feeling towards me in the same way that you feel about mother, i.e., silent, angry and defiant and expecting a scolding, and yet at the same time you treated me as father by in fact coming and talking to me. To get the feeling of defying mother you had to persuade yourself that you had arrived late. To secure help and support from me as father or T. you had to see to it that you arrived on time. I think that you are trying to change your experience of your mother and father through me. So you relive your passive defiance towards mother and yet try a different way of relating to her by being more open with me. You relive the feeling that your father was very little help by treating me as if I can't help, but at the same time you hope that, unlike your father, I might be able to help. This attempt revived the memories in today's session that you had never told me before.'

My patient said, as she left at the end of the session, that she felt this was very important and that she felt different inside. Behaviourwise, what was noticeable to me in the session was that, side by side with being 'stuck' at times, she also more often quietly, freely and intimately spoke to me out of herself.

Lack of space makes impossible an elaboration of the details of the sessions that followed. In the next session she reiterated what she said at the end of the previous session. She also said that she had arrived home feeling happy and 'deep in the session', but that there she lost her peace of mind and panic set in because she had mislaid some cheques. She got into a confusion. Were they made out to her or to someone else? Perhaps she was embezzling money. She went on to remember that she never had pocket money because, as mother said, she would lose it, but she remembered also mother sending her out to shop and threatening her if she did not come back with the exact change. She had a sore feeling inside herself about it all. She sighed and went on to say that she sometimes wished she had not got her big house to sit in all alone.

I knew that this was not strictly true, of course. The house was not so big and she always had plenty of people living in it as lodgers and/or friends. So I reconstructed: 'You were feeling just like the little girl you were when your parents left you alone in their country cottage to visit people across the valley. You screamed and screamed till they heard you and came back. You felt I had abandoned you as a little girl after the last session and left you alone in the big house, and you felt how could you deal with money and pay bills. A little girl has no right to all this money and so you screamed inside and got confused, angry and panicky.'

Later sessions were leading on to the overwhelming envy that sometimes paralyzed her, both in the transference in respect of myself and also in relation to good friends of hers, but above all in countless ways with reference to her parents from early infancy and cumulatively through the years. A final point should be mentioned out of a mass of material relating to her feeling like a small child with no sense of space and time. She got feelings occasionally as if she were a child finding it really impossible to look at or read a watch or public clock when on the way to a session. It sometimes turned into a panic about telling the time and a feeling of simply making a blind dash for it and arriving on my doorstep as if to throw herself on my mercy.

Discussion

Enough has been written to demonstrate the seriousness of the effects of the cumulative series of traumata to which my patient had been subjected as a result of the disastrous mutually destructive relationship that arose between her mother and herself, the inability of her father to intervene and the inadequate content of her parents' marriage. The reconstructive effort in the analysis uncovered a good deal of the earlier patterns that still unconsciously over-determined the patient's transference and everyday behaviour. Even in the two or three sessions described above, we can see clearly in the transference and understand reconstructively the following points, i.e., the negativistic sulks linking up with paralyzed panic; the driving of mother into states of angry desperation by the child's blocking of her perfectionist aims; her envy of her parents, combined with feeling expected to perform tasks and functions beyond her ability, including being left alone in the house at an early age; her fear of her mother, her feeling of violent impingement and the difficulty about planning ahead; her affectionate love for her father coupled with her angry despair at his (and T's) ineffectiveness and the feeling even of being exploited by them in oedipal terms; and her longing for a fresh start and a freer expression of anger and aggression and an ability to stand up to someone.

Certainly my patient began to get a sense of herself in a new way, and certainly she relaxed and became both more real and less withdrawn and suspicious. She realized more and more how angry she had always been, and how defiant and non-cooperatively destructive she had quite unconsciously become. She was on the way to rewriting her history and realizing that she was not a quiet, gentle, defeated, dim, victimized little no-good, but actually a tough, angry rather violent little woman with a lot of potential aggression and gifts and a love of life—in fact, paradoxically, much more a 'chip off the old block' and a partaker of her parents' positive feeling for life than she had thought.

These were positive gains, but they became countered by the onset of a pre-senile dementia in which her intellectual and mental performance began to decline. It appeared that this was what had happened, to a degree, with her mother, but I think it may be true to say that the psychological gains she made were not rendered worthless.

References

BION, W. R. (1963). *Elements of psychoanalysis.* London, Heinemann.

FORDHAM, F. (1964). 'The care of regressed patients and the child archetype', *J. analyt. Psychol.*, **9**, 1.

FORDHAM, M. (1966). 'The limits of analysis' (unpublished personal communication).

FREUD, S. (1909). *Notes upon a case of obsessional neurosis.* Standard Edn., **10**. London, Hogarth.

—— (1937). *Constructions in analysis.* Standard Edn., **23**. London, Hogarth.

JUNG, C. G. (1921–28). *The therapeutic value of abreaction. Coll. wks.*, **16**.

—— (1935). *Principles of practical psychotherapy. Coll. wks.*, **16**.

KLAUBER, J. (1968). 'On the dual use of historical and scientific method in psychoanalysis', *Int. J. Psycho-Anal.*, **49**, 1.

KLEIN, M. (1957). *Envy and gratitude.* London, Tavistock.

LAMBERT, K. (1962). 'Jung's later work: historical studies'. *Brit. J. med. Psychol.*, **35**, 3.

McLUHAN, M. (1967). *The medium is the massage.* London, Penguin Books.

NOVEY, S. (1964). 'The significance of the actual historical event in psychiatry and psychoanalysis', *Brit. J. med. Psychol.*, **37**, 4.

RUBINFINE, D. L. (1967). 'Notes on a theory of reconstruction', *Brit. J. med. Psychol.*, **40**, 3.

WINNICOTT, D. W. (1965). *The maturational processes and the facilitating environment.* London, Hogarth, for the Institute of Psycho-analysis.

The management of the counter-transference evoked by violence in the delusional transference*

RUTH CAMPBELL

1967

Introduction

This paper is an account of an adolescent boy in whom the turmoils and stresses of adolescence were exaggerated and augmented until his aggressive feelings boiled over into violence against his parents and his home, and necessitated his committal to a mental hospital.

On his discharge his parents consulted an analyst, Dr A, for help with their son T and it was agreed that T should have an analysis, for which he was referred to me. It was also agreed that the parents would keep a regular contact with Dr A for discussion on any problems that arose and, further, that they would not make any approach to me. It was hoped by this arrangement to safeguard T's analysis from any pressure of parental anxiety.

I am writing this report on T because he exhibited obsessional defences against omnipotent psychotic-like affects that focused with particular clarity on a number of problems characteristic of the treatment of adolescents as a whole:

1. How to manage a negative delusional transference by using (*a*) flexibility in times; (*b*) deep interpretations.
2. The inability of the parents to tolerate the child's increasing independence as he grows healthier.
3. The tendency to evoke a counter-transference.
4. The need for the management of the reality situation.

* First published in the *Journal of analytical psychology*, 12, 2, with the title 'Violence in adolescence'.

Description

T was nearly sixteen when he came along, and he made his initial appointment himself. I did not see the parents at all—the boy's history was put together from the fragments he let fall. I knew from the referring doctor that his violence and destructiveness had greatly alarmed his parents, and that he had been committed to a mental hospital a few months before.

He arrived, as he said, for one appointment only. He was an attractive, well-built boy, quiet in manner, anxious and very suspicious that I would be 'fed a pack of lies' by his parents. I said I had not seen them and would not, that I knew very little about him but left it to him to tell me what he wanted. He said: 'Fine', but did not believe this, as the other psychiatrist had listened to his father's 'lies' and he could not accept help on these terms.

In these initial interviews I said as little as possible; the boy very easily became persecuted and twisted my words into accusations that he was 'nuts' and that I would probably join with his parents in putting him away again. He realized he needed help, he said, because his home was a madhouse, and his father a devil who yelled and knocked him about. His mother was 'neurotic' and yelled too, and then he became angry and yelled back, or broke things, or hit her. He was very dependent on her good feelings towards him, but when she yelled he hated her and panicked.

T cherished a belief that she loved him more than his dad; she had said so, and also said that she did not have sexual intercourse with his dad—'perhaps she did, though, just once a year'—that she was undersexed, and that she only stayed with dad to keep a home for him, i.e., my patient.

When I did not say anything here, he asked angrily: didn't I believe him, did I think he was a liar or nuts? I now said that he was afraid he had been sent to the hospital because he *was* nuts and that he was trying to tell me about this frightening experience, because he dreaded it happening again, and that was why he had come to me.

He exploded into a shout of, 'Yes, of course that's why I come for the treatment, so that I don't have to be sent back to that hospital like that bugger (father) threatens. Whatever

the treatment does it must *not* change my hatred for my father.'
On this he was adamant—he did not want to be changed into
the good little grammar-school boy who would love his father.
His school was 'okay', but the boys were drips and had no
guts; they loved their fathers.

He got on 'okay' but he kept apart, he did not want to get
'roughed up' or especially have his hair touched. This was his
most vulnerable area, and he spent much time when he
arrived and departed in puffing up his hair. When it was
puffed up, and remained so, he felt handsome and sexually
powerful. When it went flat he felt defeated, dejected, and ugly.
He sometimes accused me on wet days of having made him
come so that I could see him ugly and powerless.

T personified these two aspects of his feelings as 1, *Antonio*,
the assertive, powerful boy with the puffed-up hair, who
would be irresistible to any woman he chose, and have sexual
intercourse with all the beautiful virgin vaginas. 2, *Herr
Guttman*, with the deflated hair, who mumbled and bumbled
and was stupid just like his father. The persecuted part had no
name, because when he was in the grip of his persecutions he
lost all sense of identity and hit out blindly.

He was anxious about the treatment, because it seemed so
slow—he thought I could hurry it up if I wanted, and felt it
would progress if I made out a list of what was wrong with
him, so that he could try and get it right. I said he had some
such list himself, and he reeled it off. 'Yes, I want to get better
and enjoy myself. I want to buy my clothes, to have sexual
intercourse, to go into politics, to be a leader, to marry a
Duke's daughter so money would never be a problem.'

T's behaviour in my room soon became more open. He would
wheedle and cajole me for favours, as he did with his parents,
or lash out at me in fury as at his demon father, when frustrations
came upon him, as they inevitably did with the insatiable greed
of his demands. Sometimes he would be early and pace up and
down in the waiting room above my head, bang doors or whistle.

When I fetched him he would become like an omnipotent
baby and rage furiously at me for having kept him waiting and
wasting his precious time. I interpreted his anger as his hunger
for the good food from me, which he couldn't bear to wait for:
'Yes, yes, let's get on with it—cut the cackle.'

If he came late or very late, which was more often, he would demand straight away an agreement on extra time, otherwise he was sure I couldn't possibly care about him—and how could he get better if I didn't?

The end of each session was stormy. He found it very difficult to leave, and I always had to give him extra time. When I eventually interpreted his separation fears in terms of wanting to remain sucking at my breast, and not be wrenched away and thrust out into the cold, he became furious and said he did not want to suck the breasts of an ugly, old, disgusting woman, and he stalked out. But the doorbell rang almost immediately and he was there, begging me to forgive him and not cast him out.

At the next appointment T was on time and had had a 'stupid dream about all that feeding stuff'. 'I was in this room and you were feeding me forcibly from your breast. It was not pleasant. I thought if it had to be, I wish it were from my mum. I could take it from her.' I said he had to be sure it was good milk before he could take it from me.

After this dream his incestuous feelings were related to me in a more florid way. He would come in, and instead of pouring out a torrent of words in his usual obsessional style—brooking no interruption—would sink down in his chair, purse out his lips and say with a flourish of his hand, 'Breast forward' and start to suck in fantasy with loud sucking noises and a look of pleasure and contentment on his face. He felt the treatment to be good at these times. He was sure he could get better and become a leader, i.e., become truly male.

By now, T had revealed the following history. The breakdown had started at boarding school to which he went for a term. His mum had said the boys were mostly queers, and he was to keep away from that sort: homosexuality led to madness. His homesickness and loneliness and the ragging he got revived her admonitions, and he began to have phobias of faeces and semen smeared everywhere, so that he could not bear to touch anything, and spent most of the breaktime washing his hands. This made him late and he was beaten. He tried to run away but was caught. Eventually he became so disturbed he had to leave boarding school. He hated it and the boys, and feared having his good body damaged by them. He was afraid of germs, not only from hands via penis and anus, but also via spit from colds and coughs.

The return from boarding school brought the persecutions of his oedipal fears into the home. He felt his father was hostile, and soon became convinced that he was not his real father, and went off to find somewhere else to live—with a nice old woman, as her gigolo, he thought. He saw a priest and then the probation officer, who, realizing he was ill, got in touch with his parents. T felt betrayed by the probation officer and became violent towards him and his parents, and then found himself being manhandled into an ambulance. At this point he became very depressed: he didn't want to go on with the treatment if the illness came back.

Things had now become better at home, mainly because he kept out of his father's way. He felt he was improving, but the treatment was so slow, and I would not make out a list. I reminded him of the list he felt his father had given to the other psychiatrist. But my list, he thought, would be a good one, made with him and connecting things up. Then he had a rush of words about 'queers'. 'I suppose I thought I was mad because of all those dirty, repulsive boys. I thought they did all those things Mum said.' He was frightened he was losing his sexual power, because he had tried to masturbate that morning and couldn't, told his mum and she said, 'Not good to do it too much; it gave one St Vitus's dance.' But he did do it later, and it was 'okay'.

He thought his illness had come about in the weak part of himself. 'What am I afraid of?'

I said he had been telling me he was frightened of losing his sexual power, and of having thought himself mad, and also of those repulsive queers who were trying to push their faeces into him.

T became very angry and yelled at me for my stupid ideas, and then almost as quickly he subsided and said: 'In the school the chaps did things with their behinds, so that germs got everywhere from their hands. I tried to control my fears but I couldn't.' I said he was afraid of the messy faeces that came out of him and got smeared everywhere, even in my room. He had previously yelled about my room, saying the colours were like faeces.

He said, shuddering, 'You go too deep—come off it.' I said it was frightening, but also a relief to find someone who did not feel his inside was poisonous. He said quite quietly, 'You don't think it is, then?'

At the next appointment T was very aggressive, accusing me of interrupting and of never saying anything positive. Why couldn't I say he was getting on well and soon would not need to come? Couldn't I imagine how great an ordeal it was for him?—he had to concentrate every minute on what he said or I said, or else he got confused. I said he was afraid of the love he was beginning to feel for me, and reminded him of what I had said the previous time, and he shouted, 'Shut up. If I don't want you to talk then you can't, because I'm nuts, not you.'

When the boy was anxious, his attempts to control me became more marked. He mocked my voice, called me 'Victorian capitalist', criticized how I sat, ordered me to uncross my knees, as I was in no danger of sexual desire from him. On one such occasion, when the shouting died down, he produced a flood of his masturbatory fantasies, which he did not tell Mum. He saw that it made her mad. He prefaced these by saying he did not care what I thought, as I was only a machine and did not have feelings. *He* had none, and could say anything because of 'the treatment'.

I was old and ugly, and he could say these things. If I were young and beautiful, it would be different. I said when he was anxious about things they became ugly, and when he had ugly feelings he felt uncomfortable and put them outside himself onto me. 'Yes, yes, you crazy old thing.' But he was apologetic when he went and was sure, because he had been so rude, that I would not want him again.

T's parents' anxiety now came into the picture. His mother telephoned to say that though he had improved he was shutting himself off from her, and was that a good thing? I advised her to have a talk with the other analyst as had been agreed, but the next day father telephoned for a written report. He did not think his only contact with T's doctor should be by cheque alone.

When T came next, I told him of these talks and what had been said. He said his parents thought I was no good and only did it for the money. He thought I was genuine, but how could he be sure?—he was nuts. He was afraid they would not let him continue the treatment.

He was feeling better—but did things change for people according to how they felt, or was beauty a thing in itself?

I tried to link this with his fear of losing his good beautiful self in all the rage and yelling that went on inside him and his fears that, if he did not hate his father so implacably, he might find he wanted to love and be loved by him. At this he lunged over to me screaming: 'I'll bash your face in if you talk like that'. He was frenzied and I realized that he wanted to strike me, and that I must say something quickly, both for his sake and mine.

I said: 'It is right to bash me if by doing so you can silence all the yelling going on inside you.' He stopped, stared at me and went back to his chair, and after a while said: 'You make me mad if you say things like that.'

I realized later that, in my anxiety to prevent his parents stopping treatment, I had made a statement that made him feel I was ganging up with his parents against him, and I also realized that he had felt fear at my discovery of his homosexual secret.

But at the time I remained silent. I listened to a dream that he did not really want to give. 'There was a middle-aged woman. She was the Queen of Heaven, not ugly or beautiful— quite attractive, perhaps like you. She had a group of angels in her charge, and was sending four boy angels down to Earth. I was one, and we had to get a piece of hardboard. We got it and flew up to her, and she said it was the wrong sort. In handing it over, it fell to earth and shattered into four. She said we must go back to earth and get the pieces for her. I thought it was stupid. If it was the wrong board, what was the point of getting it up again? But we or I flew back and scrabbled in the earth for the pieces; it was a dark unpleasant feeling, like the messy feeling of crayons.'

He asked what it meant, but without pause for a reply said, 'Well, if the great psychiatrist can't tell, I will, even though I'm nuts. I suppose the old woman is you. It's the sort of darn stupid thing you would say, to bring back the wood, I suppose you will guide me to pick up the pieces, but I don't like doing this.'

During these first six months he was also preparing for the General Certificate of Education and wanted to get through. He took the examinations and now felt he had more time to look into himself and find how to get back his power and leadership with my help. He had dreamt he was back in the mental hospital with that 'stupid old doctor with my father's list', and suddenly remembered I was alive and would not let him remain there. He woke happy and reassured.

He began tentatively to ask how he could get on better at home. Would he have to become a 'yes-man'? His attacks of rage were now much reduced, and he had been able to have a discussion with his father about an allowance. He wanted to buy the clothes that would symbolize his recovery. He had never been aggressive at school, but had kept aloof from his companions. Now he began to make relationships, was the leader of a group of four, and was venturing out with them in the evenings, instead of shutting himself in his room.

His contamination fears were still there, but he saw they were selective and that his hand-washing rituals wasted a lot of time. He began to speculate that it was linked to his homo-sexual fears and connected up his powerful penis 'with his puffed-up hair' (also beautiful hair with his good, beautiful vagina). When he felt on terms with himself, he had a fantasy of himself as an amalgam of the powerful leader (father) and the seductive female (mother), both under his control and therefore not frightening.

He had now had treatment for just over 14 months, and then I moved house. He was pleased with the new place, which was smaller and made him feel at home. His erotic fantasies were that I had a tired, worn-out Victorian husband, not good at sexual intercourse, so a young handsome Antonio would be better for me. He wanted to climb into my bedroom at night, knock my husband out, and present me with the deeds of my house, like the Prince Regent, and have a blissful time sucking my breasts. No sexual intercourse, because I was not a virgin.

About this time T became troubled because on the way to me he had had a disgusting fantasy. His father's penis was coming into his mouth and he was wanting it there. As if the penis could also feed like the breast, I said. For the first time he began to wonder about his feelings for his father, and whether the fear of his father's bad penis stayed with him to prevent these other feelings. He allowed this link and then became frightened and then angry and yelled: 'You stupid old thing—you put these horrible thoughts in my head.'

I made an interpretation about his discomfort with feelings that frightened him so that they turned ugly and were hurled at me, and I stressed the defensive quality of his rage against his father. He took this without further explosion, but said he did not think it would do any good for me to see his father.

T was doing more outside the house, meeting friends, going to dances. He had also taken a holiday job to earn money and had now bought his clothes. He wanted to wear them for me, and would do so any day now. He did, and was reassured by my approval. He had been afraid that a Victorian, i.e., me, standing for father, would not accept his need to be himself. These special clothes angered father, who forbade them, and T became violent again, so much so that his father wanted to remove him from my care and to have him leucotomized to make him more amenable. This I learned from the family doctor, whose concern for the boy prompted him to telephone me, and whose subsequent intercession at this point with the parents enabled treatment to continue.

T's new clothes made him more confident of his appeal to beautiful virgin vaginas. On the way back last time he had found a girl who had run away from an approved school. He had befriended her and given her money. What was she in for—was it sexual intercourse? She said, Yes, but what daft words he used. He became bold and asked if he could have a 'little muck about' with her. She agreed, and he took her up to his room, but became frightened because she was not a virgin. Wouldn't all virgins be deflowered long before he was well enough and able to enjoy himself?

These last sessions were in T's summer holidays. The examination results were now known, and T had been successful in the eight subjects he had taken, thus gratifying father, who at first was more tolerant. His anger had now been rekindled against T because of his son's increasing assertiveness and flamboyant clothes. He threatened to stop T's treatment unless he conformed. T refused and his father retaliated by discontinuing his son's treatment.

Discussion

1. *The transference*

T's management in the consulting-room milieu was a problem. He came for help shortly after his discharge from hospital, when his persecutory fears were so severe that they invaded his early contacts with me. His obsessional need to control his fears showed itself in his attempts to manipulate me in omnipotent ways. He made few concessions to my time or to other commitments of my professional and private life, and I had to learn to adapt to his needs, as far as was possible, so as to contain him within the analytic relationship. As part of this management, interview times had to be used with great flexibility. His fear of faeces and dirt could arouse contamination feelings in him on his way to me, and the subsequent obsessional washing delay him, so that he was often very late for his appointment. I had to allow for extra time on either side of his interview hour so as to meet these needs.

Because of his severe persecutory anxieties and compulsions I was cautious at first in the use of interpretations, for he tended to use these, and even the sound of my voice, as equivalent to aggressive attacks upon him. He mocked and jeered, or shouted at me to shut up. He was afraid I was trying to provoke him into behaviour that was mad, so that I could send him back to the hospital.

His fear of germs and infection might seize him at my front door or the hall outside my room. I once observed him pressing the door bell with his elbow so as to avoid germs; on another occasion he took a deep breath and held it throughout his passage through the hall, so as not to breathe in 'bad air left there by contaminators'. In my consulting-room it was generally safe unless I had offended him by speaking out of turn or making interpretations that proved persecutory. He would react to these by anxiety and distress: he exploded into rage.

The interpretation of his separation fears in terms of wanting to remain sucking at my breast, though experienced as persecutory at the time, was mutative. He came on time the next day and brought the dream 'all about that feeding stuff'. His hungry, greedy feelings for me expressed in this dream could, however, be denied because I was, he said, 'feeding him forcibly'.

Later, when his fantasies of breast feeding from me became enjoyable and good—'he was sure he could get well and become a leader'—he was able to see these fantasies, the hungry way in which he used his sessions, and the difficulty of leaving, as representing his longing for union with the good breast.

He told me about his hospital experiences with nightmare-like intensity. He said that he was willing to 'endure the treatment' if the illness did not come back. As his persecutory fears of me lessened, his fears of his parents' hostility increased. He felt his treatment was threatened by them: he said he was sure they would not allow his analysis to continue. As it happened, these fears were justified.

2. *The parents*

The ending of his analysis raises the question of the anxiety aroused in parents when a severely ill adolescent is under treatment and they are necessarily excluded. The one condition upon which T always insisted was that I should have no contact with his parents. He could not take the risk of my 'being fed a pack of lies' and thus influenced against him, as he felt the doctor at the mental hospital had been.

At first the parents adhered to their agreement not to contact me, but, as T began to benefit from his treatment and became more confident and independent, his mother's anxiety increased and she was driven to ask for reassurances from me. She disregarded my request that she and her husband should have a talk with Dr A: there followed the telephone call from the father asking for a written report, as he said he could see 'no point in talks with a doctor outside the situation'.

As long as T could accept his role of the sick boy and allow his mother to continue in hers of the good mother who understood, supported and comforted and mediated between him and the other members of the family, his behaviour was tolerated—destructive or aggressive as it might be towards her.

Once he had begun to transfer his infantile incestuous wishes and feelings onto his analyst, and no longer intimately discussed his secrets with his mother, she became troubled and anxious. 'He is shutting himself off from me—is that a good thing?' she asked. At this juncture, had she not felt her position threatened she would have continued her support of T at home, especially in the confrontation with his father over the new clothes, and she would have deflected the resultant anger. A. J. Ferreira discusses these factors in his paper 'Family myths: the covert rules of the relationship' (Ferreira, 1965). The family myth for the father would have been, I think,— 'Head of the family'—'provider'—'law-giver'. He had in his youth suffered a similar nervous illness from which he had emerged by his own struggles, will-power, and force of character. His conscious wish was that T would recover as he had done—recovery on the father's pattern, adopt the same profession and become a partner in the firm that his father had established and in all ways conform to the conduct befitting the son of a professional man.

T was aware of this when he demanded that his feelings of hatred for his father *must not* be changed. He would not become the 'good little grammar-school boy who loved his father', at the cost of losing himself.

It would seem that the anxieties aroused in the parents of a near-pyschotic child carry a psychotic-like potential for themselves; it is quiescent while the sick child accepts his rôle, but it begins to manifest itself as the child starts to get well. Hence the inability of the parents to tolerate their child's growing health and independence. The views of Searles (1965) may be cited in support of my interpretation of the workings of anxiety in T's parents, and the destructive effect of this anxiety on his analysis. He writes: 'My clinical experience has indicated that the individual becomes schizophrenic partly by reason of a long-continued effort, a largely or wholly unconscious effort, on the part of some person or persons highly important in his upbringing, to drive him crazy' (*ibid.*, p. 254).

Searles quotes Arieti as explaining that in acted-out or externalized psychoses ' . . . These persons often create situations which will precipitate or engender psychoses in other people, whereas they themselves remain immune from overt symptoms'.

He also refers to the work of Johnson and her co-workers (Beckett *et al.*, 1956) on concomitant psychotherapy of schizophrenic patients and their families, which emphasizes 'that in some cases parental expression of hostility through a child might both determine psychosis in the child and protect the parents from psychosis' (Searles, 1965, p. 255). Had T's parents been able to consult Dr A, as agreed, their anxiety and hostility might have been sufficiently relieved for them to have allowed T's analysis to continue.

3. *The counter-transference*

The counter-transference evoked by T was important in

initiating the changes occurring in him. Jung stated, as early as 1929, that

> For two personalities to meet is like mixing two different chemical substances: if there is any combination at all both are transformed. In any effective psychological treatment, the doctor is bound to influence the patient; but this influence can only take place if the patient has a reciprocal influence on the doctor (Jung, 1929, p. 71).

Other and later authorities hold similar views, even when they express them in different terms. Heimann, writing directly on the subject of counter-transference (Heimann, 1950, p. 81), holds that 'the analyst's emotional response to his patient within the analytic situation represents one of the most important tools of his work . . . [it] is an instrument of research into the patient's unconscious'. Another psychoanalyst, Rosenfeld, writes that 'the unconscious intuitive understanding by the psychoanalyst of what a patient is conveying to him is an essential factor in *all* analyses, and depends on the analyst's capacity to use his counter-transference as a kind of sensitive "receiving set"' (Rosenfeld, 1955, pp. 192–3). And, from Searles again, writing on the value of counter-transference feelings, there is the view (in which Jung's word *reciprocal* reappears): 'First . . . may be mentioned the analyst's feeling-responses to the patient's transference . . . the analyst will experience, to at least some degree, responses reciprocal to those of the patient' (Searles, 1965, p. 298).

Coming back to analytical psychology, Fordham's concept of the syntonic counter-transference and deintegrating self was particularly useful in helping me to understand what was happening in me. Fordham (1957, p. 97) says:

> There are two ways of behaving [as an analyst]: (1) trying to isolate oneself from the patient by being as 'integrated' as possible and (2) relinquishing this attitude and simply listening to and watching the patient, to hear and see what comes out of the self in relation to the patient's activities, and then reacting. This would appear to involve deintegrating; it is as if what is put at the disposal of patients are parts of the analyst that are spontaneously responding to the patient in a way that he needs.

Considering my feelings of involvement with T evoked by his need for it, it certainly seems to me that parts of the transference were introjected by me, to emerge as the deintegrates—the parts of me that T wanted—through the spontaneous activity of the self in the counter-transference. The transference and counter-transference belonged together (and were the inseparable halves of the whole). It was possible to influence T because I also could be influenced by him.

4. *The need for the management of the reality situation*

I found it absolutely necessary with T to tell him what I would and would not do. I accepted his demand for no contact with his parents and subsequently, when they telephoned, I told him of their calls and what had been said. When he became convinced that I was absolutely straightforward and honest with him—that I was reliable—he became willing to commit himself to the 'treatment', to endure.

Conclusion

The breakdown of T's analysis was caused by the parents' anxiety operating in the ways discussed above. Had T's parents been able to remain in contact with Dr A, as had been agreed, they would have obtained support for the difficulties they were experiencing, and might not have needed to act out their hostility to T and his analyst by ending the relationship.

Reviewing the situation, it seems to me that T's struggles to free himself from his feminine identification and become a leader, i.e., truly male, had been too threatening a situation for his parents, particularly his mother. She felt deprived of the intimacy of the former relationship with T and was able to influence her husband by reinforcing his unconscious fears of T's assertive behaviour. She described T in a final telephone call as 'a rough lout, violent, and looks dreadful in the clothes he has bought, only worn by criminal types'.

The father, though more temperate in his language, was nevertheless adamant in his decision that the treatment must be stopped. This being so, there was no alternative. To continue treatment without T's parents' support, and in the face of their opposition, would have been impossible.

References

BECKETT, P. G. S. *et al.* (1956). 'Studies in schizophrenia at the Mayo Clinic —I, The significance of exogenous traumata in the genesis of schizophrenia', *Psychiatry*, **19**.

FERREIRA, A. J. (1965). 'Family myths: the covert rules of the relationship', *Proc. VIth International Congress of Psychotherapy, London 1964*. Basel/New York, Karger.

FORDHAM, M. (1957). 'Notes on the transference', *New developments in analytical psychology*. London, Routledge.*

HEIMANN, P. (1950). 'On counter-transference', *Int. J. Psycho-Anal.*, **31**.

JOHNSON, A. M. *et al.* (1956). 'Studies in schizophrenia at the Mayo Clinic— II. Observations on ego-functions in schizophrenia', *Psychiatry*, **19**.

JUNG, C. G. (1929). 'Problems of modern psychotherapy', *Coll. wks.*, **16**.

ROSENFELD, H. (1955). 'Notes on the psychoanalysis of the super-ego conflict in an acute schizophrenic patient', *New directions in psychoanalysis*, M. Klein, P. Heimann and R. Money-Kyrle (eds.). London, Tavistock.

SEARLES, H. F. (1965). *Collected papers on schizophrenia and related subjects.* London, Hogarth.

On terminating analysis*

MICHAEL FORDHAM

1969

During the last ten years or so I have become more and more impressed with the importance of how an analysis ends. Since my ideas have not crystallized sufficiently, I have made a framework for discussion to take place: sometimes I shall simply make headings and sometimes expand briefly.

To start with, the distinction between an analysis that stops and one that ends is helpful. What is the difference?

1. Stopping

By stopping is meant a one-sided separation. The following factors may enter into it:

(a) Financial stringency. In this situation the patient will not or cannot continue to pay money for what he receives;

(b) Change of work essential to the patient's career, involving moving to a place from which the analyst cannot be reached;

(c) Overt or latent delusional transference;

(d) Overt or latent delusional counter-transference;

(e) Termination by the analyst because further analysis is known to be fruitless.

2. Ending

Ending, on the other hand, is separation to which both analyst and patient agree. The nature of the agreement will emerge as the discussion proceeds. But, to start with, here is an idealized and very much over-simplified version of an end, to illustrate how it could take place.

* This paper, hitherto unpublished, was originally delivered to the Analytical Group of the Society of Analytical Psychology, London.

The patient's contributions to the analysis become thinner than heretofore, and not very much new is brought to the interviews. The intensity of the transference becomes progressively less and the patient's recognition of the analyst as a real person increases. The patient is able to manage what comes into his mind without much help. Concurrently his life outside the analysis becomes richer and more satisfying—difficulties and conflicts can be managed and, if not mastered, tolerated and worked on.

Both analyst and patient start to think of, and reflect about, ending and one or other starts communicating with the other about the question of doing so. It seems sad that such a long partnership should end just as the patient becomes truly viable, but both analyst and patient recognize that to go on with analysis would be less fruitful than ending it. After a variable period, separation occurs with regrets on both sides. (For ever? I leave that as an open question for the time being.)

The memory of the analyst and what he has done persists in the patient, and so an ongoing internal analytical process continues, not so much consciously as unconsciously, and what the analyst has learnt from his patient becomes gradually assimilated into his work with others. So each needs to work on a mourning process, not only before but also after the analytic contract has ended.

In the rough-and-tumble of a psychotherapeutic practice, endings like this are not frequent, but the feelings of separation that I have described may be there all the same.

Reasons for ending or stopping psychotherapy are various, and Jung gave a list of nine in *Psychology and alchemy* (1944). They include a piece of good advice, presumably after one or two interviews, lack of money, a change in fortune for the better, freeing from childhood fixations, forming a philosophy of life, a religious conversion. He is left with those patients who 'hang on': these he values highly, saying, 'It is just this hanging on which can lead to the union of opposites and so of wholeness', and later, '[It] represents a unique situation that demands the maximum effort and therefore enlists the energies of the whole man'.

He was not always so positive about 'hanging on'. Elsewhere he also calls it a disease, a state of dependence that calls for reduction in interviews. He showed ambivalence to the end, but I think it is safe to understand that his psychology of the transference refers to the patients who hang on. If this be so, ending could be defined as related to wholeness, i.e. the unification of the personality based on the self.

An example of how this looks in practice is to be found in *Two essays on analytical psychology* (1916). There he describes how a transference was gradually undermined. 'Dreams,' he says, 'continued to disintegrate the person of the doctor and to swell him to ever vaster proportions', and so 'when the time came for leaving me, it was no catastrophe, but a perfectly reasonable parting. I had the privilege of being the only witness during the process of severance. I saw how the transpersonal *control-point* developed—I cannot call it anything else—a *guiding function* that step by step gathered to itself all the former personal valuations' (p. 134).

If severance depends upon a 'transpersonal . . . guiding function' then it is this that will determine ending rather than the exertions of the analyst and patient. Therefore analysis continues until the self ends it; that seems the logical conclusion. So the analyst need not do much about it; indeed, he can remain relatively passive. I have inserted this note on Jung's ideas partly because I think we should be conscious that they do not seem to encourage thought about ending. I am reasonably convinced that they contain the reason why I, and probably others, have paid so little attention to it. So it is not surprising that little work has been done. Indeed, apart from this contribution, only Henderson and Ruth Strauss have published anything relevant.

In constructing a view of ending, Jung clearly had an aim in mind. He also thought it was related to resolution of the archetypal transference through the activity of the self. I think we can see that this picture of ending is incomplete and there is plenty of room for further study of it. I have set it beside my own idealized picture of ending, as a contrast: the one is worked on, the other is fateful. I will now consider mine further, and make a list of six points in it that seem particularly important:

1. The ending is a true end—it has not been decided by pressing environmental factors such as lack of money, change of work to a place that renders further analysis impossible, etc.

2. The analysis has been conducted under conditions that have made the time available unlimited.

3. Knowledge of the patient's psychodynamic structures is sufficient to understand them thoroughly.

4. Ending itself is made into an aim to be worked on.

5. Neither the patient's nor the analyst's psychopathology is so severe as to make continuation impossible.

6. For a variable time after ending the process continues in the life and work of analyst and patient.

Headings 1, 2 and 3 I shall take as axiomatic and so shall now only discuss 4, 5 and 6 further.

4. The idea that ending is a phase in analysis to be worked on I conceive as follows.

When a patient brings up the idea of ending, it is very unusual for ending to take place then. It needs to be worked on. Ruth Strauss published an interesting account of how work on ending may look, in her paper 'The archetype of separation'. Her patient first brought up the idea in a very neurotic context, but as the analysis proceeded it grew in strength till eventually she felt bound to agree—nine months after the subject was first broached.

I should like to link this way of ending with Jung's. At first sight Ruth Strauss's description is very different, especially because there was an on-going conflict between her and the patient before agreement was reached. Nevertheless, I think the growth in certainty that her patient achieved may have been dependent on something that is very difficult to define and that Jung called the transcendent function or self. Over and over again the idea of ending may recur in any patient. At first it may be feebly cathected but as time goes on it becomes an increasingly firm proposition. It feels as if the patient were growing a centre hard to locate, hard to express in words; it is neither conscious nor unconscious but nonetheless convincing enough to act upon. Recognizing this ought not, however, to prevent us looking for criteria with which to reassure ourselves that our impression is securely based on evidence.

When the idea of ending comes forward we want to estimate its relevance, and we can do so under the following headings:

(i) How does the patient start and end the interview? Has this stable characteristics or are they variable?

(ii) How does the patient tolerate weekend breaks?

(iii) What about holidays? Are they or are they not well tolerated and enjoyed?

(iv) Is there information about how the patient imagines his analyst uses weekends and holidays?

(v) What has been the patient's experience of previous separations such as birth, weaning, birth of a sibling, loss of one or both parents through death or other eventuality? What has been the patient's reaction to them and how can ending be arranged so that traumatic situations are not repeated?

Upon the answers to these questions much of the course of the ending will depend. Probably the patient will not be able to make a judgment based on the assessment of these factors, but the analyst needs to do so. If he thinks a real ending is in sight he can start paying special attention to associations, dreams and fantasies.

5. Although the analyst's (and patient's) psychopathology is really a large subject, I assume, so far, that the case had been well selected by the analyst (and the analyst by the patient, but less so) at the start, so that analysis can proceed well and the analyst can work through conflicts with the patient. But there are some patients with whom ending becomes difficult because all the way through the analysis, or at some period of it, the analyst has made mistakes that have not been retrieved. Ruth Strauss wrote a paper in which she described how a mistake can be used fruitfully, but I am not referring to such faults. The mistakes I am referring to are essentially different. They are the ones that, as it were, drop under the table, though not necessarily out of sight. For instance, when I was working on the delusional transference, I could not discover how to deal with a patient who had said things about my interventions that I thought were true but that had left me feeling there was something wrong with this conclusion. I could not manage this feeling and so could only react by thinking of them as factual. The patient kept bringing up my faults but each time nothing could be done about them, so they formed a sort of nexus, bits of herself and bits of myself that had become fused. It was only when I recognized that they were true in their manifest content but untrue if their

latent content were examined that I had room to move about and began to reduce and then stop the growth of a gradually accumulating pile.

In other cases I found similar features, but this one was particularly difficult and so the patient forced me to recognize what could often be overlooked. Another patient had to work over **my** faults and test me again and again to find out if I knew about them and whether I was still like that. This may happen but it may not be necessary. If, however, a patient looks ready to leave and yet does not do so, it may be worth while looking out for these bits of fusion. The patient I have cited stays, I am increasingly convinced, because of them. She thinks about ending and once wrote a longish poem about how it must happen and the feelings she would have; they were rather well-integrated feelings and I thought: 'Well, why not do it, if you can feel like that?' But the pathological nexus that has been largely resolved for me is still actual for her.

I think this must happen to some degree in every case. The traumatic situations in our childhood and infancy are always there to be reawakened if regression takes place, and if we are going to analyse a patient in regression a comparable and transitory regression is required from the analyst. The early traumata that we meet are, however, made available during regression for fusion to take place. It would have to be a very odd patient who did not recognize his analyst's faults at some time or other.

6. Post-analytic phase. A patient who has finished coming for regular interviews communicates with me from time to time and occasionally comes to see me. She is a singer and writes to tell me how she is getting on. There may be a problem or a crisis of anxiety for which, when in London, she comes for an interview. Each time it is easy to get to the core of her situation and interpret it; she seldom needs a second interview, and has recently taken a two-year job in Switzerland. She could never have done this when she ended her regular interviews (four times a week, tailing off to once a week, then once every so often). Symptomatically the result was moderate, but she had been regretful about ending and so the way was open for her to return.

This example illustrates the importance of working at how ending takes place. It also indicates that ending does not necessarily happen because a therapeutic result has been achieved; indeed symptoms may finally go after and not during analysis.

I believe it is a matter for satisfaction if a patient behaves like this one and that it is more favourable than with those who terminate contact altogether. Perhaps you may hear of them later from somebody else, and to all appearances their lives are going on well, but one cannot tell.

It may seem that the post-analytic phase could go on indefinitely. I have heard analysts express concern lest contacts with a patient after the end will initiate further analysis. I agree that sometimes they do so, but the post-analytic phase seems to me different from more analysis. It is like a convalescent period which, under optimal conditions, will terminate itself. Systematic analysis is like a radical operation because it causes damage to defences. To be sure, these have been badly constructed and need taking to pieces, but as more is learned about ego-psychology it is increasingly understood that nobody can do without them. Perhaps post-analytic work can be understood as giving time for defences to become reconstructed and is like the final healing of a wound.

Theoretical Reflections

In the literature, the end-point of analysis varies according to the views of the analyst. Examining the nine ending points that Jung defines, they correlate closely with his theoretical position, even though they appear as a series of observations on what happens. The same applies to my own position. It makes a great deal of difference whether the self be conceived as a system that only integrates the personality or whether it be conceived as one that deintegrates as well. I should not think it adequate to end when the patient is capable of managing the inner and outer worlds and I should look rather for evidence that he can also work through periods when he, i.e. the self integrate, is not in charge. This idea provides a rationale for not ending because everything is going well and suggests the importance of using the ending period to test the patient's capacity to work through an especially stressful situation that can reach the level at which it is a matter of life and death.

The ending period gives room for mourning to be reached and this involves a post-analytic phase, as I have already suggested, in the self-analysis of the patient and the use the analyst makes of what he has learned from his patient, and in a variable number of meetings after ending.

The importance and severity of stress that ending involves vary within wide limits. I would understand this in terms of the patient's psychopathology or, to translate into psychodynamic terms, the degree of regression necessary for the patient to reach the traumatic situations in his early life. If the on-going individuation processes have been distorted from the start a different ending may be expected from that which takes place when the traumata have occurred later on.

In the former case, a patient may have dreams of ending as an invasion, with himself holding out, as it were, in the bits of the self left intact, or there may be a much more explicit statement of the patient's belief that his whole life depends upon blissful union with his analyst.

If the traumata have occurred later on, sadness and grief may be available and then the ending period will be much shorter. In both cases a recapitulation of the analysis, implicit or explicit, is usual and the analyst may sometimes expect attacks on the way his analysis has failed. They represent the patient's final disillusionment about what analysis can do, but some of them may combine with a dawning recognition of the 'human' failings of the analyst.

References

JUNG, C. G. (1916/1928). *Two essays on analytical psychology. Coll. wks.*, 7.
——(1944). *Psychology and alchemy. Coll. wks.*, 12.
STRAUSS, R. (1964). 'The archetype of separation'. In *The archetype*. Basel/ New York, Klarger.

PART II

Transference

Notes on the transference*

MICHAEL FORDHAM

1957

PART I. INTRODUCTION

In his foreword to 'Psychology of the transference' Jung says:
'The reader will not find an account of the clinical phenomena
of the transference in this book. It is not intended for the
beginner, who would first have to be instructed in such matters,
but is addressed exclusively to those who have already gained
sufficient experience in their own practice.' (Jung, 1946, p. 165).

It is nothing short of astonishing to find how little has been
published in the past about the clinical transference experiences
that Jung presupposes in his essay. There is no reference to the
subject in the index of Baynes's comprehensive series of case
studies, *Mythology of the soul*, nor does Frances G. Wickes make
specific reference to it in her book, *The inner world of man*, while
J. Jacobi devotes to it only a cursory discussion in her authori-
tative work, *The psychology of C. G. Jung*. Recently, however,
papers by Adler, Henderson, Moody, Plaut, Stein and myself
(1957a) have appeared, and these have begun the filling-in of
Jung's outline, which this essay continues. Here I shall discuss
those aspects of the transference that have struck me as especially significant because they have given rise to discussion among
trainee analysts and colleagues. I have not attempted to define
the term in detail, since this has been done already by Stein
(1955a), and it is only necessary to state that it will be used here
in a wide sense to cover the contents of the analytic relationship.

Jung, in his writings upon the transference, lays special
emphasis upon the part played by the personality of the
analyst in any analysis. This was first expressed when he was a

---

* First published in *New developments in analytical psychology*, 1957. London,
Routledge.

psychoanalyst; he then proposed that all analysts should undergo a training analysis, and he has since stressed it over and over again. His view appears to have stemmed from the association experiments, for Baynes, who should be in a good position to know, says (1950, p. 108):

> Jung discovered the unavoidable influence of this personal factor when experimenting with word association tests. He found that the personality and sex of the experimenter introduced an incalculable factor of variation . . . Jung realized that it was quite impossible to exclude the personal equation in any psychological work. He accordingly decided to take it fully into account.

Much of Jung's behaviour arises out of this 'discovery': the relatively informal setting, the use of two chairs with the analyst sitting in front of the patient [since modified], and the axiom that the analyst is just as much in the analysis as the patient, lead inevitably, in any thorough analysis, to his divesting himself of his persona; he is enjoined to react with his personality as a whole to the patients in analysis. It is manifest that only those with a differentiated personality can do this without making nonsense of the whole procedure, for an analyst's attitude and behaviour need to accord with what he says and, since he will be drawn into the state of primitive identity with his patient, it is essential for him to be conscious of his primitive reactions. It is this that makes a long and thorough personal analysis an absolute prerequisite for all analytical psychologists who wish to become practising analysts.

It is Jung's thesis that there is a therapeutic content in the analyst's personality. This cannot be just his consciousness; indeed, it is the unconscious that is far the more important in this respect, and so his theory of transpersonal archetypes may be expected to orientate us here. With it we can explain why the patient apparently calls out suitable or adapted therapeutic reactions in the analyst which, together with the unadapted ones of the patient, form the main substance of all intense transferences. It is, further, the analyst's archetypal reactions that form the basis of his technique, which without them must lack all true effectiveness. Thus Jung's theory has deepened our understanding of the 'incalculable factor' to which Baynes referred, converting it into a definable class of personal and transpersonal functions whose further investigation is thus made possible.

The distinction between the personal and the transpersonal unconscious, made by Jung in order to demarcate his investigations from those of Freud, is extremely subtle, and it is impossible to agree to the setting up of a clear dividing line between the two, for many personal relationships, particularly those of the transference type, express archetypal forms, and *vice versa*. Consequently, though the distinction is useful in other fields of study, I have found it better, in describing the transference, to conceive of a single unity that appears in consciousness in either personal or transpersonal form, or in both. The objective quality of experience, described as part of the numinous archetypal images, cannot be overlooked in any of the transference manifestations, and this is true in whichever form they appear. It is this that makes the study of the analyst-patient relationship so fascinating and rewarding.

From this complex relationship it results that both analyst and patient are laying the foundations of an increase in consciousness of all the innumerable psychic experiences that emerge out of the unconscious within the transference. By being analysed, all the patient's personal relationships are affected, particularly his capacity to handle interpersonal affects more fruitfully, by distinguishing between what is within and what is beyond the powers of his ego to control and manipulate.

Those outside the control of the ego comprise the contents of the transpersonal or objective transference that forms the subject-matter of Jung's essay on the transference in the individuation process. Yet even though they may be recognized as transpersonal they frequently, indeed more often than not, are first experienced personally.

The recent renewal of interest in the transference among analytical psychologists has given rise to uncertainty as to its place and importance in the analytical process. This would appear to centre on whether there are psychotherapeutic methods in which it does not occur.

Studying Jung's ideas on this topic makes it clear that he believes the bulk of psychotherapeutic procedures do not involve transference analysis, and in many of his essays the argument does not take the transference much into account.

He divides treatment up in various ways and specifies his own contribution in a variety of styles, but he is consistent in holding that methods and techniques such as confession, suggestion, advice, elucidation, and education all aim at making the patient more normal, and he links this up with the needs of the majority of patients and particularly those in the first half of life. These, if they need analytic treatment, should be treated by the methods of psychoanalysis, which is classed as a method of elucidation or interpretation of the unconscious process, based on a general theoretical outlook, or individual psychology, essentially an educational procedure aiming to socialize the individual.

But these methods are not valid with the class of patients to whom normality is meaningless and of whom individual development is, so to say, demanded. With these patients all methods must be abandoned 'since individuality ... is absolutely unique, unpredictable and uninterpretable, in these cases the therapist must abandon all his preconceptions and techniques and confine himself to a purely dialectical procedure, adopting the attitude that shuns all methods'. (1935, pp. 7, 8). Then the patient's psychical system becomes 'geared to mine [Jung's] and acts upon it; my reaction is the only thing with which I as an individual can confront my patient' (*Ibid.* p. 5).

For a long time Jung found great difficulty in describing what happened when the patient's and the analyst's psyches were geared together. In 1931 he wrote (p. 51): 'Although I travelled this path with individual patients many times, I have never yet succeeded in making all the details of the process clear enough for publication. So far this has been fragmentary only'. Later on this gap was filled in to some extent by 'Psychology of the transference'.

I surmise that Jung's difficulty arose from emphasizing the highly individual nature of the process; indeed, if the individuality is 'unique, unpredictable and uninterpretable' it is also indescribable in general terms. When, therefore, Jung wrote an essay on the transference in individuation, using alchemical myths to do so, he must have decided that it was possible to generalize. His decision can be understood only by realizing that as the result of abandoning preconceptions and setting the individual in the centre of consciousness a very general process begins to operate, as indeed the theory of compensation postulates. It is the general processes that he describes.

In various places Jung recognizes that the transference can become a central feature in any analysis, for instance in his qualified agreement with Freud that the transference 'was the alpha and omega of the analytic method' (1946, p. 172), but he came to regard the transference in psychoanalysis as different from that which developed in the individuation process because of the different attitude of the analyst towards the patient.

The value of Jung's differentiation between patients who require treatments that aim at normality and those who seek individuation is useful, but has its limitations. It could blind us to realizing that in the first class of case individual characteristics cannot be lacking, and that the individuating case not infrequently shows signs of needing to be more normal. My analytic studies of children forced me to see this in a surprising way, for I found that the attitude that Jung defined as correct for patients embarking on individuation was just the attitude that led to developments in the ego in children. A direct relation between analyst and child was indeed essential. This consideration, first based on individual analysis of children, was then supported by an opportunity provided during the last war when hostels were organized for difficult children. There I was fortunate enough to observe the remarkable work of one matron whose capacity for establishing a direct therapeutic relation with the children in her care rendered it possible for her to relax imposed discipline to a far greater extent than would otherwise have been possible. She became a 'fellow passenger in the process of individual development' that occurred in each child.

These observations naturally surprised me, but then I began to see that there was something essentially the same in all my analytic procedure. I had a basic 'belief' in the individual of whatever age, and began to criticize the attitudes described by Jung as methods or techniques of interpretation and education because they seemed to be imposed on patients. I came to consider that it was not necessary to impose adaptation on a younger personality or an unadapted one, because the aim of the young individual or the unadapted person was in any case to do what other people did, i.e. his natural aim was to become normal or adapted.

Later I came to see that the archetypes have a special relation to ego development (1957a), and this led me to examine closely the significance of archetypal forms in the interpersonal transference relationship formed by younger people. I soon realized with particular force that archetypal activity in a young patient took on a more personal form than in the second half of life, and that in consequence it was to be found in the transference projected on to the analyst. These projections call forth a response in the analyst that leads to the condition of primitive identity with the patient, out of which a stronger ego can develop (*ibid.* p. 108). This conclusion led to my giving more emphasis to the value of analysis in the first half of life than is generally current in analytical psychology.

The position would seem to differ where individuation in its proper sense begins, for this process presupposes that the problem is not one of developing the ego but of differentiating it from and bringing it into relation with the unconscious, out of which the self appears as an experience apart from the ego. It presupposes that the patient has reached the stage at which his vocational aims are satisfied and spiritual problems are pressing to the fore (cf. Henderson, 1955). In these circumstances the transference can take on the more obscure, less intense, more collective, transpersonal, even social form. But even here the reactions of the analyst, while they are different because inevitably orientated in the direction of individuation, are no less important.

It appears to me consistent with Jung's position to state the basis for my own analytic work by asserting that 'I believe in the individual'. This gives me a certain detachment from my belief and makes it possible to develop it into a theory and then proceed to investigate the transference in the light of it. For if my theory be correct, then absence of manifest transference in younger people must be due to insufficient appreciation by the analyst in the first place and later by the patient of what he is doing.

That the transference develops under special circumstances will be generally agreed. In this paper these will be considered first, before the content of the relationship between analyst and patient is gone into. Though I recognize that there is no clear line of demarcation between the formal setting of analysis and its content, and that the two interact, yet this distinction is useful. Thus the frequency of interviews, the naturalness or artificiality of the situation, the way in which the patient's libido is deployed (discussed below under the heading 'Energy distribution') all depend upon the transference of the patient and the reactions of the analyst, to be discussed under the heading of 'Counter-transference'. None the less I have designed this paper with the contrast in mind, as the reader will find if he follows the headings of the sections into which the text is divided.

PART II. GENERAL CONSIDERATIONS

The Analytic Interview

Analytic interviews consist in the regular meeting of two people for an agreed period, it being assumed that one of them, the patient, wants to come enough to repeat his visit, while the other, the analyst, agrees to put himself, his experience, his knowledge, and all his attention at the patient's disposal for this agreed period. The analyst was once himself a patient; he has been analysed as part of his training experience, and through this experience he knows what it is like to be on the other side of the bargain. He also has knowledge, acquired during his training, and techniques that are going to be useful in what follows. It can be assumed that his training will have made it possible for him not to use his techniques to interfere in the 'alchemical' process that will gradually involve patient and analyst more and more. The analyst will know that every single statement he makes is an account of the state of his psyche, whether it be a fragment of understanding, an emotion, or an intellectual insight; all techniques and all learning how to analyse are built on this principle. It is thus part of the analyst's training experience to realize that he is going to learn, sometimes more, sometimes less, from each patient, and that in consequence he himself is going to change (cf. Jung 1931a).

The patient's position is in many respects similar to the analyst's, for everything he says will be treated as an expression of his psyche; he also will be using techniques, though less refined ones; he also will be using his understanding and employing his insight, in relation not only to himself but also to his analyst. The essential difference between patient and analyst is to be sought not in these spheres, but in the patient's greater distress, his lesser awareness, and his greater need to increase his consciousness so as to change himself and his way of life. It is not to be sought in the absence of involvement in the process on the part of the analyst. Analytical psychologists all follow Jung in rejecting the idea that the analyst can possibly act only as a projection screen.

Though the analysis starts on a simple basis, the interviews soon become filled with the complexities that form the subject of the bulk of this paper. Here it need only be said that the complexity is brought about by the specific aim of investigating the unconscious. This conscious aim has archetypal roots and so has a long historical background, originating in the earliest initiation ceremonies and proceeding through religion, mysticism and alchemy to their more scientific, analytic equivalent. It is, however, important to keep firmly in mind the simple basis of the interview and to maintain it by such arrangements as keeping the time and frequency of interviews relatively stable. The stable form then becomes an expression of the analyst's reliability when all else is in a state of flux. The simple outline gives a frame of reference to which fantasies, projections and speculations can be referred.

'Naturalness' versus 'Artificiality' of the Transference

The definable basis of the analytic interview may be seen as embodying the naturalness with which the analyst meets the patient, but the recurrent discussion of whether the transference is natural or artificial covers a wider field. The constant preoccupation of analysts with 'naturalness' springs from the ascetic nature of analysis. Analysts are subject to the reproach of unnaturalness because of the sexual tensions aroused in the patient, who reproaches the analyst for his 'unnatural behaviour'. This reproach, however, usually springs from a projection of incest fantasies, which the patient misunderstands and wishes to act out. The antithesis could be stated in another way by considering how far the analyst's technique induces the transference and how far it is the inevitable consequence of two people meeting together under the conditions just described. Since the meaning of technique will only appear later the vaguer definition of the issue will here be adhered to.

In the essay already referred to, Jung makes it clear that he regards the transference as a 'natural' phenomenon, by which he means that it is not peculiar to the analytic relationship, but can be clearly observed in all social life. Jung's view is without doubt supported by many observations and by comparison with other relationships all confirming the application of his theory of archetypes to the transference: since archetypes occur within the transference and in many spheres of life, so that they are general phenomena, the transference must partake in this general phenomenon. Yet in regarding analysis as the equivalent of these social situations, it must at the same time not be overlooked that in none of them is so much attention given to the psyche of two persons under relatively standard conditions, and in none of them is so much effort expended in undoing resistances. Furthermore, in other personal relations and social situations little effort is devoted to finding out what is going on in them, and so the main bulk of the energy bound up in them remains unconscious. In this sense the word 'artificial' might be appropriate, but only with the qualification that the patient comes because of the distortion of his personality, which has been induced by failures in his development. It is this 'artificial' distortion that analysis of the transference seeks to correct, and therefore what is 'artificial' in the analysis is more than matched by what is distorted in the patient, particularly at the beginning of any analysis; but the distortions progressively lessen as the analysis proceeds, until at its ideal termination all residues of frustration will be dissolved by the patient leaving his analyst. Then the simple basis of the whole process from which the analysis began can once again be clearly envisaged by the patient.

Analysis and Life

Closely related to the discussion of whether the transference is 'natural' or 'artificial' is the question of how it is related to something broadly termed 'life', by which is usually meant all the patient's everyday activities, other than his analysis, which get related to what is 'natural'.

Henderson (op. cit.) implies that almost the whole psyche of a patient becomes concentrated in analysis, so that 'life' would theoretically almost cease while the personality is being transformed. Because of this he finds it necessary to posit a post-analysis period in which a new adaptation to life by the new personality is achieved.

My experience does not accord with this view. It is true that if a satisfactory result is to be achieved, many changes in the life of the individual are inevitable; but these take place step by step during the analysis rather than after it, and life continues, reflecting the changes that are continuously taking place within the analytic transference. The type and degree of change vary according to the subject's character; the outward changes are likely to be greater in younger persons and in the more severely neurotic or psychotic patients, whose aim, as Henderson has pointed out, is vocational rather than spiritual. It is in the patients for whom individuation or the formation of a philosophy of life is the main issue that outward changes tend to be less in evidence.

There are two basic considerations that need to be taken into account.

1. The patient comes with a presenting symptom for which he seeks a solution. It is the aim of the analyst to elucidate this, and one of the results of this process is the development of a transference in which the energy previously directed into the symptom is now transferred to the person of the analyst.

2. The problem then is how to handle and ultimately resolve the transference.

As we shall later detail, most of the material revealed in the transference is not of a kind that could lead to satisfactory living, for otherwise it would not have given rise to the symptoms, but rather is made up of just those parts of the personality that are unadapted to life. Therefore when Jacobi (1951, p. 85) states that Jung ' . . . holds an "attachment" to a third person, for example, in the form of a "love affair", to be quite a suitable basis for the analytical solution of neurosis . . . ' she appears to misunderstand the nature and importance of the transference and its relation to 'life'. In general, if a patient is capable of sustaining a satisfying 'love affair', then the libido invested in it is not of the kind that needs development through transference analysis. Over and over again patients come for analysis just because their erotic experiences do not produce a solution of their neuroses, and only when the illusions contained in these 'affairs' are lived through in the transference, and nowhere else, can a solution be found.

I have taken up the supposed dichotomy—'life' and analysis—because it is current among analysts, but it is only a rough distinction, for one of the essential qualities of the transference is its living dynamism. Here the question arises of whether analytic phenomena are induced or released. My contention is that they are released, and upon this view my thinking about transference is largely based.

Energy Distributions

A study of the distribution of manifest energy released by analysis in relation to the interview bears upon such questions as interview frequency, fantasy, and active imagination, all of which are particularly relevant to analytical psychologists, if only because they have no prescribed standard of interview frequency, but rather relate it to the varying needs of patients under different circumstances.

My usual practice is to start with three interviews a week, increasing or reducing the number as occasion requires. Jung has prescribed specific frequencies for his individuating cases, whom he aims at putting in a position to conduct their own analyses under his supervision. This subject will be taken up later, though his definite statement that he aims at reducing interviews in his cases has led me to the following considerations.

Let us now consider two extreme cases, one in which the main bulk of the analysis is conducted in the interview, the other in which the interview is supervisory and the main bulk of the manifest activity is expressed in active imagination and dream analysis outside the interview. Since the duration of an analysis can be important, the comparison is useful in seeing that the time available for study of the imaginative and dream products is vastly greater in the second case, and it might be thought that the analysis would be shortened. Since, however, all the time spent on dream and fantasy may depend upon an unrealized projection upon the analyst, and since this drives the patient to produce enough material to fill the interview with reports of dream and fantasy, the duration of the analysis can easily be considerably increased rather than shortened, as is sometimes held by analytical psychologists.

It is the consideration of these defensive uses of dream and fantasy that makes it useful to distinguish between behaviour in the interview and the reporting of what has gone on outside it; this covers all that the patient tells the analyst about himself, his relation to other people in his environment, his dreams, his inner world as exemplified in fantasy, day-dreaming, or active imagination. Using this distinction it is then easier to perceive when the patient is referring to the analyst in talking about somebody else, or when what he tells is conditioned by his attitude to the analyst, so that sometimes the very reporting of material is conditioned solely by the patient's attitude to the analyst.

A young man who was having difficulties in talking during his interviews reported that between them he could converse easily with an imaginary analyst whom he identified with me. In these conversations he would prepare what he was going to say to me in the interview, but when he attempted to put his plan into operation, the thoughts were replaced by various other interests, or there were no thoughts at all. It would seem that most of what is usually called analysis in its positive sense was, in his case, conducted outside the interview, the whole time in the latter being spent in analysing the resistance that conditioned this state of affairs. Since this was very strong no apparent progress was made for a long time.

This example shows clearly how much more energy can be expanded outside the interviews than in them, but as the analysis of my patient's resistance progressed the situation began to change so that the imaginary figure became a less prominent feature and it became easier for the patient to talk openly to me. He then spent less time conducting his analysis outside the interviews. This I regarded as a favourable development.

Gerhard Adler, in his paper 'On the archetypal content of transference', describes the phenomena in reverse. He cites a woman patient whose relation to him during interviews could be divided into two parts; the first positive, in which she played the rôle of a good daughter, the second negative, in which she entered into an aggressively-toned conflict with him. She then went away into the country, and there painted a picture in which a sado-masochistic pattern was depicted; this led on to an animus figure that revealed a vision of the self as a fantasy of the inner cosmos; all these developed away from the interviews. Adler believes that the transference, which continued between interviews, acted as a container (transcendent transpersonal temenos) inside which these events could happen.

Because Adler was aiming to show how the personal was transcended by the archetypal transference, and because the case was one in which the individuation process had been constellated, there was no necessity to enter into the motives for experiencing fantasies away from the interview. But had an analysis of these been necessary he would have been led to consider the tendency of depressive patients to split their love-hate conflicts so as to internalize the aggressive components that were so manifest in the picture and seemed to have disappeared from the transference. This might very well have proved important in leading to new developments in the transference of his patient, had he wished to investigate them.

It can happen that, if experiences of this type are not considered, the archetypal contents of the transference can dissolve the personal aspect of it, thus leading to depersonalizing defences. This is particularly liable to happen when the unconscious is active enough to give rise to frequent disturbances in consciousness during the patient's life away from the analytic interview. Probably the most important single consideration in avoiding such defences is for the patient to see that the image of the analyst does not disintegrate, melt away, or otherwise become inaccessible between interviews; none of these things appears to have happened in Adler's case or in my own.

To illustrate this depersonalizing defence I may instance a patient who had used active imagination in a previous analysis. She would come to see me with a book in which her dreams and active imaginations were written down, and would read out the experiences she had recorded and the thoughts she had accumulated, thus following a recommendation of Jung's (1931, p. 47f). When I came to make an interpretation I encountered strong defences, and I soon began to suspect that this technique was a means of ensuring that my influence was neutralized. Among the figures with which she conversed was a venerable 'wise old man' who almost invariably supported the patient in her own views and would sometimes tell her that what I had said in the last interview was wrong. It was not this, however, that struck me so much as the nature of the thoughts 'he' produced; they were in no respect unusual, so I asked why she could not think them for herself. My question led the patient to reveal that her 'active imagination' had started from a seminar at which she had been present, in which it had been asserted that active imagination was the be-all and end-all of Jungian analysis. As she had always, from childhood onwards, spent part of her life in an inner world, she took to this technique like a duck to water. She had further gained the impression that all Jungians thought better of people who presented their ideas in this form and that it was easier to contradict the analyst if she got a 'wise old man' to do it, as he would then be more impressed. Once this was revealed she was able to be more open with me, to react more immediately to my interpretations, and to spend her time outside the interviews in more useful occupations than making up fantasies with a view to controlling her analyst.

It will now be clear that, when we draw attention to the distribution of energy released by the analysis in relation to an interview, we are doing so with a view to studying the nature of the transference more carefully. The motives for this distribution are only to be brought to light in the end by realizing the nature of the face-to-face behaviour of analyst and patient in the interview itself; if this is overlooked it is only too easy for an impeccable 'technique' to become a defence against the very aim it was designed to achieve.

The whole trend of my patient's analysis was changed by the revelation of her defensive use of dream and fantasy; it turned into a process of testing what I could love, endure, or hate, while at the same time the trend of her life changed radically and her personal relationships were deepened and extended.

Such experiences have led me to consider all energy distributions and reporting in relation to the transference, and to believe that the omission of motives for telling anything to an analyst may open a rift in the analyst-patient relationship.

'Acting Out'

It will now be apparent that the gradual development of an

analysis can lead to the analyst's becoming the centre of it, so that the whole patient may become involved in the process of transformation. If, as sometimes happens, this concentration of libido is made into an aim, almost anything, whether adapted or not, that happens outside the transference in the life of the patient is considered undesirable. These supposedly undesirable activities have come to be termed 'acting out', and this term seems to have received greater prominence than its more vivid equivalent of 'living the shadow'.

The term 'acting out' is borrowed from psychoanalysis, in which it is used to cover the acting of unconscious experience in an appropriate setting; Fenichel (1945, p. 375) says: 'Under the influence of transference, everyone whose infantile conflicts are remobilized by analysis may develop the tendency to repeat past experiences in present reality, or to misunderstand reality as if it were a repetition of the past, rather than to remember the repressed events in their appropriate connection'.

A male patient telephoned to tell me that he was dissatisfied with his analyst and wanted an interview with me for various reasons, which he stated. I replied that I would see him if his analyst agreed. His analyst told me that she was quite prepared for her patient to consult me, but she did not think he really meant what he asked for, because he had not raised the matter with her.

When he arrived at my consulting room he seemed in a somewhat confused state. He repeated what he had said to me over the telephone, and then became relatively incoherent. I gathered, however, that it was his relatives as much as he who wanted the change. So I told him that I thought his relatives had played on some doubts he had about the goodness of his analyst, which he really hoped were not true. At this he became coherent and told me that this was indeed the case, so I went on to tell him that I had no intention of suggesting a change, since I thought his doubts were part of his relation to his analyst and needed working through with her. He left my consulting-room, so far as I could see, completely reassured, and I heard later that he returned to his analyst forthwith. In this example the act was not seriously intended.

If the patient means what he does, then it is not acting out, however socially undesirable his act may seem to the analyst or to those in his environment. It would seem probable that the patient cited by Gerhard Adler was acting out, though nothing undesirable in a social sense occurred. If, however, she was acting out, the fantasy that determined the experience, which occurred during the week-end, did not appear. It is not essentially a question of whether the behaviour occurs in the interview or outside it, for many patients—hysterical ones in particular—dramatize their affects in the analytic hour and thus prevent unconscious fantasies or memories from becoming conscious. Acting out is a special form of defensive behaviour wherever it occurs, and is based, as my example indicates, upon a projection to which neither analyst nor patient has been able to gain access. It will have been observed that the contents of the patient's doubts did not come into consciousness at the time he was interviewed by me.

Acting out in the interview has been described by Stein in his article, 'Loathsome women'. There he found that two of the patients ' . . . walked round the analyst's chair in a menacing manner. They described increasingly narrow circles, reminiscent of the "hag track" . . . in order to try and stir him up' (pp. 69–70). Stein found that they were aiming at getting him to 'man-handle' them. Here he suggests that a primitive drama is being enacted and this is not realized at first, either by him or his patients. They are 'living their shadow' which contains an archetypal image.

In using a psychoanalytic term, *acting out*, it is necessary to realize that it is being altered in the process and at the same time extended, to cover and emphasize the purposive aspect of the act in question, i.e., the attitude that Stein emphasizes in using the phrase 'in order to stir him up'.

In psychoanalysis, acting out is a replacement activity and as such needs to be reduced to its source. It is therefore undesirable, inasmuch as it is inadequate as a form of expression.

Living the shadow is likewise considered undesirable in analytical psychology, but for the added reason that it is acting in a primitive manner and is undesirable because it is consequently unadapted. For instance, the aim of getting the analyst stirred up with a view, as Stein remarks, to induce him to 'man-handle' the patients will not succeed, and they do not really want this to happen, for they have come to the analyst just because of the failure of their primitive and guilt-ridden activities to produce adequate satisfaction.

A Projection-Perception Scale

Though transference can only partly be described in terms of projection, yet this mechanism has the advantage of being easily defined, and furthermore it can be analysed, though not thereby necessarily dissolved.

Alongside projections the patient makes observations that turn out to be objective. Both processes are recognized by repeated tests on the part of the patient, who sometimes as if by revelation, sometimes by slow laborious analysis, comes to realize their nature. As the analysis proceeds the patient may be expected to get an increasingly true view of the analyst, so that a progression can be defined from illusion, due to projection, which may very well be creative, to reality based upon perception of the analyst as what Fairbairn (1952) calls a 'differentiated object'.

The patient's perceptions lead, in any thorough analysis, to his becoming aware not only of contents in the analyst of which the analyst may know, but also of those of which he is unconscious. If, under these circumstances, the analysis is to proceed it must be recognized that the patient gets into a position from which he can make the analyst aware of a part of his personality that he himself had either not seen or not been able to integrate with his ego. If the analyst can recognize it and benefit from it, all is well. Analysts find it difficult to do this.

But this is not all: an interesting situation arises when the patient makes a true projection on to the analyst, and again he may be conscious or unconscious of the situation. Where the patient's projection corresponds to an unconscious conflict of the analyst, the analysis may terminate if one or the other does not become aware of it in time; it is not necessarily the analyst who is the first to make the discovery. A patient of mine with a particularly strong father fixation told me she had to wait for two years in order to take up her problem because she saw that I was not ready to handle it. On looking over the period I had to admit that her view had substance, even though the subsequent analysis showed that this waiting was an ego-defence on her part. It is one of the advantages of the analyst's sitting in full view of the patient that these difficulties can be more easily handled than if he is out of sight and uses that position to maintain a supposed anonymity.

I mention these limiting problems because it is necessary to understand that the concept of a projection-perception scale has complications, but they do not invalidate the general idea, which is of value in considering such problems as the relation of active imagination to transference.

Jung has pointed out that the content of some projections can be dissolved, but that finally the projected archetypal images cannot; they only become detached from the person of the analyst. If there appears to have occurred at the same time an increase in positive perceptual awareness of the analyst, then it may be said that the projection has not only been withdrawn, but has become adequately integrated, inasmuch as the ego of the patient has become strengthened. If on the contrary this does not occur, it is almost certain that either the projection is still active or else that it has led to a fascination of the patient in another sphere; either it has been projected on to another person, or it has led to his becoming fascinated by the image in his inner world. In this case nothing has been gained and much may have been lost.

The interrelation of projection and perception is therefore a useful indicator of progression and regression of the ego.

PART III. PARTICULAR TRANSFERENCE MANIFESTATIONS

The Dependent Transference

The state of dependence arises when repressed infantile contents are released and the analyst seems to fulfil the imagined rôle of parent. Then projection predominates over objective perception.

During this period, in which the infantile patterns predominate (they never disappear), the analyst will refrain from compulsive attempts to control the direction the analysis should take, from giving advice, and from behaving too much in the many ways in which parents behave to their children. Unless he does this he will be dramatizing the transference projections and interfering with the aim of analysing them. However attractive this activity on the part of the analyst may be, and however therapeutically exciting and successful over a short term, it endangers the ultimate development of the patient's relation to the analyst. For this reason also social contacts between analyst and patient outside the analysis will be avoided.

The adoption of a parental rôle takes many subtle forms. It is even hidden in the implications of being analysed, when this means being subjected to a process understood by the analyst but not by the patient. Under this assumption all kinds of aspects of the parent imagos hide, and these have to be unearthed and analysed so as to reveal the true state of affairs.

The withdrawal of projected parent imagos is an essential prerequisite for the emergence of the self and its realization in consciousness. Analyses that give continued space for the emergence of the self are almost invariably long, because of the need for gradual maturation. Indeed I am inclined to believe that length is one of the essential features of radical analyses that lead to self-realization. It is useless to object because an analysis goes on so long, and equally futile to know what is best for these patients who cannot 'live'. They can live only in the transference, and to try to break it by any means only leads to probable disaster.

In an ideal analysis the analyst would not need any defences, nor would he display counter-transference illusions, in the sense to be defined later, but his reactions of whatever sort would be *adapted* to the patient's requirements at every point.

These requirements are manifestly complex, but they may usefully be classed under two headings: (*a*) those belonging to the transference neurosis and the repetition of infantile patterns of behaviour, termed by Freud the repetition compulsion, and (*b*) those belonging to the archetypal transference, in which the analyst can become more openly involved with the patient. The dependent transference is caused by the predominance of class (*a*), and it is often assumed that to interpret it induces an undesirable regression. The disorientation among analytical psychologists in this sphere appears to derive from the neglect of a very useful concept put forward long ago by Jung in 'The theory of psychoanalysis'. In this essay he criticizes psycho-analysts for their too great fascination with infantile sexuality, which came to be investigated in its own right, so that the importance of the present came to be neglected. He introduces the idea of the 'actual situation', which he defines as the cause of neurotic conflict and of regression to infantile patterns; he thus seems to deny the importance of fixation points. In his later writings, however, it is clear that he still adheres to the relative importance of arrested development in the genesis of neurosis, though without relating it to the concept of the 'actual situation'.

The important issue that Jung raised has not yet been settled. It is still an open question how to evaluate two evident causal elements: those that lie in the present and those that lie in the past. If, however, the actual situation is defined as the totality of present causes and the conflicts associated with them, then the genetic (historical) causes are brought into the picture, inasmuch as they are still active in the present as contributing to the conflicts there manifested. If we keep to this principle fruitless regression will not occur, because past and present are constantly kept in relation with one another and only those causes that actually operate in the present are taken up by the patient.

Where then does the transference come into the picture? It provides good conditions for investigating this 'actual situation', so long as the essential simplicity and sufficient 'naturalness' of the interview is maintained and the analysis conducted with regard to the true relationship factor as well as to the illusions that appear alongside it. These conditions provide the best chance of induced or artificial regressions being avoided and fixation points, to which little attention has been paid by analytical psychologists, being *revealed*. The fixation theory has been overlooked, as has also the contingent problem of the relation of the self to ego development. Far from being only 'biological roots', the zones and fixation points are, in my view (cf. Fordham, 1957), also centres of developing consciousness round which archetypal motifs, as deintegrates of the self, centre in alluring profusion. The magical sense of the anal zone has recently been interestingly discussed by Whitmont (1957), who has brought the whole problem into closer relation with recent developments in psychoanalysis.

The analysis of the dependent transference, which invariably leads into the infantile relation to the mother, is a lengthy and painstaking procedure. Yet it is essentially constructive since it is the only way in which many individuals can reach the growing points of their ego and so rebuild the previously inadequate structure.

The Objective Transference

In 1935 Jung wrote that

All methods of influence, including the analytical, require that the patient be seen as often as possible. I content myself with a maximum of four consultations a week. With the beginning of synthetic treatment it is of advantage to spread out the consultations. I then generally reduce them to one or two hours a week, for the patient must learn to go his own way (p. 20).

And again (1935a, pp. 26–7):

The psychoanalyst thinks he must see his patient an hour a day for months on end; I manage in difficult cases with three or four sittings a week. As a rule I content myself with two, and once the patient has got going, he is reduced to one. In the interim he has to work at himself, but under my control. ... In addition I break off treatment every ten weeks or so, in order to throw him back on his normal milieu. In this way he is not alienated from his world—for he really suffers from his tendency to live at another's expense.

I now wish to bring these statements into relation with another and later statement (Jung 1946, p. 71): 'The bond [of the transference] is often of such intensity that we could almost speak of a "combination". When two chemical substances combine both are altered'. The question that must spring to mind is how, if the relationship is so intimate, it can be desirable for meetings to be so infrequent.

There have always been certain implications in Jung's concept of a transpersonal objective psyche, which Robert Moody expresses very clearly in relation to the transference when he says of a case (1955, p. 537): 'Once the animus figure had been formulated by the unconscious, it played the rôle of a function that led the patient step by step, and *often regardless of the analyst* [italics mine], towards the various problems that stood between her and a harmonious relationship to the unconscious'.

If the unconscious is transpersonal and operates 'regardless of the analyst' and if the object is to bring the ego into relationship with it, it is clearly sensible to implement this idea by giving it technical application. It is common knowledge that Jung did this, and reference has already been made to it. He enjoined his patients to write down dreams, keep records of them and associations to them in a book, to start painting, drawing, modelling, and extending this to active imagination. All this is based on the empirical evidence that, in suitable cases, it leads to individuation. Once this process is set in motion interviews with the analyst become supervisory. The aim of these techniques was defined by Jung in his essay 'The aims of psychotherapy' (pp. 46ff.). There he says: 'My aim is to bring about a psychic state in which my patient begins to experiment with his own nature'. For this is needed 'not only a personal contemporary consciousness, but also a suprapersonal consciousness with a sense of historical continuity'.

Jung frequently states that his patients are of a special kind, i.e., those who have already been analysed and whose special difficulty is expressed in the symptom of a life lacking in meaning, a depressive state to which an individual solution is demanded. He claims that their problem is misunderstood if it is interpreted in terms of genetic psychology or of social adaptation. It is their individuality that needs emphasis, and therefore they may be expected to have an ego strong enough to stand the impact of the unconscious without too intense an 'alchemical' transference. For these already developed personalities the tendency to 'live at the analyst's expense' in a dependent transference must be undesirable because it derives from a misunderstanding of their problem. Breaking off treatment therefore aims at breaking up the dependent transference, which makes no sense. Jung's action therefore corresponds with his view of their problem, and not with the compulsive dramatization of the parent imagos, as is sometimes claimed.

This interpretation of Jung's statements means that there is no justification for erecting them into general rules, but they must rather be viewed as technical recommendations for the treatment of a special kind of case.

When I was learning to become an analyst in 1933, however, little reference to the transference was to be heard, and it seemed to be agreed by implication that if the patient's ego was brought into relation with the objective psyche a solution to his problems would appear and the transference would resolve itself without its being made more than vaguely conscious. Thus, Jung's statements had become erroneously generalized and even dogmatized without justification.

Jung's method must depend upon the patient's ability to introject his projections and 'raise them to the subjective plane'. Out of this grows active imagination, which has become the means by which the ego is brought into a vital relation with the archetypal images. It is under these conditions that it may be assumed that the transference would become less intense; they might even signalize its termination. It is here that Jung gives only general statements such as the one already quoted: 'With the beginning of the synthetic treatment it is of advantage to spread out the consultations. I then generally reduce them to one or two hours a week, for the patient must learn to go his own way' (1935, p. 20), a statement that has been interpreted in various ways, leading to considerable confusion. This I will illustrate by discussing two views on the place of active imagination in analysis.

Gerhard Adler in his paper, 'On the archetypal content of transference', says (p. 286) of his patient that she 'soon learned to use her fantasy constructively and to practise what analytical psychology calls active imagination'. But there is no mention of the transference diminishing in intensity; indeed it would seem to have gone on as before, for he says the patient (*ibid.* p. 288) 'felt her relationship to me—i.e. her secure positive transference—as a kind of temenos, of protective magic circle, inside which she was safe enough to endure this intense inner experience'.

Henderson (1955), in a comprehensive review of the subject, takes up quite a different position, from which he states that active imagination occurs after analysis of the transference has been completed. He defines four stages in the development of individuation, which begin only after the dependent infantile transference has been sufficiently analysed.

1. The appearance of the self symbols while the transference is at its height.

2. Resolution of the infantile transference and achievement of what Henderson calls 'symbolic friendship'. This term expresses the condition in which the analyst is built into the

psyche of the patient as a permanent internal 'friend'. Because this has happened the patient no longer needs regular interviews with the external analyst.

3. Post-analysis period in which a new adaptation is achieved with or without the analyst's help.

4. Discovery of archetypal symbolism through active imagination, providing a means of self-analysis without the analyst's help.

It is therefore clear that analysts do not agree as to the place of active imagination in the transference process. The drastic difference in view could spring from a variety of roots.

(a) From differing concepts of active imagination. There is indeed a tendency to regard almost any fantasy as active imagination, a tendency which I have commented upon elsewhere (1956), and I have suggested that the term should be used only when the fantasy takes on an object quality to which the ego consciously relates.

(b) From differences in the transference phenomena due to typological differences between patients.

(c) From differences in analytic procedure arising from differences in the personality structure of the analysts.

(d) From inadequate study of the motives for differing distributions of energy.

The confusion appears to me, however, to stem mainly from differing understandings of when the synthetic process begins, and from misunderstanding of Jung's sharp distinction between methods of rational influence and those in which the dialectical relation applies, i.e. his individuation cases. In the general run it is by no means easy to distinguish this clearly. In all analyses synthetic processes are continuously in evidence and, further, in my experience, an objective transpersonal quality attaches itself to the vast majority of all transference phenomena, even when they are expressed most personally by the patient and whether they are more or less intense. When the former, the alchemical combination takes place. However, there are certainly patients whose capacity for imaginative activity either dissolves or masks the personal aspect of the transference, so that it can only be detected with difficulty. These cases could very well develop into Henderson's fourth stage, which would seem to belong to Jung's special sphere, but they might equally well continue after the pattern of Adler's case. As far as my experience goes, the transference cannot be left out, and it will sooner or later form the central feature of any thorough analysis, and though Jung seemed at one time to believe that this was not so, his later work points in the opposite direction. In 'Psychology of the transference' he expounds his view of the 'alchemical' nature of the transference with the reservation that this need not always occur. In my view it always occurs, only with varying intensity. As we have seen above (pp. 123f), an apparently weak transference can be converted into a strong one by analysis. I have given this example because I believe that the indiscriminate application of Jung's thesis has led to strong transferences being too frequently overlooked because they are masked. In this connexion it appears to me that there is a point in Moody's statement that is liable to a rather serious misunderstanding. It implies that transferences only occur when the analyst participates in some unstated manner and that they never arise 'quite regardless of the analyst'. This is far from the truth; indeed most transferences have the quality of autonomy sooner or later, and they all occur without anybody's willing them.

It may well be reflected that Jung's aim of getting the patient to experiment with his own nature can occur just as well through his imagination playing on the person of the analyst, who is then the equivalent of the paintings and dreams. This has to me the following advantages: it links the whole process up to a human relationship without divesting it of its trans-personal quality; it also increases the possibilities of sorting out projections and perceptions after the manner described above under the heading of 'Projection-perception scale'. But Jung, as is well known, prefers a mild transference (1946, p. 172), and this may be one of the reasons why he takes steps to prevent a stronger transference where he conceives that the alternative method is just as much in the patient's interest. I cannot believe, however, that preferences of this kind make much difference to the development or non-development of the objective transference, which goes far deeper than conscious feelings.

PART IV. COUNTER-TRANSFERENCE

(*a*) *Use and definition of the term.*

So far we have concentrated on a number of features of the transference that are displayed by the patient either spontaneously or as the result of techniques used by the analyst. But this is only part of the analytic process, since the analyst soon becomes involved himself.

Because it was originally hoped that the analyst's personality would be eliminated from the analytic process, the counter-transference was the first class of reaction by analysts to be studied. It was soon found that the patient's transference stimulates the analyst's repressed unconscious, which becomes projected on to the patient so as to interfere with the way he conducts the analysis. Efforts were therefore made to eliminate this.

The thesis here put forward postulates that the whole personality of the analyst is inevitably involved in any analysis, and so the counter-transference is viewed from a different basis. This must lead to reconsideration of the term. A review of it is especially desirable because it has come, as a consequence of Jung's thesis, to cover more of the analyst's reactions than emanate from the repressed unconscious. Indeed it sometimes covers all the analyst's conduct in his analytic work.

In his interesting paper, 'On the function of counter-transference" Robert Moody describes how his unconscious led him to a reaction that seemed exactly adapted to a little girl's need, without his altogether knowing at first what he was doing.

His description, of how erotic instinctive processes were mobilized within him and brought into play, would seem, according to the present view, to indicate a good analytic reaction. It arose first out of Moody's unconscious archetypal response, only later to become related consciously to the patient. The idea implied in the original theory of psychoanalysis that the analyst can only safely react to his patient with his ego alone is here shown to be certainly erroneous.

It is here contended that each interpretation or other response, if it is to have validity, needs to be *created on every occasion* out of the unconscious, using material provided by the patient to give the unconscious content adequate form, and this is just what happened in Moody's case. The fact that the analyst's reactions are repeated in a similar enough form, in relation to sufficiently similar behaviour on the part of patients, for them to be called a technique does not invalidate their being created on each occasion, for there are always differences enough to necessitate an individual form for the same familiar themes. The fact of the analyst's reacting to a patient is maintained by Jung to be the essential therapeutic factor in analysis; the reaction differs from the patient's transference in that it has a less compelling character and is capable of integration; in other words, the analyst has a living relation to the unconscious at those points where the patient lacks it. This it is that facilitates the cure. Moody's behaviour was his spontaneous archetypal response to the sexual transference manifested by his child patient. If this is counter-transference, then it could be argued that all analyses are based on counter-transference, and so the term would take on a new and very wide meaning. At first I was inclined to think the extended usage was objectionable, because it blurred its original negative meaning and so opened the door to almost any unconscious behaviour by the analyst. Yet the change in our understanding of transference as a whole is better reflected by the wider usage, for *participation mystique*, projection and introjection can play valuable, even essential, parts in analytic procedures (cf. Money-Kyrle, 1956).

A solution to the quandary is made possible by dividing the general heading into two and referring to counter-transference illusion and counter-transference syntony. This differentiation is especially justified because there is a need to indicate the direction in which to look in order to become conscious. In analysis there are reactions on the part of the analyst that are syntonic and can make the patient more conscious, but these are different from the counter-transference illusion, where the increase in consciousness will come about only if the analyst himself examines his own reaction.

(b) Counter-transference illusion

The use of a recording apparatus reveals very neatly how counter-transference illusion can arise from projection. To be sure, I had found that some patients before ending their analysis would review those parts of it in which they believed I had made mistakes, and I could see that they were often right, but by then the details had escaped me; in addition, dreams about the patient give another clue, and it is possible to realize that wrong or mistimed interpretations spring from a repressed source. However, an accurate verbal record shows up the phenomena far better than anything else, for it can reveal without any shadow of doubt what can happen and how the analyst's own psyche can replace the patient's by projection.

Thus one day I ended a recorded interview with mixed feelings. It seemed on the one hand remarkably successful, but there had been a part early on when I had not succeeded in making progress. The patient was a boy of eleven who had problems over his aggressive feelings. The problems were related to his school work, in which he was not being as successful as his intelligence would warrant. The relevant part of the interview ran as follows:

John: 'Why did they block that door up?' (Referring to an area in the wall of my room where the doorway had been built up.)

M.F.: 'Imagine.' (Long silence, then M.F. continued) 'I expect to keep somebody out!'

John: 'I don't!' (then, after hesitations and much fidgeting), 'Better to have the door there' (i.e. where it is at present, leading into the passage).

M.F.: 'I suppose you thought my idea wasn't sensible. I think that from the way you went so quiet.'

John: 'They could have easily come that way' (referring to where the door is now).

M.F.: 'I still think I am right in believing you thought your remark was more sensible—you didn't think I would agree— you didn't think I would make *stupid* remarks!'

John: 'Beg pardon' (followed by long silence).

M.F.: (Repeats statement).

John: 'It isn't really stupid. It could have been. It's unlikely.' (After a further silence he went on to talk about electric trains, implying by asking me questions that I was ignorant on this topic.)

M.F.: 'You must think I'm an *awfully ignorant boob* if I have not heard of Meccano, because everybody has.' (And later on I made a more elaborate interpretation in which the phrase occurred.) 'You didn't know you had a secret feeling that *I was a fool and ignorant* and that you were more sensible than I in some respects.'

John went on to talk about Meccano and became technical in his conversation, and gradually I was able to stop over-acting and make interpretations that did not simply increase his resistance; for example:

M.F.: 'I wondered whether your questions were not some-thing of this sort: "Well, here's something I'm likely to know more about than he does"?'

Next I began to see that it was better to be even less active and point out that in his silences he was having secret thoughts. Only when I arrived at this formulation could the analysis of the thoughts proceed.

Listening to the recording made clear to me what I had vaguely felt during the interview. My aggression against this boy had interfered with my getting to understand what was going on in his mind. I had misinterpreted the child's feelings, replacing more subtle ones by a cruder statement, owing to the repression of memories relevant to a particular period of my own childhood. Then I used to attack my mother by calling her 'stupid', a word that I had repeated in my transference interpretations to John. Evidently I had identified with the memory-images and John had represented myself as a child while I, ceasing to be the analyst, represented my mother. Only when I had circumvented this reaction could I frame interpretations that brought me into relation with the boy's 'secret thoughts'; only from then onwards was I able to proceed with the analysis, understanding the child well enough for him to go on to reveal himself more and more fully.

It is to this class of phenomena that the term *counter-trans-ference illusion* applies. The example manifested the following characteristics: (1) there was an unconscious, or rather vaguely conscious, reactivation of a past situation that completely replaced my relation to the patient; (2) during that time no analysis of the patient was possible.

If we transpose this concept to the archetypal level, then the events would have to possess the same characteristics, i.e. the archetypal reaction would not be related to the state of the patient and the analysis would stop until the analyst was able to become conscious of the archetype in question. It is not so easy to find an illusory archetypal counter-transference, especially as a syntonic counter-transference is not necessarily positive. In his paper on 'Loathsome women', Stein has given the content of his counter-transference, apparently partly syntonic and partly illusory, based on a negative anima possession, to a type of woman patient. In this paper he formulates his affective attitude, dreams, and some of his personal experiences. In doing so he has contributed towards objectivity concerning the conflicts in which an analyst can become embroiled. In my experience, when the illusion of the analyst does not become conscious for too long, the analysis ends altogether, and the patient becomes acutely aware of what is happening. But when the analyst realizes what is going on, even if he cannot resolve the projection, a more favourable issue may be expected.

A frequent counter-transference manifestation is the tendency of analysts to make personal confessions to patients on unsuitable occasions. When I have objected to this practice or attempted to draw analysts' attention to their motives, I have been asked: 'Why do you find it necessary to withhold information about yourself from the patient?' Assuming that this question is not aimed at what is usually covered by discretion, and has not behind it the naïve belief that personal confessions in answer to questions improve the personal relationship between analyst and patient, which usually they do not, I reply that I do not find it 'necessary', but that I consider it essential to relate the question to another because of the special liability of confessions to cover counter-transference illusions: 'What do you want to give information to your patient for, in view of the fact that in doing so you usually give a report about yourself as you are, or conceive yourself to be, while this is not at all the person he necessarily imagines you to be?' This question often disposes of the first, but leads to another, for it is then said to be only 'human' to make confessions and also to err. The term *human* is contrasted with *divine* and *animal*, and if translated into psychological language refers to the ego.

My answering question now changes to: 'Why do you want to introduce your ego, i.e. personal consciousness?' If the answer is that the patient wants it or needs it, then we can go on to try to define the conditions under which it is desirable: when is it adapted to the patient's requirements and when a projection? I agree that it may be correct procedure, but I must reiterate that confessions by the analyst are far more frequently obstructive than otherwise, not only because they introduce projections but also because the information is only too often liable to drastic elaboration or distortion owing to the activity of fantastic projections arising from archetypal roots. In these circumstances the analyst as a human being (an ego) is of little consequence. It is then that we are exposed to reproaches of inhumanity and the like, but this is not to be dissolved by trying to be human, i.e. by making confessions, etc. Analysts are inhuman because of the transference, and we need to know *how* to be inhuman; this is surely one of the main reasons for undergoing an analysis, so that we may understand the patient's need and, at the same time, maintain our humanity.

But as the patient's ego becomes more established, towards the end of the analysis, it is relevant for the analyst to introduce more and more of himself—not only his ego. Then it is possible and satisfying to both parties to conduct conversations, and to interact in a more and more complete and spontaneous fashion.

Though I have never heard it stated, I have certainly thought that the introduction of the analyst's ego, as I maintain often at the wrong time, has the aim of reducing the transference, but it really avoids its transpersonal aspect by pretending that to introduce 'personal and human feeling helps'. Much more effective in reducing the transference is the method of recording dreams and teaching the patients to work them up before coming to the analysis, and getting them to paint and start on active imagination. The danger of this procedure, however, needs to be kept clearly in mind: as we have seen, it is liable to create an illusion that the transference does not exist when it is in reality just as big but is concealed in the method, which does not by any means prevent 'big transferences'. If it is not taken up by the analyst it only too often turns against him or the patient in the environment, or creates a situation for which there is no means of a decent solution.

All this does not overlook the need for the patient as well as the analyst to distinguish between the transpersonal objective transference and the conscious situation. This criticism of many personal confessions made by analysts is based on their ineffectiveness in attaining what they aim at, not to mention exploiting the patient's belief in the truthfulness of the analyst! If, however, a statement that can be checked by direct observation of the patient can be introduced, this is much more likely to continue the analytic aim of strengthening the patient's ego and helping him to gain greater control in the transference.

A female patient was attacking and at the same time trying to seduce me because I would not stop 'being an analyst' and live with her so that she could have day-to-day 'ordinary' relations with me. She attacked me as unfeeling, heartless, and indifferent to her distress. It was as fruitless for me to deny this as it would be for me to inaugurate a more personal kind of approach, to meet her outside the analysis, for instance, or to start those personal confessions for which she asked because she was the victim of a projected hermaphroditic figure. It was not until I took the bull by the horns and asserted that she overlooked that my interpretations were an expression of my concern for her condition, since they were attempts to bring her relief from it, that I made any progress. This I regard as an open statement about the main root of my making the interpretations she did not like; she can confirm my motive by numerous observations of my behaviour if she wants to make them. One of these is that I will go on meeting her poisonous attacks in a friendly way and seeing their positive content.

In voicing the attitude that lay behind my interpretations I am also expressing the fact of my being involved. It was only when I had said this that I broke through her defences and was able to press home my interpretations so as to relieve her of some of her anxiety, for she had been convinced that I was using concepts in order to destroy the mature love she felt, as well as to analyse its fantastic and infantile contents.

(c) *The syntonic counter-transference*

The extension of the term counter-transference seeks to undermine the idea that the transference consists in projections from a patient upon an analyst who never reacts spontaneously but remains as a kind of impervious reflector in which the patient can see his projections. This thesis holds no charms for Jungian analysts, who unanimously reject it. They hold that because of the archetypes the analyst inevitably becomes sooner or later involved with the patient in an unconscious process, which is first experienced as a projection and then further analysed.

Since the aim of analysis is realization of the self by the patient, whether it results in ego development or individuation, and since the analyst aims at performing a mediating rôle in this realization, all his syntonic reactions will ideally relate to the self, i.e. to the essential wholeness of his nature. Yet it is evident that the self as an integrated whole is seldom in the forefront of the analyst's behaviour, which is more often based on other archetypal forms. Yet it may be discerned obscurely by patients in their experience of their analyst as a god of one kind or another. This easily induces resistances in analysts, but it has indeed a basis of truth, since all the analyst's reactions, whether interpretations, questions, comments, or acts, are operations of their own natures.

The danger associated with the emergence of this archetypal form is inflation. But it is not necessary for analysts to feel any particular merit when this comes into the patients' consciousness, since awareness of the self is no individual achievement but a historical process, as Jung has clearly shown in 'Answer to Job'. The objection to being seen as a god is surely as narcissistic and dangerous as being inflated by it; indeed it reveals a negative inflation. Therefore if a patient dreams or feels I am a god, saying that it is ridiculous, I usually ask him: 'How do you know it is?' This question has behind it the idea that the self is the prime mover behind every analytic procedure, and is a recognition that the patient's 'projection' has a basis of truth in it. My question aims at leaving the door open to a wholeness that transcends consciousness and at the same time expresses my transpersonal involvement. It is therefore appropriate or syntonic.

It is commonly believed that consciousness is one of the great aims of analysis, but this is only partly true if the analysis is based on the self. Then consciousness is the instrument we use in the analytic process; it does not embrace the whole of it any more than the self can be identified with consciousness.

As I have suggested elsewhere, the self is a dynamic structure, having two definable functions (cf. Fordham, 1957); it integrates and deintegrates, and I have shown that this view of it can be used to explain how consciousness is produced and how an ego is formed in early infancy. This concept arose partly from studies in child psychology and partly from reflection upon my behaviour as an analyst. There were two ways of behaving: (1) trying to isolate oneself from the patient by being as 'integrated' as possible; and (2) relinquishing this attitude and simply listening to and watching the patient, to hear and see what comes out of the self in relation to the patient's activities, and then reacting. This would appear to involve deintegrating; it is as if what is put at the disposal of patients are parts of the analyst that are spontaneously responding to the patient in a way that he needs; yet these parts are manifestations of the self. It was this that led me to see that what Jung describes as the dialectical relationship is based upon processes that neither I nor my patient can control consciously, and that analysis depends upon the relatively greater experience of the analyst in deintegrating so as to meet the patient's disintegration. Moody (1955a) describes the feeling accompanying this experience very well when he says (p. 54): 'I decided . . . to allow myself to be drawn into whatever kind of relationship I felt her [his child patient] to be silently demanding of me'. When he did this, he remarks: 'I was somewhat at sea as to what was happening, but I realized that some important development had begun to occur from the time when I allowed my . . . reactions to express themselves freely'.

This experience accords with Plaut's view of incarnation. In his paper on 'The transference in analytical psychology', he asserts that there are two ways in which analysts handle the projected image: 'One', he says, 'will deal with it by educative procedure centred on the elucidation and differentiation of archetypal contents', while others 'will accept the projection in a whole-hearted manner making no *direct* attempt to help the patient to sort out what belongs to him, what to the analyst, and what to neither as well as to both. On the contrary they will allow themselves to become this image bodily, to "incarnate" it bodily for the patient'.

It will be observed that the way of incarnating the image leads to what is described as primitive identity, a condition that Jung has called preconscious and which I have incorporated into the theory of the deintegrating function of the self by pointing to primitive identity as the manifestation of deintegration. It follows therefore that if any new consciousness is to arise and to lead to differentiation of the ego, a lowering of the conscious threshold is inevitable and desirable. This leads to a view of archetypal projections somewhat different from that frequently held. In the case of repressed material emerging from the patient there is less difficulty in detecting projections, because they are more immediately related to memory images, but where archetypes become active, giving rise to 'fantastic images', the position is different for, owing to the concurrent primitive identity, the images can be expressed by the analyst or by the patient. This means that it can be just as valid for the analyst to know of the projection through registering its impact upon himself and perceiving it first within himself, as it is by listening to the patient and realizing it as an inference from what the patient says. Thus if a patient presents infantile material to the analyst, the latter can find out the appropriate reaction from himself, i.e. whether it be a mothering or fathering attitude that he can go some way towards meeting and out of which he can make an interpretation when the patient is ready for it.

At this stage in the transference the affective stability of the analyst is crucial; he must be able to rely on the deintegrates, knowing that consciousness will inevitably arise from them. It follows that he *will inevitably find* the right form or response so long as counter-transference projections do not obstruct its development.

It is on the basis of 'incarnating' the image, which should obviously be distinguished from acting out, that explanations and interpretations can begin to find their right place, for without them the patient will sooner or later become disorientated. If, however, the analyst keeps himself apart from the patient by adopting an explanatory or superior rôle without incarnating the image, he does nothing but isolate the patient at just the point at which he needs a primitive form of relationship.

Interpretations are therefore to be regarded as an end product of the analyst's syntonic counter-transference. They stand, as it were, on the basis of less definable affective preconscious experiences out of which they are distilled.

Some analysts depreciate the value of interpreting the transference, but in many places Jung emphasizes the importance of making the transference conscious. For instance, in 'Psychology of the transference' he says (p. 219),

As this [breaking infantile projections] is the legitimate aim and real meaning of the transference, it inevitably leads, whatever method of rapprochement be used, to discussion and understanding and hence to heightened consciousness, which is a measure of the personality's integration. During this discussion the conventional disguises are dropped and the true man comes to light. He is in very truth reborn from his psychological relationship and his field of consciousness is rounded into a circle.

This clear statement that it is necessary and desirable to bring the transference into consciousness requires amplification. What does this 'discussion and understanding' involve? To some extent this question has already been answered, but the question of interpretation, the most powerful instrument in the hands of the analyst, needs special consideration.

The great majority of the statements made by the patient, including those reported, are made to a projected figure, and it is evident that the analyst needs to be constantly on the look-out to recognize who the figure may be that he incarnates. This constitutes the major problem of transference interpretation for, if it is not defined, all that he says is reinterpreted by the patient in the light of projection, and misunderstandings inevitably arise. It is for this reason that the patient is introduced to the desirability of saying all that he can about his analyst as it occurs to him either outside the analysis or during his sessions. For this reason also the analyst introduces as few complications as possible, for how he behaves is as crucial as what he says. Therefore, in order to follow what he is doing, the advantage of keeping the essential framework of the interview simple is self-evident. The simplicity also facilitates the detection of projections, which can be interpreted when sufficient material has accumulated.

It follows that the interpretation of patients' material must be regarded as incomplete if its transference content is not referred to when it is sufficiently near consciousness. This applies to all reports embodying present or past occurrences, even to such simple phenomena as bits of history revealed by the patient; they all have reference to the 'actual situation', which in the case of analytic interviews is to be found in the transference.

It is sometimes held that no rules can be made as to when an interpretation should or should not be given, but this is not my experience. The following principle can certainly be formulated: when the patient has brought enough material for the analyst to make the interpretations in such terms that the patient can understand them, the interpretations can be given without hesitation. Under these conditions the patient's ego is mobilized, the reality content of the relationship is increased, and so regressive trends are brought more under control by coming into consciousness.

There is this to be said, however, against a rule—it could prevent the interpretation from being a creative act based on the analyst's past experience combined with the new experience he has of his patient; and it could short-cut the analyst's feeling of concern for the patient, the best safeguard against the use of theoretical interpretations as defences against unconscious activity within the analyst. An interpretation that violates the relationship clearly does not subscribe to the above rule, which aims at maintaining and improving the relationship between analyst and patient.

In 'Psychology of the transference' Jung says (p. 178): 'Even the most experienced psychotherapist will discover again and again that he is caught up in a bond, a combination resting on mutual unconsciousness.' It is out of this unconscious bond that, in my view, interpretations best arise, for if they do not they easily become impositions of the analyst upon his patient. But this bond is not stable, because of the 'ever-changing content that possesses the patient', which Jung compares to Mercurius who, in uniting all opposites in himself, appears 'like a demon [who] now flits about from patient to doctor, and as the third part in the alliance, continues its game, sometimes impish and teasing, sometimes really diabolical' (*ibid.* p. 188). Whether the 'demon' becomes a source of consciousness or of confusion all depends on how he is handled. One useful means is to try to start every interview as though a new patient were entering the room, for this helps in getting into relation with the patient's mood of the moment.

Amplification

In 'The aims of psychotherapy', Jung says, (p. 45): ' . . . It is particularly important for me to know as much as possible about primitive psychology, mythology, archaeology, and comparative religion because these fields offer me invaluable analogies with which to enrich the associations of my patients'. The necessity for this knowledge is generally agreed, but it needs to be borne in mind that extraneous mythological parallels, however close, can be used to obscure rather than clarify what is going on in the transference. After the myth has been developed within the transference it will naturally give the patient a special interest in the remarkable parallels that will almost inevitably be sought out in books and will be all the more striking because he knows that their substance was first revealed to him spontaneously.

It is quite clear that what I have described is at variance with the notion of introducing intellectual knowledge when the archetypal projections are in full swing, for whether the analyst likes it or not he will inevitably embody the image, as Jung clearly sees when he says (1946, p. 170):

> Practical analysis has shown that unconscious contents are invariably projected at first on to concrete persons and situations. Many projections can ultimately be integrated back into the individual once he has recognized their subjective origin: others resist integration, and although they may be detached from their original objects they thereupon transfer themselves to the doctor.

There is no possibility of explaining or getting rid of them by educative procedures; if this were possible it would only be necessary to give lectures. The ultimate resolution of these projections depends first and foremost on the analyst's behaviour and experience of his own myth. Once the parent imagos are projected they stay projected till the self appears, which initiates the 'stage of transformation' (1931a, p. 69ff.). Here Jung introduces the idea of the self-education of the 'doctor' as part of the analytic process. He does not, however, mean intellectual education but rather the analysis of the analyst as a means of introducing him to the inevitability of transforming himself as his patient also does.

The thesis of this essay is an extension of Jung's. It states that this mutual transformation extends to all the transference; it only becomes more significant in the 'stage of transformation' in which the mutual unconscious bond between analyst and patient becomes increasingly apparent. Amplification is used to elucidate the content of this, and is only valid when based upon the analyst's experience in the transference. That it can be used to support depersonalizing defences, and mask easily verbalized transference relationships when used earlier, has already been shown, and therefore I aim at using the patient's and my own experienced images first. Then if these correspond to known myths the latter can be added; then they do act, as Baynes (1955, p. 424) so vividly asserts, like the stains of a histologist, throwing obscure psychic contents vividly into relief, enriching the transference and leading to clearer definition of its contents.

Conclusion

These attempts to assess some problems presented by transference analysis will, I hope, lead to other reviews of the subject. They are especially important at the present juncture because the realization of transference analysis as a two-way process, in which the personality of the analyst takes an essential part, can lead and has led to abandoning the attempt to define and verbalize what is contained in it, because the whole process seems too individual and subjective. I believe, however, that Jung's thesis can be used to illuminate and describe its contents in a more realistic and scientific way than if the attempt be made to eliminate the analyst as a person and regard him as a projection screen.

I have made no reference to such practices as the patient going to two analysts at the same time, or to the important question of whether the sex of the analyst is significant. These issues still appear too complex to formulate. Neither have I considered the different forms of transference due to psychopathological considerations, but have rather confined myself to more fundamental clinical problems.

The general trend of my view is that the individuality of the patient cannot be overlooked in any age group, and that the process of analysis and therefore the transference is always basically the same though patients and analysts react to it differently.

In reading Jung's essays assembled in volume sixteen of the *Collected works* it is impossible to miss the changes that have taken place in the author's views with the passing of time. Jung is continually seeking adequate means of describing the remarkably complex and difficult field covered by psychotherapy. Fundamentally his view is the same, but the changes are often important. His tendency seems to have been to give more and more attention to the transference, and in 1951 he says (p. 116), 'The intelligent psychotherapist has known for years that *any* complicated treatment is an individual dialectical process' (my italics). Since the dialectical process corresponds with what I have defined as transference he would here seem to be in basic agreement with the thesis of my essay.

References

ADLER, G. (1955). 'On the archetypal content of transference'. In *Report of the International Congress of Psychotherapy, Zürich 1954*. Basel/New York, Klarger.

BAYNES, H. G. (1950). 'Freud versus Jung'. In *Analytical psychology and the English mind*. London, Methuen.

——(1955). *The mythology of the soul*. London, Routledge.

FAIRBAIRN, W. R. D. (1952). *Psychoanalytic studies of the personality*. London, Tavistock.

FENICHEL, O. (1945). *The psychoanalytic theory of neurosis*. London, Kegan Paul; New York, Norton.

FORDHAM, M. (1956). 'Active imagination and imaginative activity'. *J. analyt. Psychol.*, 1, 2.

——(1957). 'The origins of the ego in childhood'. In *New developments in analytical psychology*. London, Routledge.

——(1957a). 'Note on a significance of archetypes for the transference in childhood'. In *New developments in analytical psychology*. London, Routledge.

HENDERSON, J. L. (1955). 'Resolution of the transference in the light of C. G. Jung's psychology'. In *Report of the International Congress of Psychotherapy, Zürich 1954*. Basel/New York, Klarger.

JACOBI, J. (1951). *Psychology of C. G. Jung*. London, Routledge.

JUNG, C. G. (1913). 'The theory of psychoanalysis'. In *Coll. wks.*, 4.

——(1931). 'The aims of psychotherapy'. In *Coll. wks.*, 16.

——(1931a). 'Problems of modern psychotherapy'. In *Coll. wks.*, 16.

——(1935). 'Principles of practical psychotherapy'. In *Coll. wks.*, 16.

——(1935a). 'What is psychotherapy?' In *Coll. wks.*, 16.

——(1946). 'Psychology of the transference'. In *Coll. wks.*, 16.

——(1951). 'Fundamental questions of psychotherapy'. In *Coll. wks.*, 16.

——(1952). 'Answer to Job'. In *Coll. wks.*, 11.

MONEY-KYRLE, R. (1956). 'Normal counter-transference and some of its deviations'. *Int. J. Psycho-Anal.*, 37, 4 and 5.

MOODY, R. (1955). 'The relation of the personal and transpersonal elements in the transference'. In *Report of the International Congress of Psychotherapy, Zürich 1954*. Basel/New York, Klarger.

MOODY, R. (1955a). 'On the function of counter-transference'. *J. analyt. Psychol.*, **1**, 1.

PLAUT, A. B. (1955). 'Research into transference phenomena'. In *Report of the International Congress of Psychotherapy, Zürich* 1954. Basel/New York, Klarger.

——(1956). 'The transference in analytical psychology'. *Brit. J. med. Psychol.*, **29**, 1.*

STEIN, L. (1955). 'Loathsome women'. *J. analyt. Psychol.*, **1**, 1.

——(1955a). 'The terminology of transference'. In *Report of the International Congress of Psychotherapy, Zürich* 1954. Basel/New York, Klarger.

WHITMONT, E. (1957). 'Magic and the psychology of compulsive states'. *J. analyt. Psychol.*, **2**, 1.

WICKES, F. C. (1938). *The inner world of man.* New York/Toronto, Farrar & Rinehart.

The transference in analytical psychology*

A. PLAUT

1956

Until Jung published his *Psychology of the transference* in 1946 (now contained in volume 16 of the *Collected works*), many references and statements expressing his views on the transference had appeared in his writings. Although this exposition forms a comprehensive and significant statement, an account of the clinical phenomena of transference is deliberately omitted, and one would look in vain for a description of anything that might be called a technique. The reasons for and the consequences of this state of affairs are of great interest, and I hope to say something about both. My brief survey is divided into a theoretical and a practical part. While the former is based on my selection of quotations, I found it advisable to introduce some personal views into the second part.

Points in Jung's Theory

Jung tells us (1946, p. 172) that after his first meeting with Freud in 1907, Freud suddenly asked him: 'And what do you think about the transference?' Jung replied with deepest conviction that it was the alpha and omega of the analytical method, whereupon Freud said: 'Then you have grasped the main thing'. By 1946 Jung had modified his views, but in order to understand what he now means by the 'relative importance' of transference, we must bear in mind the evolution of his concepts.

In his correspondence with Dr Löy during 1913 (published

---

* Presented as part of a symposium on Jung's contribution to analytical thought and practice, and first published in the *British journal of medical psychology*, **29**, 1. The other contributors were Dr. M. Fordham and Dr. R. Moody.

152

by the latter in 1914), Jung stated: 'The transference is indeed at present the central problem of analysis', (Jung & Löy, 1914, p. 283) and described how he turned away from hypnosis and abreaction, because he felt that it was the patient's transference that produced the therapeutic effect in both (Jung & Löy, 1914, p. 256ff.). He also discovered in his investigation of a case of somnabulism, which he began in 1896, that he could have a 'certain formative influence' on the various types of personalities that manifested themselves in the patient during trance (Jung, 1925). In reading his correspondence with Dr Löy one notices in the following remarks that the views characteristic of Jung's attitude are already germinating: 'The patient is bound to the doctor, be it in opposition, be it in affection, and cannot fail to follow the doctor's psychic adaptations. To this he finds himself urgently compelled. And with the best will in the world and all the technical skill, the doctor cannot prevent him, for intuition works surely and instinctively, in despite of the conscious judgement' (Jung, 1916, p. 272). And again: 'Accordingly, I cannot regard the transference as merely the transference of infantile erotic fantasies; no doubt that it is from one standpoint, but I see also in it, as I said in an earlier letter, the process of the growth of feeling and adaptation. From this standpoint the infantile erotic fantasies, in spite of their indisputable reality, appear rather as material for comparison or as analogous pictures of something not understood as yet, than as independent desires. This seems to me the real reason of their being unconscious.'

There is a direct connection between the first statement concerning the doctor's (i.e. analyst's) rôle and the following (Jung, 1929, p. 72): 'Between doctor and patient, therefore, there are imponderable factors which bring about a *mutual transformation*'. As Jung sees it, the analyst's influence on the patient by virtue of his own psychic adaptations is inevitable, while in Freudian technique, Jung says, the analyst tries to 'ward off' the transference as much as possible. I quote: 'Hence the doctor's preference for sitting behind the patient, also his pretence that the transference is a product of his technique, whereas in reality it is a perfectly natural phenomenon that can happen to him just as it can happen to the teacher, the clergyman, the general practitioner, and—last but not least—the husband' (Jung, 1946, p. 171).

Since transference, like projection, is a spontaneous phenomenon it cannot possibly be 'demanded' by the analyst, and our attention is now drawn to the fact that it is the unconscious content that is transferred on to an object and then appears to be part of the latter, but ceases to be so (i.e. is taken back) at the moment at which the subject acknowledges the content as belonging to him. 'The projection ceases the moment it becomes conscious, that is to say when it is seen as belonging to the subject . . . It is indeed easy to show that the divine pair is simply an idealization of the parents or of some other human couple, which for some reason appeared in heaven. This assumption would be simple enough if projection were not an unconscious process but were a conscious intention . . . This can be seen most plainly in cases of transference where it is perfectly clear to the patient that the father-imago (or even the mother-imago) is projected on to the analyst and he even sees through the incest-fantasies bound up with them, without, however, being freed from the reactive effect of his projection, i.e., from the transference . . . We must therefore assume that, over and above the incest-fantasy, highly emotional contents are still bound up with the parental imagos and need to be made conscious. They are obviously more difficult to make conscious than the incest-fantasies, which are supposed to have been repressed through violent resistance and to be unconscious for that reason . . . '

'Someone once observed that in ordinary society it is more embarrassing to talk about God at table than to tell a risqué story. Indeed, for many people it is more bearable to admit their sexual fantasies than to be forced to confess that their analyst is a saviour . . . [The patient] may perhaps have no particular resistance to religious ideas, only the thought has never occurred to him that he could seriously regard his analyst as a God or saviour. Mere reason alone is sufficient to protect him from such illusions. But he is less slow to assume that his analyst thinks himself one' (Jung, 1954, pp. 60–61).

I have quoted rather extensively in order to illustrate the kind of evidence on which Jung's conclusion in *Psychology of the transference* (1946), was based, i.e., 'that the collective contents of an archetypal nature are the very essence of the transference' (p. 185). I presume it was this that was in his mind when he wrote to Löy in 1913 that 'infantile erotic fantasies, despite their undisputed reality, are analogous pictures of something not as yet understood, this . . . the real reason why they are unconscious' (Jung & Löy, 1914, p. 285). But before he felt himself able to substantiate and elaborate his early impressions, he had devoted much time and effort during the intervening thirty-three years to major researches into mythology and comparative religion. Aided by a wealth of clinical experience, he was then able to state his views on the transference. The following is an attempt to summarize some points of cardinal importance:

1. That the infantile sexual content of transference may conceal the patient's wish to get into intimate contact with the analyst. The feebler the rapport, i.e., the less doctor and patient understand each other, the more likely is sexuality to intervene by way of compensation (Jung, 1921, p. 134).

2. Some markedly sexual forms of transference conceal collective unconscious contents that defy all rational solution (Jung, 1946, p. 186n).

3. The symbolism (often based on sexual imagery) vested in transference phenomena is *one* of the most important means of transformation, i.e. development from an apparent to a real relationship (Jung, 1921, p. 136f).

Some Considerations from Practice

As we see, no detailed theory of neurosis emerges. Jung, throughout his writings, eschews anything that savours of a technique; the idea of a blue-print is abhorrent to him. On the other hand, he perceives and distinguishes certain recurring themes or dominants that emerge from the unconscious and are clearly recognizable, despite their innumerable individual variations. They constitute essential instruments for research as well as for therapy. In the absence of a theory of neurosis, and because Jung is so lacking in dogmatism, it is perhaps not surprising that there is no dissension among his followers over these fundamental concepts. On the other hand, even if one makes due allowance for the highly individual reactions between patient and analyst, it still begins to look as if two rival schools were coming into existence concerning the handling of transference phenomena.

To begin with, I should like to recall that in Jungian analysis, patient and analyst can see each other. This fundamental fact has far-reaching consequences on the transference situation, of which I can only mention one: the analyst is together with his patient in the analysis and therefore in the transference. He is exposed to the patient's projections, which can reach him like 'projectiles'. Despite all experience and awareness, he cannot help being affected by them. The physical situation in itself makes it clear that there can be no 'warding off', no 'blank screen' on either side and therefore also little need for the patient to 'unmask the analyst's professional hypocrisy', to use Ferenczi's phrase. The analyst is not barred from responding to the situation with his emotions. As these are touched anyhow, he need not pretend to himself that it is otherwise and he need not make any bones about it when the patient notices it.

When the content of the projected material springs from the patient's personal experience and is therefore near to consciousness, it will not be difficult for the analyst to remain *relatively* unaffected or for the patient to take these projections back, once they have been made fully conscious. It is, however, a different matter with projected archetypal images; they are not only accompanied by the intensest emotions, but are also irreducible to purely rational concepts. How then is the analyst to behave in the face of such difficulties, i.e. when such contents are projected on to him and when he becomes necessarily affected by them? The projected contents, be they gods, devils, demons or magicians, make human relations impossible. But 'What would be the good of explaining', Jung writes, 'that I am not in the least sinister, nor am I an evil magician! That would leave the patient quite cold, for he knows that as well as I do. The projection continues as before, and I really am the obstacle to his further progress. It is at this point that many a treatment comes to a standstill. There is no way of getting out of the toils of the unconscious except for the doctor . . . to acknowledge himself as an image' (Jung, 1917, p. 89).

At this point there arises the difference of opinion over the handling of the situation: while both schools of thought will recognize the transference, one will deal with it by a mainly educative procedure centred on the elucidation and differentiation of archetypal contents, while analysts of the other school will accept the projection in a wholehearted manner, making no *direct* attempt to help the patient sort out what belongs to him, what to the analyst and what to neither as well as to both. On the contrary, they will allow themselves to become this image bodily, to 'incarnate' it for the patient. I should like to add that the difference between the first and second school of thought in this matter does not consist in the timely interpretation of transference phenomena (i.e., neither too early to reduce intensity nor too late to prevent disruption of the analysis), but in a totally different attitude to the transferred image. It cannot be over-emphasized that the analyst incarnates the image *in response* to the transference situation over which he cannot exert any deliberate control, and the resultant situation has therefore nothing to do with a rôle-taking technique. It does, however, require a great deal of skill and integrity to achieve a position from which the analyst can undergo this incarnation in *comparative* safety.

Perhaps it would clarify matters if I pointed out some of the main dangers, as well as some of the requirements for this type of transference analysis:

1. Naturally, and first of all, the archetypal image that is transferred must be recognized and distinguished from the patient's conscious demands and his near-conscious personal experiences, memories, etc.

2. Because of the extraordinary attracting force or 'numen' inherent in an archetypal image, the analyst is in danger of becoming identified with it and may not recognize the danger, or, alternatively, he may sense the danger acutely and resist it. In neither case can he help the patient to achieve the desired disidentification from archetypal images or mythological motifs which—as hidden ruling forces—have no regard for the patient's welfare.

3. It follows that the analyst when incarnating such an image must be able to recognize the boundaries of his own ego as distinct from the non-ego or archetypal images.

Let us take the following representation as exemplifying what I mean. A patient insists that I am a remarkable teacher who can formulate her own confused views and thoughts in the most lucid manner. All associations and interpretations in terms of her personal history have been tried, and she now avoids expressing herself in quite the same words, showing what a good pupil she is, but the image and her feeling nevertheless persist. This makes it inevitable for me to compare what she believes with what I think I know about myself. I could then think: 'Oh, yes, there is quite a lot in what she says', and find it very agreeable. This would strengthen the bond with the animus image, with which I could then identify myself, and the analysis could stop on this very pleasant note. If, on the other hand, my reaction were to be: 'I am nothing of the kind and I loathe teachers anyhow', I should probably be inclined to express my non-acceptance by further interpretations, elucidations and—even a bit of teaching! But, whatever my personal likes and dislikes about the teacher—as animus figure—, I cannot deny that it has an archetypal or collective content and that, for this reason alone, it must have a place somewhere in my unconscious. So I had better wait and see where this transferred image impinges on my conscious ego, or, in other words, where the boundary lies. I can then become what the patient's unconscious insists I should be, or, in my own phrase, I can incarnate the image for her.

In case all this still sounds too simple and easy, I should like to add that the skill required can never be regarded as a possession of which one may be sure, but that it has to be re-learned with each case. I have come to regard a definite feeling of *reluctance* that assails me before finally allowing this incarnation to take its course as a reliable pointer to what will be required of me, and I think that this is what Jung is referring to when he says: 'Personally I am always glad when there is only a mild transference' (Jung, 1946, p. 172). Why then should one be willing to undergo this process at all, with all its dangers and difficulties? What is the object? Why should one not assist the patient in a more direct and obvious manner with explanations, etc.?

It is not at all easy to put the following into words, mainly because so much of this process cannot be directed and the dangers of over-simplification and distortion are considerable in trying to describe it. Moreover, the process has no pre-determined sequence and usually takes a long time. It is therefore with diffidence that I give the following summary.

After the analyst has been indistinguishable for the patient from the transferred archetypal image and its appropriate emotional valuations for a varying length of time, a certain 'subterranean undermining of the transference' (I am using Jung's phrase (1934, p. 131)) occurs. The patient now notices that the powerful image changes for him, not so much in appearance as in meaning and function. To put it differently: as his ego becomes stronger, so he is able to notice the symbol concealed within the image. For these concepts I must refer you back to the expositions of Drs Fordham and Moody. Once this process has been started the analyst emerges for the patient as a person, distinct from his archetypal and symbolic function. A kind of separation or differentiation has occurred between the analyst as a person and the function he has served. The fact that the patient can now distinguish between the two is, we presume, due to the development of a 'trans-personal control point' (this is Jung's term (1934, p. 231)), which frees him from personal over-valuations and assists him to discern his position between ego and non-ego or self. It is usually only from that moment onwards, i.e., when the, at first, almost imperceptible 'undermining of the transference' has begun, that the analyst can again assist with interpretations as he did earlier on, when much of the transferred material consisted of projections of personal, i.e., not archetypal, material.

So much for my summary. To refer back to my example: if I can allow myself to incarnate the animus without resistance and without identification on my part, this transference will— in the fullness of time—become undermined by a movement in the patient's unconscious. As this gathers momentum, some of the energy formerly linked to the animus image becomes freed and is now disposable, or, to put it another way, the animus can now serve her as a function rather than dictate to her. This describes the transforming process via the transference in barest outline.

There is, however, one distortion that I want to clear up before I finish. Most papers on transference leave the reader under the impression that the analyst knew all the time what was going on. I should not like to leave you under this impression. While there is an intense transference situation, one can, very often, only sort out afterwards what has happened. At the time the affect produced by the image is frequently far stronger than anyone's consciousness.

Finally, it would be misleading to give the impression that every case makes the demands I have tried to describe.

Individuation remains the goal, but not everyone travels the same distance on the road leading towards it.

The approach of the second school of thought shows some affinities to Rosen's 'Direct analysis' and Sechehaye's 'Symbolic realization'. If I am right in my assumption, i.e. that rival schools of thought are forming within the Jungian camp, I should regard this tendency as a sign of strength and growth.

References

JUNG, C. G. & LÖY, R. (1914). 'Some crucial points in psychoanalysis'. *Coll. wks.*, 4.
——(1917). 'Psychology of the unconscious'. *Coll. wks.*, **7.**
——(1921). The therapeutic value of abreaction. *Coll. wks.*, **16.**
——(1925). Seminars. Unpublished.
——(1929). 'Problems of modern psychotherapy'. *Coll. wks.*, **16.**
——(1946). 'Psychology of the transference'. *Coll. wks.*, **16.**
——(1954). 'Concerning the archetypes and the anima concept'. *Coll. wks.*, 9, 1.

Transference as creative illusion*

ANN CANNON

1968

Introduction

The startling effect of some interpretations, and the very ineffectiveness of others, made me think about the technique of analysis. One patient threw the furniture about when I pointed out how angry he was, while with another patient even the juiciest comments seemed to have no effect at all, and the analysis got stuck. Clinical papers tend to select dramatic episodes to highlight a conclusion, but this made me wonder what happens in the more humdrum daily flow of analysis. What is the aim of interpretation? Why say this rather than the other? And how account for change?

In the dramatic episodes of analysis the patient's fantasies come alive as it were, and get linked with the impulses that they mirror. Unconscious fantasy reflects instinctual wishes and impulses, and underlies conflict over such impulses. Conflicts over instinctual pressures at the crucial points of development give rise to anxiety, and the defences come into force as an attempt to deal with this anxiety. This is the psychoanalytic view, and Melanie Klein gives prominent place to conflict over aggressive impulses towards the breast as a fantasied inner object. In her view (Klein, 1952) it is fantasies about the consequences of a hungry attack on the mother's breast, and about the breast as a fantasied inner object, that give rise to anxiety in the infant and so to defences of a schizoid nature. Thus she stresses the primary rôle of fantasied inner objects in infantile conflict.

Accounts of Fantasy by Freudian and Jungian Schools

It is useful to be clear about the sense in which we are using the word fantasy. At first Freud located the origin of neurosis in an

* First published in the *Journal of analytical psychology*, 13, 2.

actual traumatic event, but this changed when he found the crux to be fantasies of such traumas in hysterical patients. The fantasies with which we are concerned are unconscious fantasies that may become conscious, and are to be distinguished from fantasies as day-dreams, or sexual wishes that may have become repressed. Fantasy in the sense of original unconscious mental content may or may not become conscious.

The recognition of the importance of unconscious fantasy is a central part of psychoanalytic discoveries. In an early paper, criticizing psychoanalysis, Jung said: 'The realm of unconscious fantasies has become the real object of psychoanalytic research for it seems to offer the key to the aetiology of neurosis' (1912, p. 139). A little later he comments on the remarkable connection of such fantasies with mythological themes.

The Kleinians' main concern has been with the operation of unconscious fantasy in young children, and the light it sheds on neurosis and borderline psychosis at all ages. In her paper 'The nature and function of phantasy', Susan Isaacs shows how the Kleinians ground their work on Freud. She says: 'A study of the conclusions arising from the analysis of young children leads to the view that phantasies are the primary content of unconscious mental processes' (1952, p. 82).

In the same paper, after stating the universality and central importance of fantasy for mental life, she shows how the Kleinian concern with fantasy is grounded on Freud's thought. She quotes from Freud. '" . . . everything conscious has an unconscious preliminary stage"' (Freud, 1900, p. 612). And: '"We suppose that it (the id) is somewhere in direct contact with somatic processes and takes over from them instinctual needs and gives them *mental expression*"' (Freud, 1933, p. 98.) (Isaacs, *op. cit.*, pp. 82–3.) (Her italics.)

Susan Isaacs goes on to say that this 'mental expression' is in fact unconscious fantasy, and as such it is the psychic representative of instinct. She says: 'A phantasy represents the particular content of the urges and feelings . . . dominating the mind at the moment. In early life there is indeed a wealth of unconscious phantasy which takes specific form in conjunction with the cathexis of particular bodily zones.' (Isaacs, *op. cit.*, pp. 83–4.)

In discussing fantasies centring on the bodily zones Michael Fordham refers to: ' . . . fantasies which are not differentiated from the physical experience. These fantasies are part of the preconscious system and must therefore express archetypes' (Fordham, 1957, p. 111).

This follows from the postulate that the archetype, with its instinctual base, will be expressed in bodily experience and in images. Here in infancy the impulses are powerful and the archetypal image or fantasy correspondingly strong. These are the fantasies with which the Kleinian school is concerned; they are the instinctual pressures writ large. The difference between the two schools here lies in the frame of reference rather than in any disagreement about the observed facts. Archetypal fantasy can be understood as part of a development which is released under instinctual pressure, and which has the function of giving form to the instinctual experience, while Melanie Klein is concerned with the origins of the conflict to which these pressures give rise, expressed in unconscious fantasy of a powerful kind.

Significance of Making Fantasies Come Alive

If these fantasies are directly related to conflict about impulses, a crucial aspect of technique is to make them live, in the sense of connecting with the impulses as well as becoming conscious. This can only be done effectively and safely within the transference. The patient first experiences fantasy, then the affects, wishes and impulses that go with it, and thus he gradually becomes aware of its origin. The guiding light is the patient's fantasies, which are reflected onto the analyst and he becomes the catalyst.

Thus the technique of analysis has two aspects; it involves drawing out the unconscious fantasy, with its attendant feelings and impulses, and then relating these experiences to their roots in childhood. The task is to let the fantasies come alive so that the patient experiences the fear, pain, anger, the impulses to hit and suck, which have lain split off. Thus fantasy becomes real and is linked to the impulse that it mirrors.

Reaching the source of the fantasy in wish or impulse, and the conflict over them, is what I shall call for short 'making the fantasy live'. This is to distinguish 'knowing about it' from the fuller 'knowing and feeling it'. It is this aspect of technique that calls for a particular art from the analyst, in entering the

163

patient's fantasy world. It is this aspect of analysis with which I am specially concerned here, bringing the fantasy alive so as to link it with the wishes and impulses from which it sprang, and these to their roots in childhood. Stage two, that of discrimination, is where these fantasies, feelings and impulses are linked with their childhood roots; this latter is usually thought of as interpretation in the strict sense.

A reductive interpretation cannot be given all at once, partly because of the need to work through defences and partly because, as a link with the early life and instinctual experience of the patient that are still alive in him, fantasy needs to be granted its own validity. It needs to become real before any connection with the past can be effectively made.

A fragment from the analysis of the patient who will be our main concern will illustrate this. Her lover came irregularly and when he did not turn up she was extremely depressed, but in a controlled way for she could not show any outward reaction. I tried connecting this with the time when she was an infant and her mother did not come, but without effect. I also interpreted her fears of rejection in terms of her own wish to push her lover away when he treated her like this.

This interpretation of the defence was of no use. Then one day when she was depressed and silent I put into words her unexpressed fantasy, and said 'So he'll never come any more'. At this she wept a little—the fantasy had come alive. Of her own accord she then made connections with the past, and recalled more about the time when her mother did not come when she cried. The living link had been touched at last, the fantasy connected with 'the cathexis of particular bodily zones' in her early life.

At one time I was so taken with the importance of making the fantasy come alive that I did not realize that it was important not to be dazzled by the startling effects of a symbolic experience in analysis. It may crystallize a development, or open up the way to further analytic work, but it is also the outcome of or preliminary to long work on the defences and the roots of conflict. Technique may be thought of as consisting of two parts: first the bringing to life of the dominant fantasies, secondly the reduction of these, relating the fantasies and affects to their childhood roots.

Jung makes a distinction between a reductive analysis and

synthesis. Reductive analysis he describes as Freud's work, while synthesis he uses to describe the conflict and fusion of two opposed forces and the new third that emerges from the tension of opposites (Jung, 1928). He is primarily concerned with synthesis. The distinction between reductive analysis and synthesis arose because Jung was less concerned with the ego and its defences than with the way the archetype gives form to unconscious wish and impulse. But this serves to overlook the extent to which the defences themselves are full of archetypal fantasy, so that any reductive interpretation of the defences has to do with archetypal material. To make a distinction between reductive analysis and synthesis is to overlook the way in which analysis works. If the fantasy is made to live, this both serves to relate it to the unconscious conflict, with its origin in the past, and at the same time prepares the way for change as the ego can relate to the feared impulses as they are experienced in the transference.

Fantasy is not haphazard, but is connected with conflict centring on the growing-points of personality. If the mother does not adapt herself well enough to the infant's needs, the personality of the child remains in part bound by unconscious fantasy related to the areas of frustration. The fantasy gives the form and attitude to the elements of the conflict. The task of the analyst is to get near the source of the conflict by eliciting the fantasy that draws near the surface of consciousness when the patient is regressed. Then he can know something of his unconscious wishes and impulses, and start to distinguish between inner and outer reality. It gives him a chance gradually to sort out his fears about his mother and what she was like, and to recognize that present anxieties and feelings, which still stir him so powerfully, may well have to do with long past experience. In this way the underlying conflict becomes accessible.

Case Material

I want to illustrate the importance of making the fantasy live, as a means of contact with the impulses so feared by the ego, and some of the difficulties in practice. The patient already referred to may be taken as an example, since her rigid defences, with the consequent difficulty of letting any unconscious fantasy come to the surface, will serve as the extreme to point the rule. In his paper, 'The criteria for interpretation in patients with obsessional traits', Libermann (1966) discusses the problem of approaching unconscious fantasy and the difficulty of getting access to an obsessional patient while he remained defended against depressive anxiety. He discusses the part played by dissociation as an attempt to deny damage and danger, the danger of what the patient's envy might do to the analyst. My patient had considerable obsessional defences, keeping everything under control by blocking or not feeling anything in response to what I said. She kept me off, and fended off her depressive anxiety.

She appeared rather normal, positive and full of life outside the analysis, and worked with children, which she enjoyed and was very good at, but she had difficulties in intimate relationships. With me she was at first silent and depressed in a quiet way, always rather 'good' and polite. There was plenty of material, memories and associations, to fill in the pattern of childhood conflict. Interpretations showing the connection with childhood could be made, but they simply went into her head and were drained of all affect. She would say in effect: 'I see that—so what?'

Unless fantasy could be made to live, interpretation was useless because it was stopped by her defences. Indeed, interpretation, in the strict sense of making links with her childhood, seemed to reinforce her intellectual defence against experience of the underlying affect. For, as she told me, to hear me make the connections with mother and childhood was sometimes a reassurance against what she felt as reality, namely that she was unwanted by me or by her lover. It seemed as if interpretations at this point only served to cover over her deepest fears.

The essential connection between the transference and making the fantasy live was brought home to me by this patient. There was little overt transference and she remained quite self-contained, neither taking much in from me, nor letting much out. She could neither feed nor eliminate nor cry about me. She had been with me for a number of years at the time of the episode I shall relate, but she persistently denied all transference affects, though there were plenty of signs of them. She said she did not care if I went on holiday—it was just part of the calendar of events—yet she was markedly more silent the few days before I went.

She rarely made any personal comments, and what went on in my house was never remarked on. If I challenged her on this, she said other people's comings and goings need not intrude on the analytical relationship, and she felt I wanted to keep it like that for her sake. I wondered about this pseudo-normality—obsessional undoing and hysterical denial one might say—yet she was more depressive in her long silences, which must conceal unbearable infantile feelings.

Implicit in her defences was a fantasy of me as neutral and uncaring. This was expressed in her comment that what went on in other aspects of my life was irrelevant to her, and that as an analyst I was merely there to reflect or comment in a neutral way on what she said. At one point she told me she had felt at the start that people 'are supposed to have a transference, so I will take care that doesn't happen'. I pointed out that she had not managed to avoid this, only hers was the so-called negative transference—just what she had felt towards her mother.

Her attitude to me was a transference illusion of a destructive kind, attributing to me her mother's attitude of 'doing the right thing' by her, without caring. This was in part a projection of her own uncaring attitude, for on the surface at any rate she was polite, cool and indifferent.

Underlying these defences there was a deep depressive anxiety. Her long silences, which often concealed hopeless feelings, stemmed from despair that there was no food for her. Much later she could say this openly, but at this time she rejected all interpretations directed at this area.

My more juicy interpretations she simply ignored. I would say that I thought she kept me at a distance out of fear that she would want to attack me hungrily if she came near, to which she would say nothing, but would start up another, more innocuous subject, some ten minutes later. She took little in, not saying a great deal, nor following up what I said—it was as if she could neither feed nor eliminate.

She felt my comments were like pebbles falling into a pond and often she had 'nothing to say'. She held my remarks in her mouth till 'after a decent interval' she could dispose of them. She agreed that this phrase referred to mourning, but there was no awareness of her hostility as such. Having killed off a comment of mine, she would start again after an interval with some mild remark, just as she kept her mother off with a false front and made harmless chatter to her.

It seemed she was cut off from me and rebuffed me stonily as if I were her mother. She understood this, but nothing changed. She felt there was no interchange between us. She began to tell me that my comments were routine, not specifically for her. She felt I just 'did my duty' by her as an analyst, just as her mother 'did the right thing' by her without really caring, and was satisfied only if she did not 'make a nuisance' of herself.

However, one break in this picture of self-sufficiency was bed-wetting in childhood. It was as if at night she secretly wept for her mother and attacked her with her tears, while by day she was cut off by what was felt as her mother's rejection and her own stony response. It was noticeable that for years she did not use my lavatory. Now small signs of hostility to me, picking holes in what I said, indicated a loosening-up, and some time before the episode I shall describe she used my lavatory for the first time.

For a long time she could not take much in or let much out. She denied any wish to be fed, and said she had 'never thought of analysis as a feeding situation'. But once on leaving me she bought and ate a box of chocolates, and she would sometimes start thinking of her next meal during a session. I said she turned away from me as if I was not there because she felt I was enjoying my own food and not feeding her. She replied with a comment from one of her children; the child had said one could be happy if one knew there was something to be happy about. This confirmed she had taken in what I said, and I replied that she felt she could be happy if she knew my breast was there to feed from. But this was too much for her. She retorted: 'I don't see what that has got to do with it', and complained at my 'making it so physical'.

It was only later that she could tolerate my interpreting her fear that her hostile attacks had destroyed any good food there might have been for her—what she felt unconsciously had happened with her mother. She had been told of a terrible rage she had had as an infant with her mother, but had no conscious memory of it. As a child she had never dared be openly angry, and especially not with her mother, who had a hot temper when roused.

At one stage her work load became less, and occasion offered for an increase in sessions from three to five a week, and to have them just after lunch. It was after lunch that her mother would invite her to sit on her lap, and she remembered sitting there rigidly, which I interpreted as fear of wetting. Now I began to notice that I was getting really quite angry with her, and it occurred to me to make use of this. I was also helped in this by my patient. She remarked that in dealing with children she had to show endless patience with the so-called 'good' child, but sometimes a bit of warm anger helped. So next time I felt angry with her blocking and niggling at me, I raised my voice and said: 'Why can't you shit—lying there like a dumb cluck!'

This surprised me almost as much as it did her—'mustn't smack patients', my ideal analyst commented—but it had striking results. She told me the next day she had felt furious with me in a helpless way she had not experienced for years; the last time must have been when she was a baby. For the first time she was aware that she hated me. She had been considering ending the analysis, but when asked later that day if she would be ending soon, she was surprised to hear herself replying tartly, 'What makes you think that?'

She felt things were starting to move at last, and at the session directly after this we had a good interchange for almost the first time. She took in what I said, made use of it, amplified it and gave me more material to go on. She said with longing in her voice that her mother had never smacked her, but that it would have been nice if she had taken that much interest in her.

When she felt that I, as it were, gave her a warm slap on the bottom, this made contact directly with her hostile impulses and her infantile rage. She felt I had been nasty and this had released her anger, making it possible for her to be nasty too. The image of the so-called good mother with the corresponding image of the falsely good daughter was now openly shifted.

It was as if I had fulfilled her fearful wish to have me approach her shit-anger which she dared not let out. For the moment I was felt as hateful, yet taking enough interest in her to have a go at her. She said her mother would threaten to 'wipe the floor' with her sister, and this saying appeared as a dreadful yet attractive threat. She had a wish to wipe me out which she lived in the way she wiped out what I said, but at the same time she felt isolated with her hostile impulses, and was almost inviting me to behave like her mother. Slapping her in a token way fulfilled her longing for me to get close to her and her bad impulses.

Discussion

In the paper already mentioned Libermann discusses the question of reaching unconscious fantasies and says that obsessional patients frequently have fantasies of dirt and chaos, and of damage and loss. The typical dissociation serves to deny the danger of the damage the patient's envy might be felt to do. This dissociation, he says, leaves the patient feeling an isolated infant, having to deal with his faeces by himself. This corresponds to my patient's sense of isolation with me.

Libermann says the most opportune moment for an interpretation is when there is a shift in the defences, as was happening with my patient, and the only chance for the patient really to listen to the analyst is when the fantasies are related to in a direct and personal way. Only then can the patient take in what is said and start to integrate the split-off parts of himself that contain the depressive experiences.

A benign illusion with far-reaching effects is described by Frieda Fordham (1964) in her account of the hungry patient who could not get enough. I would have wished to feed my patient in this way, feeling her withdrawn and deprived, but this was my counter-transference. I was also well aware of her hostility. Her problem was not then one of extreme hunger, but an inability to feed or eliminate out of fear of her hostility. Her immediate need was for contact in another area, focusing the hostility that was cut off, and it was left to me to respond to this. She needed to feel as it were a warm slap and thus to feel it was not too dangerous to come nearer. Soon after her rage she recalled, for almost the first time, some good memories of her mother. Contact had been made in this episode and the blockage was removed, temporarily at least, as the analysis went on with greater ease. She began to make comments about me and the objects in my room, was less polite and got in little digs.

She had often recalled how she sat on her mother's lap, rigid, after meals, and she would lie rigid on the couch. I had interpreted this without effect. Now I said that when she was silent she wanted to sit on my lap and feed, but was afraid of her wish to eliminate on me, and this she took in. She then recalled a good incident—sometimes she had sat on her mother's lap and had enjoyed it. This was when she had climbed there of her own accord, and not when she felt her mother was 'trying to do her good' and she had to please her. Not long after this she was able to curl up under my rug during a session as if snuggling up.

The episode described made her less defended, though it did not get to the root of her depressive anxieties. She talked more readily, was more capable of spite, sometimes was warmer, and gradually came to deal better with her relation to her lover. With this awareness of an increasing strength of ego, she began, more than two years after this episode, to look to the end of her analysis, and the sessions, which had come down to four, were now reduced to two a week. It was only then that she was able to become openly depressed with me, and to despair at how relatively little her defences had given, how she had not let go more or let me come nearer.

When I said she could be sad with me now she was thinking of leaving me, she expressed her despair by saying 'You can't be sad at what you've never had'. This at last put into words her despair at what she felt was the self-destructiveness of her defences, which had made it seem safer to deny I had anything good for her than to risk it being destroyed.

This was the underlying depressive anxiety, that her hostile impulses meant my breast got destroyed, often as soon as she arrived, so there could be no food for her. This was connected both with her mother coming too late when she cried as a baby, and with an actual separation that she had recently been told of. As she worked through this, she alternated between bitterness and anger, and sadness that she had so often kept me off.

I pointed out that she had been able to make use of me all right, having me as her rejecting mother so as to get at her own despair and indifference, at the ruthless and hopeless infant inside her, which she could not cope with otherwise. Next time she said this had made a difference in the way she felt; indeed it seemed to reach her guilt. In the following sessions she talked in a more friendly and easier way than ever before. Soon after, she dreamed she was pregnant, and at once connected this with the baby she would soon have to look after by herself.

Creative Illusion and Change

This episode made me reflect on what makes for change. If a main problem of technique is to make the fantasy come alive, how is this connected with change? There is some enactment in analysis, recalling the old traumatic situation in a new environment, but this in itself is not necessarily productive of change. The conflict often dates years back and the past as such cannot be re-lived; the patient cannot become an infant again literally.

In order to become aware of the areas of conflict, the past has to be lived through in all its depth of feeling, and experienced as both now and not-now. Then a link can be made between the feared wishes and impulses and their infantile origins, which can become conscious.

The classic account is given in the early case histories of Freud, of little Hans (1909a) and of the Rat Man (1909b), and in Jung's account (1910) of the little girl Anna. Here the important thing is to become conscious of the conflict and, as in the paper on the Rat Man, to recollect memories associated with it, so that it may be traced to its origin. Consciousness by itself is not enough, however, and his discovery of the importance of the defences led Freud to recognize the need for working through the resistances in the transference. He says:

'The aim . . . has, of course, remained the same. Descriptively speaking, it is to fill in gaps in memory; dynamically speaking, it is to overcome the resistance due to repression.' (1914, p. 148). And again:

One must allow the patient time to become more conversant with this resistance . . . , to 'work through' it, to overcome it, by continuing in defiance of it the analytic work according to the fundamental rule of analysis. Only when the resistance is at its height can the analyst, working in common with his patient, discover the repressed instinctual impulses which are feeding the resistance; and it is this kind of experience which convinces the patient of the existence and power of such impulses (*ibid.*, p. 155).

However, working through had not sufficed with my patient, and at the right moment a creative illusion proved the only way to dissolve part of the resistance and enable reductive interpretation to be tolerated.

In the transference fantasies are experienced at their strongest. Here we witness all the defence phenomena, splitting, projection, denial, dissociation. The patient attributes to the analyst all that is felt as unacceptable or unobtainable, and this can be interpreted. However, the transference may retain its tenacity for long periods despite interpretation, or the time may not have come to interpret certain aspects, or as with my patient it may resist interpretation.

Thus interpretation is not the whole story; it is as if the patient needs to regress and to experience these fantasies in all their strength in relation to the analyst before change can take place. The feared impulses and split-off aspects of personality cannot be integrated until they are experienced in the transference, where they can come alive. There may be a powerful illusion reflecting aggressive wishes in relation to the analyst, or there may be a fantasy of destruction leading to extensive blocking and holding off the analyst.

When fantasy comes alive it is tested against the reality of the analyst's person and presence, and so can help in placing the conflict where it belongs; as such it is a part of working through as described by Freud. He says (*op. cit.*, p. 154): 'The transference thus creates an intermediate region between illness and real life, through which transition from the one to the other is made'.

Freud's stress on the reductive aspects of analysis has been modified in an important respect by the Kleinians, since they lay greater stress on the importance of relating to the unconscious fantasy first. This is perhaps because they are often dealing with patients more ill than Freud felt suitable for analysis. The Kleinians are more inclined to give fantasies a run for their money, as it were, to see what is contained in them.

Winnicott emphasizes how they may operate as a bridge to reality in early life. Speaking of the importance of the mother's care, he stresses the way the infant can use illusion to relate to its first object, the breast. This illusion is, he says: ' . . . un- challenged in respect of its being created by the infant or accepted as a piece of perceived reality' (1958a, p. 224). He adds: 'We allow the infant this madness', and it seems patients are allowed something of the same sort when fantasies come alive so powerfully that for a moment or for a while their status is left open. Winnicott develops this idea in his account of the transitional object (1958b).

It is the awful isolation of such patients left alone with their fantasies that is the problem, and a creative illusion of some sort has to take place before reductive interpretations can be tolerated. Regression within the transference creates the conditions for experiencing the feared impulses as if still an infant, in a safe situation. This is the point at which the patient's fantasies may have a status that is not fixed. As Winnicott puts it, it is an open question whether they are delusion or illusion.

The purpose of such a proceeding is illustrated by Marion Milner (1955). She questions the classical Freudian concept of the transference with its attendant illusions, as simply a defence to be interpreted, and she introduces the concept of a benign illusion. She describes a boy who had lost interest in school, and how this was connected with his anxiety about his aggres- sion. His play showed great omnipotence. She interpreted his aggression towards her, but it remained intractable.

Then she began to be aware of his need to make a creative illusion of his toys and of her. The omnipotence and aggression began to lessen only when she sensed his need to fuse with her, to have her as his malleable stuff—first as his bad stuff, his faeces, and then as his lovely stuff. She says: 'When I began to see . . . that this use of me might be not only a defensive regression, but an essential recurrent phase in the development of a creative relation to the world, then the whole character of the analysis changed' (Milner 1955, p. 105). Then the boy could start to let her exist in her own right.

Marion Milner says that the origin of the difficulty was that the boy had had to face the distinction between internal and external reality too early, with too sudden an ending of the illusion of oneness with the mother. Though my patient's history was different, I was reminded of Marion Milner's comment about a too sudden ending of the illusion of oneness with the mother when faced with her omnipotence and implacable hostility, and I recalled her account of how at an early age she felt she must get on without her mother—exactly her attitude to me.

She was rational and controlling, and though she was aware of her fear of regressing she felt unable to let it happen. She was held in the illusion that I was 'out to do her good' and did not really care about her. But after the illusion of a warm contact she attacked me more freely and made more personal remarks. It was as if she was beginning to use me as 'her stuff', since I was capable of a bit of anger. Then she curled up under the rug as if she had found the lap of the good mother. It was clear my earlier interpretations were felt as separating forces, rousing her anxiety, while now she was less afraid of her hostile impulses.

Conclusion

When the fantasy is lived in the transference, the sorrow and pain, fear, anger and bliss are felt in their full depth in relation to the analyst, who is thus drawn into the patient's inner reality as good or bad object.

At the same time there is another reality that may impinge on the patient in more or less degree as he is ready for it; this is the analyst's presence and reactions. This may be poignant, as first experienced with the mother and yet so long ago, and in the first instance it may be enough for the analyst to share it. The second stage, the opportunity for fantasy and reality to be sorted out, occurs as the analyst is felt to be the origin of the grief or rage, and yet is seen not as the origin but friendly enough. Finally, the links with childhood may be made in so many words.

Only when inner reality is at last given its due can a proper distinction be made between inner and outer reality, between fantasies about the mother and how she actually was. Early on it had been difficult for my patient to tolerate her feelings about her mother when everyone said what a good and worthy mother she was, and with this fearful guilt over her hostility her false self grew. Later it was painful to her when she began to realize she was treating me with the same cold hostility as her mother. But until the patient's inner reality is given its due there can be no understanding of his own difficulties, or of anyone else's point of view.

It was only much later than the main episode described that my patient was able to say how depressed her mother must have been and what an unresponsive child she must have been for her. Only when his own fantasies have been taken for real can the patient start to take back what has been projected, and both forgive the damage done and grieve for his own destructiveness. When he can experience his own reality and know, in part at least, what is outer reality, he experiences relief.

This experiencing of the thing as a whole, with the guilt and anxiety falling away, is a sign of a synthesizing process. Synthesis follows on the two main stages of analysis; first, fantasies and affects that were cut off from the rest of the personality come alive and, secondly, reductive interpretation helps to make this conscious. With this coming together of conscious and unconscious there is relief, and the possibility of further development.

The importance of a creative illusion lies in aiding synthesis, and this is because of the very nature of unconscious fantasy, which is a living connection with the early growth and experience of the patient. When fantasy becomes alive, the instinctual roots are touched, as when the fantasy coming alive in my patient enabled her to experience an infant's rage. The ego is strengthened when this connection is made, and there is a chance for further development. For fantasies reflecting instinctual conflict, when made conscious and reduced to their origins, would be expected to give way to other more ego-congruent fantasies, reflecting further instinctual development, as the conflict is resolved. This accords with the theory of archetypal function, and the operation of the self in a releasing growth, provided the ego can relate to it. This is illustrated by my patient's dream of pregnancy, which she at once recognized as referring to her own situation and enabled her to contemplate quite calmly the prospect of leaving me.

The elucidation of fantasy not only serves to increase the area of consciousness and to strengthen the ego, but it also aids the release of further growth, with further unconscious but perhaps more ego-related fantasies. Fantasy so released offers the link with the cut-off instinctual life. Jung makes this point when he says we cannot do without the gods, or pretend they are not there, but we can take steps to attend to what they are up to in our unconscious. The purpose of analysis is to help the ego to relate to the conflict expressed in unconscious fantasy, to wrest the power from the archetype and to release the ego's capacity for growth from the point at which it was held.

References

FORDHAM, F. (1964). 'The care of regressed patients and the child archetype', *J. analyt. Psychol.*, **9**, 1.

FORDHAM, M. (1957). 'Origins of the ego in childhood'. In *New developments in analytical psychology*. London, Routledge & Kegan Paul.

FREUD, S. (1900). 'The interpretation of dreams'. *Standard edition*, **4–5**.

——(1909a). 'Analysis of a phobia in a five-year-old boy'. *Standard edition*, **10**.

——(1909b). 'Notes upon a case of obsessional neurosis'. *Standard edition*, **10**.

——(1914). 'Recollection, repetition and working through'. *Standard edition*, **12**.

——(1933). 'New introductory lectures'. Hogarth Press. *Standard edition*, **22**.

ISAACS, S. (1952). 'The nature and function of fantasy'. In *Developments in psychoanalysis*. Riviere, J. (ed.), London, Hogarth.

JUNG, C. G. (1910). 'Psychic conflicts in a child'. In *Coll. wks.*, **4**.

——(1912). 'The theory of psychoanalysis'. In *Coll. wks.*, **4**.

——(1928). 'On psychic energy'. In *Coll. wks.*, **8**.

KLEIN, M. (1952). 'Notes on some schizoid mechanisms', Riviere, J. (ed.), *Developments in psychoanalysis*. London, Hogarth.

LIBERMANN, D. (1966). 'The criteria for interpretation in patients with obsessional traits', *Int. J. Psycho-Anal.*, **47**, 212–217.

MILNER, M. (1955). 'The role of illusion in symbol formation'. In *New directions in psychoanalysis*. Klein, M., Heimann, P. and Money-Kyrle, R. E. (eds.), London, Tavistock.

WINNICOTT, D. W. (1958a). 'Psychoses and child care'. In *Collected Papers*.

——(1958b). 'Transitional objects and transitional phenomena'. In *Collected Papers*. London, Tavistock/New York, Basic Books.

Transference as a fulcrum of analysis*

ROSEMARY GORDON

1968

This paper will be concerned primarily with a discussion of the place and the function of transference analysis, and with the exploration of the parallels between the analyst's concept of human relationships—based as it is on the studies of the analytical process—and those of Martin Buber. I intend to show in this paper that the exploration of the transference that the analyst undertakes together with his patients has really as its goal a shift in the character and quality of a person's relationships away from the 'I-It' towards the 'I-Thou' attitude, as these have been defined by Buber. The parallel to which I shall point in this paper should not, of course, mislead the reader to assume that the theories of Jung and Buber are at all points closely related. On the contrary, there are very many important differences between them, but in the area of the evaluation of human relationships the correspondences seem to me worth noting and exploring.

Jung, in his paper entitled 'The therapeutic value of abreaction', which he published in the *British journal of psychology* in 1921 and which now forms part of volume 16 of the *Collected works*, discusses the origin and the function of transference in analysis as follows (I shall quote from it fairly extensively, since it is very pertinent to my theme):

> The transference phenomenon is an inevitable feature of every thorough analysis, for it is imperative that the doctor should get into the closest possible touch with the patient's line of psychological development. One could say that in the same measure as the doctor assimilates the intimate psychic contents of the patient into himself, he is in turn assimilated

* First published in the *Journal of analytical psychology*, 13, 2.

178

as a figure into the patient's psyche. I say 'as a figure', because I mean that the patient sees him not as he really is, but as one of those persons who figures so significantly in his previous history.

The transference therefore consists in a number of projections which act as a substitute for a real psychological relationship. They create an apparent relationship and this is very important, since it comes at a time when the patient's habitual failure to adapt has been artificially intensified by his analytical removal into the past.

Once the projections are recognized as such, the particular form of rapport known as the transference is at an end, and the problem of individual relationship begins.

The touchstone of every analysis that has not stopped short at partial success, or come to a standstill with no success at all, is always this person-to-person relationship, a psychological situation where the patient confronts the doctor upon equal terms, and with the same ruthless criticism that he must inevitably learn from the doctor in the course of his treatment.

Before embarking on a general discussion I should first like to quote a summary of Buber's ideas regarding relationships, written by a Christian theologian, John MacQuarrie (1963, p. 196).

> There are two primary attitudes which man may take up to the world and these attitudes express themselves in two primary words, or rather combination of words: 'I-It' and 'I-Thou'. There is no 'I' taken in itself apart from a combination with an 'It' or a 'Thou'. The 'I' which is present in the speaking of the two primary word-combinations is, moreover, different in each case. The primary word 'I-Thou' can *only* be spoken with the whole being. The primary word 'I-It' can *never* be spoken with the whole being.

This passage points, I think, to most important and thought-provoking affinities with Jung.

The concept of transference as projection (viz. Jung, 'Two essays on analytical psychology', p. 62n) seems to have been accepted from early on by both Freud and Jung. More recently this definition has been further elaborated by Michael Fordham in his paper on 'Transference and its management in child analysis' (1963), when he defined transference as a special kind of relationship. He described it there as 'the projection of split-off or unintegrated parts of the patient onto or into the analyst. Projection being an unconscious process, the parts later seen in the analyst are therefore first unconscious.'

Transference is therefore thought of as above all character-ized by the fact that the perception of another person is determined primarily, not by that other person, but by the inner situation of the percipient—by his experiences, expecta-tions, complexes, fantasies, feelings, etc.

However, it is now generally accepted that all perceptions, and in particular the perceptions that men have of one another, are an amalgam of a reaction to a 'real' person, out there, *plus* the projection upon him of the perceiver's internal complexes, conflicts, expectations and of the *dramatis personae* that have been built up in the course of his own personal history and emotional development. For the sake of clarity I would suggest that we designate it as a 'true' relationship when awareness of the 'other' is formed, predominantly, by the facts of the real person out there, while in a transference relationship the pressures of the internal needs create distortions that do violence to the existence and to the wholeness of that other person.

The analyst in the 1960s can no longer question whether or not transference exists, whether or not it is a valuable concept or that it must be central in the analytic work. That is now taken for granted. But what does concern him is the whole problem of how to increase the understanding of the roots of the transference phenomenon and of its manifestations and of how to develop ever more refined and efficient techniques that will then help him use these discoveries in the service of the patient's recovery and growth. It is concern with these particu-lar clinical and therapeutic problems that raises such issues of whether, what and when an interpretation of a transference situation should be made to the patient and what forms such interpretations should take.

It is, I think, justifiable to claim—and it would indeed be sad evidence of passivity and stagnation if we could not—that analysts today possess more detailed and accurate knowledge of the transference than was available in the lifetime of the pioneers, Freud and Jung. We now have access to many clinical case studies; much information has been gathered through the development of child analysis; cross-fertilization has resulted from collaboration with workers from different disciplines or different schools of thought. All this has contributed a great deal to our knowledge of the experiences of childhood, what effects they may have, what defence mechanisms exist and how they may be deployed, and what personality patterning can result when historical situations are sifted through the filter of internal fantasy systems. Consequently we might expect that our methods of analysing the transference relationship between analyst and patient have become increasingly sensitive and perceptive.

Adjoining the development of transference analysis is the whole topic of the analyst's counter-transference; that is, the analyst's feelings in relation to the patient: hence each analyst must constantly ask himself whether what he feels in relation to the patient stems from his own still unconscious and unintegrated conflicts or whether it is a necessary and matching reaction to the unconscious drama the patient needs to re-enact. And he must decide whether to communicate to the patient his own emotional reactions and, if so, in what form and when. Fordham (1957) has written at some considerable length about the problem of the counter-transference but a discussion of this topic goes beyond the scope of this short paper.

Once transference has been truly recognized as the fulcrum, as the central focus of the work of analysis, then the analyst offers to his patient both his knowledge of the dynamics of the psyche and also himself, as a person who is willing to carry, and even to incarnate, his patient's projections. He does this and yet keeps all the time intact his rôle of observer of what is going on and also keeps in touch with his own personal and essential reality as he knows it from inside himself. As a result of these complex transference transactions, the patient may get to know the personages that inhabit him; experiencing these internal personages in and through the analyst may then help him to differentiate himself from them. This will then increase his capacity to relate to the new and to the real persons he meets in his world *now*.

Analysis of the transference—in other words the observation and the interpretation of the unconscious themes as these are experienced in the relationship to the person of the analyst—re-creates in the analysis all the turmoils of the patient's actual life problems. But this happens in a context in which the affective encounter of the person of the analyst with the person of the patient helps to differentiate the past from the present and the inner-world figures from the external ones. Such concentration of the analytic work on the actual emotional transactions between patient and analyst is likely to discourage the former from using the analysis either as an escape route into cogitation about his past or else as a sort of non-participant observation of his internal fantasy systems.

How the analyst can helpfully enter and participate in these inner world dramas has been well described recently by Dorothy Davidson (1966) in her paper on 'Transference as a form of active imagination'. Active imagination was regarded by Jung as a process through which a person enters consciously into the happening of a fantasy and takes part in its development, reacting to this fantasy and yet allowing complete autonomy to the fantasy images. Dorothy Davidson suggests that the transference/counter-transference relationship between patient and analyst is in fact an enactment, in the here and now, of the unconscious drama in which the patient has been held prisoner.

Transference analysis can, therefore, be thought of as 'lived-through' active imagination; that is to say, the active imagination is carried on—not within a person, between his ego and one or more unconscious complexes—but between one person and another, that is the patient and his analyst. And, one might add, as the drama unfolds and is brought to some sort of resolution, the analyst becomes progressively freed from the limitations of having to fill one or two rôles only, and instead becomes increasingly acknowledged as the person he is.

Case Material

To give a short example: a patient, a man of 32, became extremely disturbed, angry and hostile whenever the problem of money was touched on. He had been married for five years to a woman who brought two children from a previous marriage. They had one child together. His analysis was paid for in part by an uncle on the understanding that sooner or later he might be able to pay for all of it himself. He had worked in the family business for a time but then lectured in the evenings to adult education classes. He also wrote poetry and short stories and began to publish while in analysis. Though quietly spoken and having an air of vagueness about him he had, in fact, a lot of energy. But he seemed to need me to look on him as 'inadequate', 'ineffectual' and 'poverty-stricken', a useless person, ignorant, uncouth and helpless. In contrast to him I was thought of as infinitely rich, as quite unable even to imagine what it is like to be poor, and as ruthless in my implicit demand that he should earn more money so that he might contribute more to the cost of his analysis.

Obviously the problem of money carried enormous symbolic significance and was the focus of a great many deeply-experienced conflicts. One reason why these seemed to have constellated themselves around the theme of money was the historical fact that this was the ever-recurrent theme of his parents' rows. He described his mother as a quiet, withdrawn woman who felt that but for her marriage she might have carved out for herself a career as a singer or a novelist. She had brought most of the money into the family but was excessively mean with it. His father could earn only a moderate amount, but as a person was more dominant and ebullient.

The patient was the second of four boys. There were no girls. He remembered that he and his brothers seemed often to be used as a reason for the parents' arguments because the money for their education could be provided only by his mother. He felt that mother might have thought of it all as 'the males ganging up on her' and wanting all her money for themselves; but that it might have been different had he been a girl, which he thought his mother wanted him to be. His envy of women was in fact expressed in periodic aggressive outbursts against his wife.

Thus the rage, hostility and the sense of being victimized, which he experienced in his relationship to me whenever money emerged as the major theme, was a partial enactment of the parental quarrels, which he witnessed with much fear. He enacted them with me, I think, because they became a valid expression of his own conflicts concerning envy, greed, omnipotence, passivity and the longing to make a baby.

Most of the time I felt myself to be experienced as if I were the attractive and rich but mean mother, whom he desperately wanted to seduce and whose resistance to his seduction he felt as evidence of a mean lack of care and concern. But when actual money matters came to be discussed in the session, then, so it seemed to me, I became the greedy, demanding father who had deprived mother of her true vocation.

Only after several years of analysis, during which time the emergence of the money theme had led nearly always to a markedly delusional transference, did the patient begin to differentiate himself—and me—from the quarrelling parents inside him. And as this differentiation developed and became more certain so he became progressively able to earn more money by getting a better and more secure job, and to pay me with less sense of persecution or personal damage.

Discussion

The value of transference analysis is, I think, intimately linked up with its potentiality for stimulating the development of the symbolizing process, or, as Jung has called it, of the transcendent function. This function enables the psyche to form and to relate to symbols. Symbols act as bridges between pairs of opposites and so link the conscious to the unconscious, the strange to the familiar, soma to psyche, and the fragment to the whole. Francis Bacon regarded myths or 'fables' as 'a transparent veil occupying the "middle" region that separates what has perished from what survives'. One might say that analysis strives to help a patient develop such a middle region, so that, as in the case of my patient, what has perished (i.e., the quarrelling parents of the past) will cease to be confused with what survives (i.e., the patient himself, who needs to gain access to his potential to grow and to create).

When 'transference' rather than 'true' relationship predominates then the symbolic function has most likely remained immature. For then past and present cannot yet be seen as related but different, nor can the object perceived be recognized as other than the object desired or feared. In a previous paper I have suggested that the transcendent function can develop only when a person has become able to confront three major life problems: death, mourning and separation, and greed.

The very context and circumstances of analysis inevitably

evoke these fundamental anxieties—which the history of the patient may have made too overwhelming and unbearable for him to contain. Through the constancy and reliability of the analyst, the rhythm of his presence and of his absence, and the perception, verbalization and interpretation of the fears, rages, loves and hates the patient experiences, the disintegrating ferociousness of these anxieties may be diminished sufficiently for true symbolization to develop.

I should now like to return to Buber in order to discuss how some of the analytical observations and some of the analytical goals might be related to Martin Buber's concepts of the 'I-It' and the 'I-Thou' attitudes. To recapitulate: Buber believes that in the 'I-It' attitude the object remains 'objecti-fied', and is never spoken of—or to—with the whole of one's being. The object is perceived in only some of its aspects and functions, and it is thought of as something one uses or does something to. In contrast, the 'I-Thou' attitude involves 'relationship', which Buber characterizes as 'meeting', as 'encounter' and as linking a subject not to an object, but to another subject. Such relationship, he claims, is direct, is mutual and includes reciprocity.

I should like to suggest that the 'I-It' attitude has much in common with what I have described as 'transference' relation-ship. For where transference relationship predominates the other person is likely to feel himself treated as an object that is of use only in some particular way. Only certain of his qualities are recognized or responded to and many of his characteristics may, in fact, be perceived in a distorted manner. But such distortion will, I believe, be experienced by the analyst as having a certain 'rightness' about it—if, in Fordham's terms, the counter-transference is syntonic. This 'rightness' will need to be communicated to the patient at the appropriate time. But it is also the analyst's job to recognize that this is necessarily a temporary phase.

This 'I-It' relationship is perhaps what Melanie Klein has designated as a 'part-object' relationship. Thus to the greedy infant nothing about his mother matters but her breast, and the presence or absence of that breast is all that he can be con-cerned with. Equally, the greedy adult patient may relate to his analyst as if he were an inexhaustible feeding machine. The hungry longings for the analyst at weekends or during holidays are then experienced as an unbearable mixture of sorrow and rage, and the analyst's non-presence is felt unconsciously as a hostile withholding of himself. Again, the patient with identity problems, experiencing his ego boundaries as fragile and unreliable, may, in his need to keep the analyst at a safe arm's length, perceive him as a 'juggernaut, cold crushing and ruthless'.

Buber himself acknowledged that both attitudes are necessary if, as he puts it, 'we are to find our way around the world and yet retain our humanity'. And, indeed, it is clear that, for the sake of survival and growth, relationships in life and in analysis may have to be at times ruthless and primarily determined by internal needs. Indeed, the baby's survival depends on his primary concern with his mother's breast as the provider of food and thus of life. And the adolescent, in the throes of an identity crisis, may have to withdraw into secrecy and come to regard those closest to him as potential enemies.

The presence of such intense and single-minded relationships to the external world depends on the differentiation—or, to use Fordham's now accepted term, 'deintegration'—out of the self of the various archetypal patterns. Their presence constitutes both a safeguard of man's personal survival through the creation of focused and urgent needs and, because of the numinous quality that characterizes one's experience of them, they also act as 'agents of the synthetic process'; agents, that is, that make a bridge between the world of soma and the world of psyche, between the individual and the species as a whole.

Stein's concept of 'good' and 'bad' structures, which he developed in his paper, 'In pursuit of first principles' (1965), is of value in helping us to conceptualize the rationale for the different stages in analysis, and to understand the need for both the 'I-It' and the 'I-Thou' attitudes. He has suggested there that such 'good and complex' structure comes into being in two phases. First, archetypal elements emerge as a result of de-integration—a process facilitated when the analyst participates in an 'I-It' attitude relationship. In the second phase, each of these archetypal elements becomes limited and restricted in its function, so that no individual archetype can predominate at the expense of the welfare of the whole organism. This second phase characterizes the analytic work when the 'I-Thou' attitude is mediated.

The goal of analysis, in Stein's terms, is thus the facilitation of the development of 'good' structure, and this involves a growing predominance of 'I-Thou' attitude relationships; relationships, in other words, that are characterized by mutuality and respect for the other's otherness, which can develop only when symbol formation has become possible and when a certain amount of wholeness and integration has been achieved.

My experience of myself in the relationship to my patient is sometimes the first hint I get that the pressures inside him have become less destructive and fragmenting. During the initial and central stage of an analysis I may feel that only parts of me can be used or responded to by the patient. In fact, I often suspect that my very body movements, my gestures and my vocabulary may be limited and restricted. But when I begin to notice that I respond in the sessions with, as it were, a wider spectrum of myself, then I take this as a sign that the patient's internal world has become less stressful: and then, so I believe, there is now more of him there with which to respond to more of me, and a shift from a predominantly 'I-It' to a predominantly 'I-Thou' attitude is in the making.

References

Buber, M. (1937). *I and Thou.* Translated by Ronald Gregor Smith. Edinburgh, T. & T. Clark.

Davidson, D. (1966). 'Transference as a form of active imagination', *J. analyt. Psychol.,* 11, 2.*

Fordham, M. (1957). *New developments in analytical psychology.* London, Routledge & Kegan Paul.*

——(1963). 'Transference and its management in child analysis'. *J. Child Psychother.,* 1, 1.

Jung, C. G. (1917/1928). *Two essays on analytical psychology. Coll. wks.,* 7.

——(1921). 'Therapeutic value of abreaction'. In *Coll. wks.,* 16.

MacQuarrie, J. (1963). *Twentieth century religious thought.* London, S.C.M. Press.

Stein, L. (1965). 'In pursuit of first principles', *J. analyt. Psychol.,* 11, 1.

Transference as a form of active imagination*

DOROTHY DAVIDSON

1966

The ideas in this paper are based on my having become aware of a certain type of counter-transference activity which, in turn, has led me to the central idea that during analysis a hitherto unconscious drama in which the patient has been held a prisoner is enacted in the here and now; he finds himself repeating the same type of relationship, or non-relationship, like 'a stuck gramophone record', as one patient put it. The record can become unstuck if the enacting of the drama has been, so to speak, realized by being lived through and worked through within the transference. The patient is then freed to possess and use his own emotions and imagery instead of being compulsively driven by the unconscious drama within him. It is in this sense that I think a successful analysis can be thought of as a lived-through active imagination.

Jung described active imagination as follows:

> By [active imagination] I mean a sequence of fantasies produced by deliberate concentration. I have found that the existence of unrealized, unconscious fantasies increases the frequency and intensity of dreams, and that when these fantasies are made conscious the dreams change their character and become weaker and less frequent. From this I have drawn the conclusion that dreams often contain fantasies which 'want' to become conscious. The sources of dreams are often repressed instincts which have a natural tendency to influence the conscious mind.
>
> In cases of this sort, the patient is simply given the task of contemplating any one fragment of fantasy that seems

* First published in the *Journal of analytical psychology*, 11, 2.

significant to him—a chance idea, perhaps, or something he has become conscious of in a dream—until its context becomes visible; that is to say the relevant associative material in which it is embedded. It is not a question of the 'free association' recommended by Freud for the purpose of dream analysis, but of elaborating the fantasy by observing the further fantasy material that adds itself to the fragment in a natural manner.

This is not the place to enter upon a technical discussion of the method. Suffice it to say that the resultant sequence of fantasies relieves the unconscious and produces material rich in archetypal images and associations. Obviously it is a method that can only be used in certain carefully selected cases. The method is not entirely without danger, because it may carry the patient too far away from reality. A warning against thoughtless application is therefore in place. (1936, *C.W.* **9**, 1, p. 49.)

Again Jung says:

[Active imagination] is a method (devised by myself) of introspection for observing the stream of interior images. One concentrates one's attention on some impressive but unintelligible dream image, or on a spontaneous visual impression, and observes the changes taking place in it. Meanwhile of course all criticism must be suspended and the happenings observed and noted with absolute objectivity. (1941, *C.W.* **9**, 1, p. 190.)

It will be noted that Jung presupposes the presence in the patient of a relatively strong ego and that where this prerequisite is not found he says that the practice of active imagination is not to be recommended.

I think, however, that there are other reasons, too, why active imagination in the context in which Jung defined it is rarely practised among latter-day analytical psychologists. The reasons are largely a matter of history. When Jung and Freud were formulating their own ideas and concepts of the unconscious and its contents, their concepts must have been by comparison no less dangerous, exciting and startling than the modern concept of man in space.

It has sometimes been said of Jung that he appeared to have

been more interested in his concepts of the unconscious than in his individual patients, or rather that they served as a means of testing out his ideas, particularly as evidence of the collective unconscious. This is often the impression some of his writing creates, but since he 'invented' the collective unconscious it is hardly surprising that he should want and need to amplify and test out the validity of his theoretical model, just as any other scientist would.

We who follow him in time have grown up heirs to these ideas and tend to take them for granted, as well as being able to adapt ideas and models from other schools. The dimension and perspective this affords inevitably puts us in a different relation to the theory and practice of analysis. Jung has, as it were, already made a map of the ground-plan of the psyche and shown us how the unconscious works. Because the idea of the unconscious is now unquestioned it seems to me that there has been a correspondingly greater interest in how conscious-ness develops—in ego development and integration.

This shift in emphasis has, I believe, been evoked by the type of patient now coming into analysis. These patients seem to reflect in a different form a malaise similar to the patients in Jung's day. The malaise has as its background modern problems that are portrayed through such collective expressions as nuclear war, the population explosion, the affluent society, over-permissive parents and 'Beatlemania'. The malaise seems to be expressed in doubts about identity, a sense of apathy and futility, a feeling that someone else has already written, painted, acted, filmed or televised every idea anyhow and that therefore the individual is valueless.

Peter Hall, in his address to the Stratford Theatre Company last year on his production of *Hamlet*, said:

> *Hamlet* is one of mankind's great images; it turns a new face to each century, even to each decade; it is a mirror which gives back the reflection of the age that is contemplating it. It is one of the darkest and most penetrating statements of the human condition and the play is a product of a time of doubt. . . . There is never an ideal production of *Hamlet*, any interpretation must limit. For our decade I think the play will be about the disillusionment which produces an apathy of the will so deep that commitment to politics, to

religion, to life is impossible . . . this negative response is deep and appalling.

It is out of this context that our modern patient steps. Unlike many of the patients Jung (1943, *C.W.* **7**, p. 72) described as being 'firmly rooted in their ego function', he is still in search of an identity.

This search has had a profound effect upon analytical psychology and on us who practise it. The problems of the modern patient are to do with the first, not the second half of life. Unfortunately for us, this covers the area in which Jung was least interested: in fact he recommended psychoanalysis for those in the first half of life. Thus we are faced with the necessity to adapt Jung's methods in order to give the maximum assistance to our patients.

I want now to amplify and explain why I think there is a parallel between Jung's idea of active imagination and an essential feature of analysis itself. In my view it is the analyst, in the first instance, and not the patient who needs to have the attitude favourable to active imagination. The analyst has to act as the carrier, or holder, of the patient's potential integrating ego function. There has to be someone there—an entity—into whom the unconscious drama of the patient can be projected. Jung (1946, *C.W.* **16**, p. 178) says:

> The only way to get at [unconscious contents] is to try to attain a conscious attitude which allows the unconscious to co-operate instead of being driven into opposition.

It is, I believe, the same attitude that Joanna Field describes in her book *On not being able to paint*. It is a letting go—an openness of mind—which allows the painting to come through and in a sense paint itself. In the same way, I think, in analysis the unconscious contents, if they are not 'driven into opposition', will enact themselves in the form of a drama that will go on being enacted until such time as it *comes through* to the analyst—in exactly the way Jung has described the fantasies coming through to consciousness in active imagination.

Once the drama is understood inside the analyst he can respond correctly, in the sense that the patient's unconscious will have evoked in the analyst the response he basically needs—not the one he is consciously clamouring for, but a response to the emerging drama, which is the opposite of that which the patient thinks he wants. This attitude is also a technique that facilitates the analysis.

To give an example. A woman patient complains that I am not human—she might as well talk to a chair. At the same time I feel strongly that I am not able to be human—something seems to be at work in my patient that prevents this—in fact I get the feeling that it is vital for her that I should, at this level, remain non-human.

Harold Searles (1960) says:

The non-human environment provides a relatively pure culture medium in which the child is both helped and required to see himself as he really is, to a greater extent than is true in the much more complex medium of the interpersonal world.

Later on he says:

In normal ego development also, the non-human functions as a kind of shock absorber upon which the child can project various part-aspects of himself to integrate them into his developing sense of self.

It seemed that I was responding syntonically (Fordham, 1957) to my patient's need for a 'relatively pure culture medium'. Later on in her analysis my patient used to lament that I no longer seemed to her like a chair and, when she finally ended her analysis, she said sadly, 'How much easier it would be to say goodbye if only you were a chair still.' She had reached the stage of inter-personal relationships and so could feel sadness and grief about loss, as well as pleasure about feeling prepared to live her own life.

Now although I had found myself responding in the opposite way to her conscious demand that I should be more human, at the same time I was not, in contrast to the other people in her life, drawn into the projection sufficiently to re-act altogether blindly; I could sense that something important was going on and I could allow it. The difference was that I began to understand and recognize—as her drama began to come through—what she needed to do and feel about me, without my feeling that I was being used as an inanimate object. So I could gradually interpret what seemed to be happening.

My patient spent many sessions in silence; the atmosphere was not hostile, but peaceful and restful. However, if I commented on this she seemed to feel interrupted. She explained she was remembering times when she had been happy and these were all times when she had been alone in the country. She told me that she had always sympathized with the line in one of Rupert Brooke's poems, 'You came and quacked beside me in the wood'—which seemed to sum up very neatly what she felt about my interruptions.

I began to see much more clearly why my patient had unconsciously wanted me to be inanimate. She had had a particularly deprived babyhood and childhood, and it seemed that in the silent sessions with me she was reliving an early stage of her babyhood that had not been successfully accomplished and I thought it belonged to the stage of omnipotence when the baby needs to feel it is he who has created his mother or hallucinated the breast at just the right moment (Winnicott, 1958).

As she began to grow through this stage she became exacting, controlling and demanding in an attempt to regain her omnipotence, which she now projected on to me: she said I was her jinx. As time went on she became aware that there was a jinx inside her who seemed to act like a sort of blind fate—she felt jerked this way and that by the jinx, who pulled strings like a puppeteer or manipulator.

The jinx had many associations and meanings for her but the prevailing one seemed to be that it represented her father. She had been afraid of him and experienced him as rigid, stern and controlling; he could 'quell you with a look'. She fought and rebelled against me in a way she had never been able to do with her father. Having lived through this on the objective level, she gradually realized its subjective contrast—that it was *she* who was always trying to quell people, particularly her own children, who rebelled violently. Then she could see how she had been identified with the jinx and compulsively driven by it and how, as long as she had been able to feel manipulated and manipulating, she was saved from the difficulties of being herself.

By this stage my patient no longer needed me as the carrier of her potential ego. She had acquired an awareness of her own intrapsychic drama or, as Jung would say, she understood on the subjective level and could relate to it with her own ego. She felt, as she put it, 'more the mistress of my own life'.

This patient had unconsciously tried to fix and silence people, quell them, turn them into puppets (chairs) in an attempt to try to get hold of the quality of mothering she needed in order to be able to relinquish her infantile omnipotence, and she had been caught in a sterile, vicious circle. She cast me, willy-nilly, into the rôle of the chair or puppet. My understanding of this enabled the fantasies to emerge, become conscious and be lived through with me. It then became safe enough for her to pass into the next stage and express against me the aggression that belonged to her relationship with her father, the jinx or negative animus, who was also the fantasied embodiment of her infantile omnipotence.

I have chosen a child for my second illustration. This child, whom I shall call Clare, was nine years of age, and although chronologically years younger than the patient just described, was in fact held up at a later stage in her psychological development.

Clare was an adopted child living in the position of an only child with her elderly parents. She had become uncontrollable and had violent outbursts of rage against her mother, alternating with fits of despair in which she wished she could die. She was unable to make friends with other children. Notes I took early in her treatment describe how she presented her problem:

Draws a picture of two little girls—one is called Juliet—if she had a baby she would call her Juliet—ask if Juliet is her favourite name and she nods—does she know anyone of this name? 'Yes, Romeo and Juliet—it's my best story'.

A session two days later:

Draws another picture of Juliet standing by a tree. Juliet has no arms—she says the tree is really a bear who wants to eat Juliet—she makes clawing movements with her hands as she says this—says she often dreams about bears who chase her—if she can't go to sleep she goes into her parent's room—or sometimes they are still sitting downstairs and then she creeps in—she wants to know what they are talking about—I ask her what she thinks they would be saying—

after some hesitation says she thinks they are talking about her being naughty. 'What sort of naughty?' She replies: 'I rant and rage at mummie.' She is afraid her parents will creep out of the house and leave her.

Gradually Clare substituted playing for drawing and talking to me. The game developed with a strong urgency and intensity and lasted over a period of months. Clare would rush into the playroom and pretend to telephone a boy-friend; she would speak only her end of the imaginary conversation and it is difficult to convey how vivid and implicatory she managed to make this sound.

She was flirtatious, coy, giggly and possessive. I said she was trying to make me jealous and she was clearly delighted. She continued to do all in her power to create jealousy-making situations. The pretend boy-friend turned out to have four names and was alternately John, Paul, George or Ringo, the respective names of the four Beatles. Sometimes she would come into the playroom and say significantly, 'I spent the weekend in Liverpool with *them*.'

She would pretend to invite the Beatles to supper—I was allocated the rôle of the small girl who had to go to bed before they arrived. She would then enact the whole scene—greeting them, kissing them, making them pay her compliments—and this was interspersed with instruction to me to cry and be angry and jealous. She explained to her guests that I was too rude and naughty to be allowed up—sometimes she pretended to hide with them so that I would think she had left me.

It seemed she had by this means reversed her own painful situation *vis-à-vis* her parents. She pushed into me the jealousy she had not been able to stand, together with her fears about her parents deserting her. Later I had to take the rôle of the screaming fans, while she was one of the Beatles. She told me to pretend to pull her hair out—then she would have to go to hospital as an injured Beatle. Here, through my enacting the rôle of the overwhelming love of the fans, it seemed I was carrying for Clare her own fears about the damage her love would do and the screaming was as when she 'ranted and raged' at her mother.

Here is another extract from my notes, which shows how the game worked.

Says she has something terrible to tell me—Ringo is in hospital (this was an objective fact at the time, which she knew). First she is a nurse mixing medicine for Ringo—there is doubt about whether it is good or poison. She lies on the floor and I have to be the nurse giving Ringo his medicine —it is still doubtful whether it is good or poison. Then she says 'When can Ringo leave hospital?' I say, 'Four o'clock' (when the session ends).

She smiles and writes on the blackboard 'beastly pig'. I say, 'Ringo is cross with me.' She says, 'He's going to run away.' She goes to the door, opens it and comes straight in again as the nurse who tells me Ringo has run away and she will have to 'phone the police. Tells me the police say they will search the airport—goes out and comes in again saying 'They've found Ringo—here he is', lies down and is Ringo back in bed. I say, 'I think he may have run away because he was afraid I would be cross with him when he called me a beastly pig—just as a part of you gets afraid I will be cross with you if you say Ringo sort of things to me.' She nods and says, 'Ringo says he will stay in hospital until four o'clock and then he wants to take some of your medicine home.'

The intensity of the play gradually faded and culminated in a wedding scene between Clare and Paul (another Beatle). She had a baby called Juliet who was treated lovingly by both 'parents' and also handed to me to be minded when they went out. It seemed that we had, as it were, gone full circle and returned to the starting place. Clare had lived through one round, so to speak, of her oedipal conflict. After this she spent most of her sessions drawing and talking to me and it was now possible to make more complete interpretations. She could talk directly about her parents and her relationships at school.

I hope my analogy between the dramatic component in analysis and active imagination is now clear. I have tried to show how, as the analyst, I related to the different characters in Clare's drama and was the carrier or holder (Newton, 1965) of the emotions she was then unable to stand. My containing them and holding them for her made it safe enough for her to live out in the game the fears and fantasies which appeared to be the content of her nightmare. In this way she became conscious and was able to integrate the part-aspects of herself into her ego.

Although in the later sessions we referred back to the game, Clare never played it again. I realized with a part of myself that I was delighted at her independence and progress, but I was aware too, at another level, that I felt wistful and sad. We had been through a symbiotic experience. I had been a part of her inner world, inside her dream, but now I was no longer in it. She had a separate identity of her own.

I have found what Fordham has said about the syntonic or archetypal counter-transference very helpful in coming to understand this phenomenon. He says (1957, p. 98f.):

> . . . It can be just as valid for the analyst to know of the projection through registering its impact upon himself and perceiving it within himself, as it is by listening to the patient and realizing it as an inference from what the patient says. Thus if a patient presents infantile material to the analyst, the latter can find out the appropriate reaction from himself, i.e., whether it be a mothering or a fathering attitude that he can go some way towards meeting and out of which he can make an interpretation when the patient is ready for it.
>
> At this stage in the transference the affective stability of the analyst is crucial; he must be able to rely on the de-integrates, knowing that consciousness will inevitably arise from them. It follows that he *will inevitably find* the right form or response so long as counter-transference projections do not obstruct its development.
>
> It is on the basis of 'incarnating' (Plaut, 1956) the image, which should obviously be distinguished from acting out, that explanations and interpretations can begin to find their right place, for without them the patient will sooner or later become disorientated. If, however, the analyst keeps himself apart from the patient by adopting an explanatory or superior rôle without incarnating the image, he does nothing but isolate the patient at just the point at which he needs a primitive form of relationship.
>
> Interpretations are therefore to be regarded as an end product of the analyst's syntonic counter-transference. They stand, as it were, on the basis of less definable affective preconscious experiences out of which they are distilled.

Having read Fordham I realize that it was this type of counter-transference activity—which I referred to at the beginning of this paper—that led me to the idea of the drama of analysis being itself a form of lived-through active imagination. It can no doubt be argued that I am emphasizing one aspect of analysis at the expense of others, and because I am aware of this danger it is necessary to try to clarify my statements a little further.

In 'real' life, that is life outside analysis, if two people each get into the dream of the other, or if their dreams coincide and they become characters in them, and if the experience is mutual, total and unconscious we call this falling in love or fusion. It may or may not be possible for these two people eventually to find each other as separate individuals. The difference in what I have been describing as my experience as an analyst in taking part in a kind of active imagination is that I have been more aware than the patient of the four-fold action going on in the transference/counter-transference relationship (Jung, *C.W.* **16**, Part 2, 3).

In the case of Clare, I did get into her dream and at times the experience was intense, even breathtaking, but it was never total on my side. Her romancing intimacy with the Beatles could not arouse in me the jealousy that would have been appropriate if I had *really* been the small girl whose rôle I had to take. Intense though the play was, Clare knew we were pretending and knew I was not really herself reversed. Yet, as another child once put it, 'It's pretending, but it's real.' My turn for feeling jealous came when she could be separate from me and have a baby—Juliet—(ego) of her own. If I had not been conscious of my jealousy I would have acted this out and would have become to her the terrible mother-bear of her nightmare.

With the adult patient my counter-transference activity was more severely taxed. In the first instance it was difficult to stand being shut out and accused of being inhuman. At the same time as I was the 'chair', I functioned for her as something that represented her mother's body and I was gradually included in her dream of the country—which had represented for her the good idealized aspects of her mother in a non-human form. During her long attacks on me as the jinx, I once or twice reacted in a total response and behaved exactly as she did.

This was fairly disastrous and took a lot of careful analysing before the drama could proceed.

It will be apparent that I am really talking about relating at a pre-verbal level and of course this is more necessary with some patients than with others. At the same time, I think there is probably a part of every analysis where this must happen and it is the soil out of which true interpretations grow.

I hope I have made it clear that I am extending the use of the word interpretation to include the way (ideally) the analyst responds to the basic unconscious needs of his patient, both through his behaviour and through the verbal interpretation he is eventually able to make. It is for this reason that I have found it illuminating to consider aspects of 'analysis' as a form of lived-through active imagination.

References

FIELD, J. (1950). *On not being able to paint*. London, Heinemann.

FORDHAM, M. (1957). 'Notes on the transference' in *New developments in analytical psychology*. London, Routledge.*

JUNG, C. G. (1917). 'The psychology of the unconscious', *Coll. wks.*, **7**.

——(1936). 'The concept of the collective unconscious'. *Coll. wks.*, **9**, 1.

——(1941). 'The psychological aspects of the kore', *Coll. wks.*, **9**, 1.

——(1946). 'Psychology of the transference', *Coll. wks.*, **16**.

NEWTON, K. (1965). 'Mediation of the image of infant-mother togetherness', in *Analytical psychology: a modern science*. Library of analytical psychology, vol. I, London, Heinemann, 1973.

PLAUT, A. (1956). 'The transference in analytical psychology', *Brit. J. med. Psychol.*, **29**, 1.*

SEARLES, H. (1960). *The non-human environment. Monograph Series on Schizophrenia*, No. 5. New York, International University Press, Inc.

WINNICOTT, D. W. (1958). 'Psychoses and child care' in *Collected Papers*. London, Tavistock.

Transference phenomena in alcoholism*

A. PLAUT

1969

The title and scope of this paper require an introduction. I
agree with the definition of alcoholism as 'a chronic disease
that interferes with the drinker's health or social or economic
functioning' (commonly all three). It is hardly necessary to
reiterate that it constitutes a far bigger problem in our society
than all other addictions taken together, estimated to affect
over a quarter of a million people in the United Kingdom.
Consequently there is a vast and constantly increasing literature
on the subject, which also extends into the past. The psychoanalytic literature is also fairly large, certainly dating back to
Karl Abraham's paper of 1908, but I could not find any
significant contributions made during the last five years and
no contribution in the literature of analytical psychology, with
two exceptions. In a paper on manic mood-disorder dating
back to 1903, Jung, then a psychiatrist aged twenty-eight,
describes cases of alcoholism connected with emotional ab-
normality instead of using the then current psychiatric terms of
'moral defect or insanity' or 'psychopathic instability'. The
relation between addiction and manic-depressive disorder is
elaborated in psychodynamic terms in Rosenfeld's (1960) paper
on drug addiction.

Whether or not alcohol is a drug would seem to me to
depend on the motive for which it is taken. Laurie (1967)
excludes alcohol on the grounds that our society itself is
dependent on it and that prohibiton has done more harm than
its legal presence. I do not think that the issue can be settled
in this way. But it is certainly true that if alcohol is a drug then
it is the only one in our civilization that has a mythology and

* First published in the *British journal of medical psychology*, 42, 313.

an established ritual. In this connection two references may be made in passing, both appearing in the same issue of the *British journal of addiction*.

One, by a Greek psychiatrist (1967), observes that, despite the vast consumption of wine in modern Greece, the number of people suffering from alcoholism is very low. He writes: 'The Greek never drinks alone. Alcohol is not used by him as a solution to his problems, which are normally solved in discussion with other people'. The other paper is by Leibowitz (1967) and is one of a series on 'Studies in the history of alcoholism'. He shows that descriptions of acute alcoholic psychosis go back as far as Hippocrates, Galen and others. When looking through the more recent literature, I came across a book written by a namesake of mine (Plaut, 1967). It is an American publication with which I decided not to compete. But I was well aware that by narrowing the focus as much as I intended to do I should be taking two different kinds of risk, which I shall now describe.

The first risk is brought out by Selzer (1957) and influences the means of my presentation. He writes:

> Since it has become fashionable to speak of alcoholism as an illness, many individuals conform by paying lip service to this concept. However, it is not unusual to hear professional persons declaim on the alcoholic as a sick person on one occasion and then intimate at other less guarded moments that the alcoholic is a wastrel who simply lacks 'will power'. This inability to accept emotionally what cannot be denied on an intellectual basis characterizes unconscious hostility toward the chronic inebriate.

I therefore decided that the usual safeguards of anonymity in reports on patients would be inadequate and that I should have to omit the contents of transferred and illustrative material from analytical sessions and confine myself to phenomenology and certain theoretical and tentative conclusions. All these are based on notes recorded as soon as possible after many but by no means all analytical sessions. The total period of observation and analytical therapy of the four patients extends over twenty-five years. As I became more experienced with note-taking, I recorded more about my reactions and reflexions on what had been going on and what puzzled me, and gave up as useless any attempt to give complete sequences of events in sessions.

The second risk in linking the specific aspect of dynamic psychology, i.e. the phenomena of transference, with an illness like alcoholism is that of mixing two frames of reference. In analysis—as I shall call it from now on—one is concerned with mental processes (e.g., projection) that may be more or less prevalent, according to symptomatology and the stage of analysis. Both of these, process and symptomatology, are present in every analysis to some degree, while a disease like alcoholism is either present or absent. It is therefore necessary to consider alcoholism as a specific expression of a psycho-pathological state of dependence on a substance that acts as a depressant on the central nervous system, facilitates regression and is always available to the patient under ordinary circumstances, differing in this respect from the analyst, who cannot be imbibed.

I wish to pay tribute to psychological studies like Walton's (Kessel & Walton, 1965; Walton, 1968) which classify 'personality of alcoholics', 'varieties of drinking patterns and causes', and correlate these. I shall refer to only two types of drinking pattern, classified by Jellinek (1960) as the 'loss-of-control addiction' and the 'inability to abstain' or 'inveterate' alcoholism, and shall not refer to other forms like 'symptomatic alcoholism', meaning symptomatic of severe psychiatric illness like schizophrenia (or manic-depressive psychosis, with which alcoholism has many resemblances), or disease of the brain. (On the other hand, I was unable to make the distinction between these two categories and others, e.g. the 'neurotic' and the 'bout' drinkers to which Walton also refers.) Of my four patients only one was an inveterate drinker, three were loss-of-control drinkers. A point of interest is, as we shall see, that one of the siblings of a loss-of-control drinker belonged to the inveterate type, while one of the siblings of the inveterate drinker was of the loss-of-control type. The inveterate drinker is less likely to accept that he is ill and in need of help.

Aim

In approaching the subject of alcoholism, my consideration was that the relatively microscopic examination of a particular aspect of dependence of one person on a substance, contrasting it with his dependence on a person, could yield results. If these were then found to be applicable on a wider scale, and with due modifications, in circumstances differing from both the analytic setting and the specific addiction that I am examining, this paper would have served its purpose. I further had in mind two patients with personality structures, shown by transference phenomena and incipient symptoms, that suggest to me that they could become alcoholics, and also two other patients against whose relatively mild but obstinate drug-addictions I had been competing for years.

There is no reason to consider, on the basis of my own experience and from my reading of the psychoanalytic litera-ture, that analysis is the treatment of choice for the vast majority of alcoholic and other addicts. On the other hand, I have some hope that something can be learned from failures. This would seem especially likely if factors can be isolated that have made some patients worse or started their addiction under analysis. Jung (1935, p. 38) wrote:

> In my psychotherapeutic practice of nearly thirty years I have met with a fair number of failures which made a far deeper impression on me than my successes. Anybody can have successes in psychotherapy, starting with the primitive medicine-man and faith-healer. The psychotherapist learns little or nothing from his successes, for they chiefly confirm him in his mistakes. But failures are priceless experiences because they not only open the way to a better truth but force us to modify our views and methods.

These statements contrast markedly with the number of published failures by any psychotherapist; it does not seem in keeping with a scientific attitude to leave it to one's detractors to point out one's failures and to justify one's own methods by returning the compliment.

A general point regarding management and technique needs to be made in this connection. Rosenfeld (1960) mentions the scarcity of psychoanalytic literature in the last 20 years on the treatment of drug addiction, and attributes this to 'it being a difficult problem'. I regard this as an understatement. He, like everyone else, agrees that such patients cannot be accepted without at least temporary residence at a nursing home or hospital, which in my view especially applies to loss-of-control compulsive drinkers (as I shall call them from now on), who have to go on until physical illness is produced. But Rosenfeld disagrees with Knight (1937), who says that orthodox analytic technique is of no avail, and states that he, Rosenfeld, found it unnecessary to modify his usual analytic approach.

One may find it difficult to combine these two statements, but I think that analysts of whatever school fall into two groups: those who can admit to modifications and those who draw more comfort from asserting that there is no necessity to modify. Going by private rather than published communications, I am inclined to the view that the two groups vary less in practice than in their published statements. Whatever position and view we adopt and however much we are concerned with psychic growth rather than the elimination of symptoms, one has to agree with Menninger (1938), who termed alcoholism a form of chronic suicide, and one has to remain mindful of the frequency with which acute suicidal attempts supervene in compulsive drinkers.

A Classification of Transference Phenomena

After some hesitation I gave up the hope that I could present a well-systematized coherent theory, and decided it would be less ambitious and possibly more truthful to proceed more or less in the chronological order in which I learned about these matters. These include what I have taken over from other schools into my own frame of reference, that of analytical psychology. (What I have arrived at is therefore unlikely to satisfy purists.)

As I have already referred to the analyst who cannot be ingested and to my having had to compete with patients' drugs, it seems logical to mention first how much I have been impressed by the applicability of psychoanalytic and notably Kleinian contributions regarding orality, greed, sadistic impulses and early ego-splitting, which Rosenfeld (1960) particularly and rightly emphasizes. The relevance of pre-analytic observers like Janet and William James fell into place as I went along. I am thinking of Janet's remarks on the interchangeability of over-eating and alcoholism as well as other habits due to 'sentiments of incompleteness', and James's remarks regarding the relation between alcoholism and religion, which I hope to put into perspective.

There is, furthermore, a relationship between the well-known symptoms of craving for specific foods and other objects and the spending sprees and debts that frequently precede drinking bouts.

The Dependent Transference

Dependence in analytical usage implies, of course, regression to infantile fixation points, thought processes and ego states. As regards thought processes, the splitting of objects—which include people, except that when so divided they no longer appear as people—into ideally good and totally bad parts is very evident in all the reported material, but it *seems* to except the analyst himself, who is treated as if he were what he may well desire to be—an altogether benevolent neutral. However, in the patient's fantasy he soon figures as an anonymous servant who is being taken for granted and who could be dismissed at short notice if he failed to give satisfaction. I am using my metaphorical description of patients' fantasies in order to indicate the defence of denial of dependence, which dates back to a time when omnipotence of thought was necessary in order to combat infantile helplessness and anxiety. (The restriction I have imposed on myself to preserve patients' anonymity, on the one hand, and the absence of an agreed connotation concerning levels of abstraction, on the other, make expression by metaphor indispensable.)

At all events the phenomenon of denial of dependence, as well as that of reversal, i.e., the analyst-servant being dependent on the patient who is master, breaks down when the analyst decides to go on holiday. The usual pattern, familiar from other cases, whereby the patient finds a reason to absent himself just before the analyst goes away or as soon as he returns, showing of how little account he really is to the patient, does not express intensively enough his denial of dependence. Many alcoholic breakdowns I witnessed coincided with my absence on holiday, but not with sessions cancelled owing to my being ill. When it first occurred, it came as a surprise to me, who had been taken in by the patient's denial of dependent transference. Inter-pretations referring to frustrations evoked punitive and sadistic reactions and were totally refuted. But as the analysis progressed and such instances multiplied, awareness of dependence and all that it entailed dawned on the patient, and this was liable to result in breaking off the analysis or in potentially fatal crises.

It is therefore essential for the analyst to have the fullest understanding of what his transference interpretations are demanding of such patients. If they are not co-ordinated with the patient's real capacity to take in and digest, he will destroy both the offered interpretation and himself by drinking himself into oblivion. In this respect the addict has the actual instrument of destruction always at hand in a way that is unrivalled by most other patients.

Wholeness and the Destructive Impulse

It is an essential assumption that the patient has a model of wholeness that he can invoke whenever the need arises. I am using a model to indicate that it is not a repressed content or an unconscious fantasy but an imageless pattern of behaviour that cannot be located in the mind. For me, the observer, this model finds expression in the concept of the archetype of wholeness. It can also be regarded as fusion of subject and object. In its unbroken state it is as compelling as it is for an infant to feel mouth-filled-by-nipple; on the more whole-object, symbolical level, images of incest and bisexuality express this kind of wholeness in a less primitive form and are sometimes the source of impulsive behaviour in the kind of patient I am discussing (Jung, 1946, p. 262).

The alternative to this wholeness by fusion with the ideal object is fusion brought about by a state of non-being or death. All consciousness, in the sense of differentiation between ego and object, I and you, constitutes a separation, an absence of wholeness, for which on an infantile level the only tolerable alternative is non-being; this would account for the alcoholic's well-known and justified reputation for self-destruction. One of the characteristics of the compulsive drinker is his striving for perfection. When the latter fails, his taking to drink is an act of despair, an inability to bear his limitations.

In his studies on archetypal images of the self in relation to Christian symbolism, and in particular the crucifixion, Jung

(1951, p. 69) mentions the opposite characteristics of and the conflict between perfection and completeness and how the passionate striving for perfection ('which constitutes one of the strongest roots of civilization') has in the end to yield painfully to completeness. 'Perfection' for Jung (1952, pp. 395–9) is a masculine desideratum and by its nature always incomplete, while completeness, a feminine principle, lacks perfection. They are compensatory to each other.

For present purposes I am equating completeness with receptivity and integration, allowing the other to exist and to be important. Integration means not only taking back and assimilating projections but also (Jung, 1948, p. 30) realization of the double aspect of unconscious contents and their feeling value. In other words, the realization of ambivalence in every subject/object relationship and the conscious acceptance of conflict.

The relevance of these remarks to the point of view I am adopting is, first, that there appears to be a complementary relationship between the compulsive and the inveterate drinker, in which the former envies the latter whom he sees as if in blissful incestuous union, against which he experiences envy and sometimes enacts hostile attacks.

The envy is probably mutual, but my experience of inveterate drinkers is too limited to be sure. My remarks in the introduction concerning siblings suggested such a complementary relationship and so does the model of the perfect fit, of imageless wholeness, with the difference that it is not felt to be complementary as, for instance, the words 'my mouth and the nipple' would imply. In addition, I found that the compulsive drinker sees the analyst much as he sees the inveterate drinker, replete and self-satisfied, like a full bottle. His striving for perfection is expressed in the drive to 'do it all myself better than anyone else'. But beneath his striving is the bitter envy of the inveterate drinker's unweaned and unrepentant 'everything is being done for me' state.

Secondly, I have come to view the model of primitive wholeness, in as much as it cannot be said to be in the patient's mind, as taking priority over the analytical reconstructions of actual events in infancy. This model is challenged by the analytical situation. The only point of practical importance that I shall make, and in fact the reason for presenting this paper, is based on this view.* This is not to say that my patient's characteristic psychological structure was not to a large extent shaped by events during infancy. But when and how these should be translated into the present by means of the transference, or the transference used to reconstruct the past, is the crucial question. At this point I want to refer to a paper by Rubinfine (1967) in which he cites the case of a woman suffering from depressions and compulsive over-eating. He concludes that the reconstruction of traumatic events was the least significant of the several themes in the analysis.

The central achievement was the reconstruction of a childhood ego-state. It is clear from what Rubinfine has to say regarding memory, ego-states and schemata, according to which sensory data are perceived and represented, that 'the past', to which analytical contents are so often referred, is a more complicated affair than we like to think. But when Rubinfine writes that 'a part of the ego remains outside this process, observing . . . ' and refers to 'the "controlled regression" typical of the analytic process' I know that he is not writing about the compulsive drinker.

If one wanted to emphasize the personal historical or 'genetic' contribution to the model on which his personal fiction, his ego-ideal, is based, one might say that his life's motto is 'death or glory'. On a deeper level it is death *and* glory, the combination symbolizing that kind of wholeness that Jung (1924, p. 325) in his earlier work called 'the merging of subject and object as the reunion of mother and child'. James (1902, p. 388) wrote, after taking nitrous oxide: 'The keynote is invariably reconciliation. It is as if the opposites of the world whose contradictoriness and conflict make all our difficulties and troubles were melted into unity'.

My reason for giving these quotations is to underline how easy it is for the analyst concerned with transference reconstructions and defence mechanisms to forget the addicted patient's condition of being passionately in love with an illusory state of wholeness, as if it could be produced like an all-powerful genie out of a bottle. It is useless to enter into direct competition with this fantasy-creation even if the means of

* Walton's (1968) investigation, based on personality tests showing that the loss-of-control or compulsive addict is more hostile and more afraid of his impulses, is in keeping with my findings.

competing are called 'analytical technique'. When he is aiming at a conflict-free state the patient cannot be reached: unconscious splitting into ideal and persecutory objects, and therefore splitting of his ego, is essential for the preservation of an illusory wholeness and omnipotence. When you try to interpret this he may appear to be deaf, actually fall asleep or resort to going off on a different tack, such as the recounting of symptoms, to which you have to listen.

When the patient has alcohol inside him, the analyst is forced to the sobering realization of this state of affairs. If he goes on to interpret, his attempt at disillusionment will be felt by the patient as persecutory and may result in abusive responses of which he is only capable with the help of alcohol.

This brings me to a brief discussion of the destructive phenomena in the analytical situation, which are usually only expressed by symptoms, perhaps an occasional slamming of the door at the end of a session, or in letters. Interpretations and 'working through' in the analytical session are firmly resisted. Guilt and anxiety about the possible eruption of hostile impulses show themselves often in bodily symptoms before and after the session and, in particular, in the way in which the compulsive drinker between bouts is meticulous about the time and money conditions of analysis—he must never put a foot wrong. He feels so bad about his wish to be destructive towards the analyst that he has to deny for as long as possible that he has resorted to the rival, the bottle, thereby destroying in fantasy every ounce of goodness in the analyst.

I agree with Rosenfeld (1960) when he says that a drug 'symbolizes an ideal object which can be concretely incorporated' but this next statement, 'He is then blissfully hallucinating an ideal object and feels united or identified with it', is only applicable to the inveterate drinker. The compulsive drinker, who is desperately and anxiously seeking oblivion, is not in a blissful state. He begins to drink when the reality of his limitations and his dependence on others, especially the analyst, are eroding his apparent omnipotence. It is true that with the first few gulps there may be a feeling of triumph, as if he had stolen the forbidden fruit, but this is not bliss and in any case only momentary.

The subsequent remorse about having destroyed the analyst's goodness is one of the most severe psychic pains imaginable, and the contempt he feels for himself equals the contempt for the stuff he has incorporated and by which he feels humiliated. Therefore he has to knock himself out and cannot stop drinking until total physical incapacity and illness supervene or someone comes to the rescue. Attempts at suicide in this state of remorse and humiliation seem very understandable; he is now in a state of almost total identification with a bad object, the destruction of which seems to offer the only route of escape. Bearing this in mind, one begins to see why all attempts at interpreting the negative, destructive transference meet with such determined resistance. Other people, mainly those who are the hands (breasts) that feed him, may be attacked openly and with violence in the intoxicated state, but not, as a rule, the analyst who has begun to function as a container for the patient. There are two aspects to this function, the first being that of a receptacle for excrement, the bad objects that constantly accumulate as the result of splitting and that have to be got rid of—somewhat unflattering for the analyst, but highly necessary for the patient.

I recount all this in support of my major contention which is that, in the case of alcoholism, too early or too insistent transference interpretations are as dangerous as unawareness of the transference. Consciousness too early awakened may not only ruin the use the patient has to (not wants to) make of the analyst, but may also load him with intolerable guilt, thus precipitating another cycle of remorse and need for oblivion.

Container and Contained

These are words I associate with Jung's paper on marriage as a psychological relationship (1925), and also with abstractions that Bion (1963) uses in his search for a system of connotations from the raw data of analysis. The only bit of common ground between the descriptive and the conceptual use of the terms is that container and contained are unthinkable without each other, and that in any analytical relationship involving repression the words automatically recall mother and child.

With a patient in whom the container-contained relationship is reactivated imagelessly, as in infancy, the analyst as container should function both for the purpose of expulsion of worthless material, as I said, but also for ingestion. Any inadequacy on this literal level is unforgivable and makes it necessary for the patient to prove his superiority to the analyst by defeating his verbal interpretations (Bion, 1962, p. 6), while use of the analyst's lavatory and the taking of snacks before and after sessions are also resorted to. In my experience of alcoholism, the way of defeating interpretations is commonly to store up the analyst's interpretations and to quote them back as accusations, thus projecting the punitive super-ego into the analyst, making him the instrument of the patient's attack on himself. However, it is no use telling him this as it only lends new fuel to the vicious cycle of attack and self-punishment. In fact, it is doubtful whether words as such can reach the container-contained situation when it exists as a thing itself, an undigested fact rather than a memory, or, to use Bion's terminology, a beta-element (the equivalent term in analytical psychology would be *archetype*, as a concept about patterns of behaviour rather than archetypal imagery). It is for this reason that I can agree with Kessel & Walton's (1965) statement that many alcoholics fight shy of an individual treatment relationship, and can see why group therapy is the more acceptable alternative.

In these circumstances I have given a positive place to the analyst's vulnerability. We know that many patients find it a great relief when the analyst has a cold, is otherwise indisposed or makes mistakes. This relief is usually looked on as a defence, as a reversal mechanism, etc. However, on the primitive level on which I am considering the container-contained relationship, there is no differentiation: the two are interchangeable. In this way the analyst's vulnerability, including his ability to make and admit mistakes, confirms and accepts the patient's state of non-development constructively.

It also arouses a positive counter-transference affect without which, in my submission, no containment and no psychic growth take place in analysis. It is, however, even more important that the analyst as container, although vulnerable, should not break down. In practical terms this means living with the addicted patient through a series of crises, which transforms the imageless model into one with imagery and/or memories, making a therapeutic alliance and further analysis possible. Integration can gradually take the place of the suicidal wholeness. The transition is, however, slow and painful for both parties. Some analysts would regard what I am describing as 'preparation for analysis', thus distinguishing it from 'the pure gold'. I do not think the distinction is tenable.

Extra-Analytical Attempts at Achieving Wholeness and the Analyst's Negative Function

I could have stopped at the end of the previous section if it were not for the fact that we have to look at certain activities of the patient as transference phenomena that are also, like the symptom itself, attempts at achieving a cure. There are, for example, the attempts to find wholeness by means of overwork or having an affair. (Both are very popular and need no exposition.) Then there is religion and Alcoholics Anonymous (A.A.) and I hope I shall be forgiven both for lumping the two together and for looking at these often much more successful means of therapy from my limited point of view. The religious and Oxford Group origins of the founders of A.A. might justify the juxtaposition, but it must be clearly understood that this aspect of religion is quite different from the mystical longings I referred to earlier, and also from religious conversions.

Sessions (1957) observes how the frequent rebellion against orthodox religion nevertheless often fails to eradicate the deeply implanted guilt and conviction of unworthiness. He gives credit to the tolerant and truly 'spiritual' religion that A.A. promotes. However this may be, it is easy to understand that the need for attacks on the container is obviously lessened by the status of equality with the contained person: to accept help from a fellow sufferer is tolerable. Neither the container-contained nor the perfection-completeness opposites are evoked by this situation.

On the other hand, the religious element in the twelve steps of A.A. specifically demands recognition as a 'power greater than ourselves which could restore us to sanity', thus taking care of any envy of omnipotence and invulnerability which the projection into an analyst would produce. The eighteenth-century prayer adopted by A.A.:

> God give me the detachment to accept those things I cannot alter; the courage to alter those things which I can alter; and the wisdom to distinguish the ones from the others

could not be better designed to facilitate the differentiation between omnipotence and reality. Together with the A.A.'s injunction to think only of the next twenty-four hours, it certainly expresses the principle of surrendering ideas of perfection and omnipotence for acceptance of limitations. But abstinence and personality growth are not the same thing, and gregariousness and public confessions are not every alcoholic's cup of tea. Like everyone else, A.A. has its failures. On the other hand, we as analysts have to admit that the pain of heightened emotional awareness, the journey from apparent adulthood to rebirth, the exchange of illusory wholeness for integration of conflicting aspects of the personality, and the ability to be alone (but not unrelated) suit even fewer patients. They also do not suit many other people and analysts know that this kind of work is never completed.

There is another bit of knowledge that an analyst has to bear without becoming masochistic: it is that by his failure—if the breaking off of analysis may be regarded as such—a very few patients (I only know of one) may have been helped indirectly to achieve a self-cure at least resulting in abstinence. I therefore suggest that analysts could with advantage modify the A.A. prayer for their own use and change the last sentence to 'and to recognize the indications and contra-indications for analysis'.

A different type of negative analytical function in the interest of therapy is described by Jung (1963, p. 142) in a case of alcoholism. The patient was a man diagnosed by an American colleague as suffering from 'alcoholic neurasthenia' and 'incurable'. Jung diagnosed with the help of association tests that the patient was suffering from a formidable mother complex. His mother, a very powerful woman, was the owner of a large company in which the patient occupied a leading post. Whenever he was with her she interfered with his work and he drank too much, yet he did not want to leave 'the comfortably warm nest'. After brief psychotherapy the patient stopped drinking and Jung warned him against returning to his former situation, which the patient promptly did, with the expected result.

Then his mother came to see Jung, who realized 'what the son had to contend with' and that he did not have the strength to resist. Jung decided that an act of *force majeure* was indicated.

He wrote out a certificate—behind the patient's back—to the effect that he was incapable of fulfilling the requirements of his job and recommending his discharge. The patient was of course furious with Jung, but left his mother's firm and struck out on his own with great success, as Jung learned from the grateful wife of the former alcoholic. Nevertheless, Jung writes that he had a guilty conscience about this patient and his own behaviour, which he would ordinarily have considered unethical and, we may add, nobody would consider analytical. Although based on analytical insight, Jung's procedure was negative in terms of the analytical situation. The reason for quoting it is that, in my submission, even 'the strong horse pill', as Jung puts it, that he administered would not have worked had the patient not had a relatively advanced but unconscious image of wholeness, namely that of incest.

Discussion

A number of addicted patients are capable of forming transferences in the analytical setting but, as regression occurs, the analyst is no longer able to be a good enough substitute for the imageless model of wholeness with which the patient's ego is fused, nor can the patient go on imagining that he is self-sufficient.

At this point he resorts to the bottle. Phenomena that precede this indicate that the patient needs to feel that the analysis is his own creation. The psychopathology at this point is similar to that of narcissism as described by Rosenfeld (1964). The point of practical importance is that transference interpretations that make the patient aware of his dependence on the analyst can trigger off the well-known vicious circle. For a modicum of integration to occur it seems to be necessary for patient and analyst to live through dangerous alcoholic crises. I further suggest that some important interpretative work can be done during crises, provided the patient allows one to be present when he is just conscious enough and thus to lessen the feelings of guilt and remorse about having destroyed the analyst.

It is only at these times that the archaic ego-state corresponding to what I described as primitive wholeness and the container and contained is reached. The patient's usual way of holding on to this state is by splitting and by keeping the analyst and himself consciously on the good side of the split. When this defence can no longer operate and the patient's misery and dependence so obviously belie the omnipotence symptomatic of primitive wholeness, the analyst's helpful presence and actions are the first and essential interpretations. Next, an analyst's admitted vulnerability is required for the patient to take his essential share in the analytical situation; he is helped to realize the equality of container and contained.

I have spoken about the model being challenged or re-activated by the two-person setting of analysis. It is necessary to add that this does not depend on the awakening of something akin to a prenatal memory, as Little's (1960) 'basic unity' seems to do. I would incline to Freud's view when he writes (1937, p. 265) that 'constructions can achieve the same result as a recaptured memory' (which, as he says, cannot always be recollected). However this may be, the important point here is that the model of wholeness that goes with an archaic ego-state has not been abandoned by those patients who are forced to return to it.

They render themselves helpless. This is the critical condition that offers a therapeutic opportunity not to be missed.

The next practical point is that the compulsive drinkers I analysed did not seem to have had an adequate experience in infancy of what Winnicott (1951) called the 'first not-me possession' (better-known as 'transitional object'). If transferences were verbally interpreted at this stage, the 'not-me' aspect would certainly be underlined for the patient, but at the expense of the 'possession' part, which is still essential to him and is likely to remain so for a considerable time. By postponing some verbal interpretations at this point the analyst can be of use by letting the patient experience him as a 'not-me' possession.

From my point of view, alcoholism may be seen as a symptomatic attempt at self-cure by the patient's diving in to the depth of his being, out of which he cannot get unaided. On the other hand, he cannot bear his need to depend directly on one other person.

References

ABRAHAM, K. (1908). 'The psychological relations between sexuality and alcoholism'. *Selected papers on psychoanalysis*. London: Hogarth, 1927.

BION, W. R. (1962). *Learning from experience.* London, Heinemann.
——(1963). *Elements of psycho-analysis.* London, Heinemann.
FREUD, S. (1937). *Constructions in analysis.* Standard Edition 23.
GREEK PSYCHIATRIST (1967). *Br. J. Addict.,* **62,** no. 1–2.
JAMES, W. (1902). *Varieties of religious experience.* London, Longmans Green.
JELLINEK, E. M. (1960). *The disease concept of alcoholism.* New Haven, Hill House Press.
JUNG, C. G. (1903). 'On manic mood-disorder'. *Coll. wks.,* **1.**
——(1924). *Symbols of transformation. Coll. wks.,* **5.**
——(1925). 'Marriage as a psychological relationship'. *Coll. wks.,* **17.**
——(1935). 'The aims of psychotherapy'. *Coll. wks.,* **16.**
——(1946). 'Psychology of the transference'. *Coll. wks.,* **16.**
——(1948). *Aion. Coll. wks.,* **9,** pt. II.
——(1951). *Aion. Coll. wks.,* **9,** pt. II.
——(1952). *Answer to Job. Coll. wks.,* **11.**
——(1963). *Memories, dreams, reflections.* London, Collins; Routledge & Kegan Paul.
KESSEL, N. & WALTON, H. (1965). *Alcoholism.* London, Penguin Books.
KNIGHT, R. (1937). 'The dynamics and treatment of chronic alcohol addiction'. *Bull. Menninger Clin.,* **1,** 233–250.
LAURIE, P. (1967). *Drugs.* London, Penguin Books.
LEIBOWITZ, J. O. (1967). *Br. J. Addict.,* **62,** no. 1–2.
LITTLE, M. (1960). 'On basic unity'. *Int. J. Psycho-Anal.,* **41,** 377–384.
MENNINGER, K. (1938). *Man against himself.* New York, Harcourt, Brace.
PLAUT, T. F. A. (1967). *Alcohol problems: a report to the nation.* New York, Oxford University Press.
ROSENFELD, H. A. (1960). 'On drug addiction'. *Int. J. Psycho-Anal.,* **41,** 467–475.
——(1964). 'On the psychopathology of narcissism: a clinical approach'. *Int. J. Psycho-Anal.,* **45,** 332–337.
RUBINFINE, D. L. (1967). 'Notes on a theory of reconstruction'. *Br. J. med. Psychol.,* **40,** 195–206.
SELZER, M. L. (1957). Hostility as a barrier to therapy in alcoholism. *Psychiat. Q.,* **31,** 301–305.
SESSIONS, P. M. (1957). Ego religion and superego religion in alcoholics. *Q.J. Stud. Alcohol.,* **18,** 121–125.
WALTON, H. (1968). Personality as a determinant of the form of alcoholism. *Br. J. Psychiat.,* **114,** 761–766.
WINNICOTT, D. W. (1951). *Collected papers.* London, Tavistock, 1958.

PART III

Counter-transference

The dangers of unrecognized counter-transference*

W. P. KRAEMER

1958

The analytical relationship consists of various layers in depth. One of these may be seen as the layer of equality, and on this the transference/counter-transference dynamism has its main field of action. The idea of the twin pair is derived from Jung's thesis in which thinking as well as feeling in opposites features. Any attempt to leave out the counter-transference in the contemplation of the relationship as a whole strikes me as alien to the way in which analytical psychologists look at things.

The psychoanalysts, who, on the whole, were much earlier aware of the counter-transference phenomenon, used to regard it as an unavoidable but undesirable element in analysis. Money-Kyrle (1956), in his recent excellent contribution to the subject, says (p. 360): 'We used to think of it [counter-transference] mainly as a personal disturbance to be analysed away in ourselves. We now also think of it as having its causes, and effects, in the patient and therefore as an indication of something to be analysed in him.' The author thus confirms the impression one gains from earlier papers by Paula Heimann (1950), Margaret Little (1951), and others, that counter-transference is, in fact, unreservedly accepted as an integral part of psychoanalytical procedure. Money-Kyrle still maintains in his article that 'the discovery that counter-transference can be usefully employed does not imply that it has ceased ever to be a serious impediment'. Yet a little later (p. 361) he describes the ideal condition of analysis as one in which 'the analyst's counter-transference feelings will be confined to that sense of empathy with the patient on which his insight is based'. I feel that this is a most important statement which,

* First published in the *Journal of analytical psychology*, 3, 1.

perhaps, shows that the author is moving towards a position where the negative aspect may eventually seem less important to him than the helpful one.

Money-Kyrle, however, in the passage just quoted, does not speak about counter-transference as such, but instead about counter-transference *feelings*. Feelings, in his sense, are on the whole consciously experienced, and therefore also much more easily under conscious control. We may expect maximal awareness on the part of the analyst regarding the phenomenon; without such awareness he is in no position to control the feeling situation and use it in the furtherance of his patient's treatment. Counter-transference is, in fact, a most powerful force, and if it remains an unrecognized element in the analysis, it can be of the utmost danger.

The argument in favour of the respectability of the counter-transference as a whole is not generally accepted, however. Michael Fordham (1956), in a private communication, objects to my way of using the term as, in his opinion, I extend the concept too far 'because it lumps together feelings which are adapted to the patient's need with feelings that are not' (cf. also Fordham, 1957). I maintain that this is true only where full awareness has not been established, in which case, I suggest, we should not speak of *feelings*, but rather of urges or drives. Once awareness has been established, the conscious control of counter-transference forces and their adaptations to the patient's need will, I think, follow suit. Fordham perhaps doubts that such an ideal state of awareness, control, and adaptation can ever exist. On the other hand, what is going to happen if a part of the analyst's archetypal relation to his patient is held back, thereby interfering with his capacity to enter into a total relationship? Eventually, *all* feelings and indeed the analyst's whole personality must be adapted to the patient's need. I suggest that Money-Kyrle's formula regarding the ideal condition I have mentioned may be fully acceptable from the point of view of analytical psychology and at the same time answer Fordham's objection.

The practical reason for my upholding the counter-transference as good and normal is that it actually *exists* and according to most authors is unavoidable. As we aim at the understanding and acceptance of reality, I cannot see how we can, for instance, on the one hand find it natural to accept the shadow, and on the other deny that of the counter-transference. Without the existence of the shadow any balance of the psyche is unthinkable. Jung as well as Freud emphasizes the necessity of making conscious and eventually controlling the unconscious contents. While Freud does not see beyond the need of unearthing suppressed and repressed material, the aim of analytical psychology is to establish a deeper and deeper balance of intrapsychic opposites from which all creativeness and knowledge spring. Thus ego and shadow are accepted as essential counterparts in psychic wholeness.

I have no wish to enter here into further discussion of a possible causal link between shadow and counter-transference, but simply to note that the analyst's unrecognized shadow may well be at the root of an unrecognized counter-transference. I am using the concept of the shadow merely as a simile, as it is a relatively simple and straightforward content *within* the psyche, and therefore may be compared to an equally simple content of the interpsychic entity that forms the relationship between analyst and analysand. Fordham writes in a private communication (1956): 'The shadow is bound up with natural spontaneous behaviour'. I quote this because I should like to think of the counter-transference in the same way: it is bound up with natural spontaneous behaviour. Most analytical psychologists aim at such behaviour towards their patients. At the same time, however, some also play the complementary rôle of conscious identification with the archetype (Paulsen, 1956). On the whole, I certainly see the counter-transference operating on a much deeper level than that of the shadow; I see it in the realm of the collective unconscious where, together with the transference, this decisive archetypal event has its rightful place of action.

The incarnation of the archetype (Plaut, 1956), which some analysts undertake for the patient, contributes the principal argument in favour of the acceptance of counter-transference. If the *opus* is to be effective, the incarnation of the projected rôles has to be genuine, and this implies that the patient must needs correspond, from time to time, to an inner figure for the analyst in the same way as the analyst does for the patient. Money-Kyrle expresses this in corresponding psychoanalytic terms when he says that the analyst can hardly fail in some degree to respond to the patient's treating him as a parent, by regarding the patient as his child. The more integrated the analyst is, however, the more will the patient's need in the drama be of primary, his own of only secondary, importance. But as both *dramatis personae* also form an indivisible whole, this distinction can have only relative validity. Yet I think this is exactly the point on which some analytical psychologists, too, base their distrust of the counter-transference. As long as the primacy of the patient's need is accepted and the analyst's reaction adapted to this need, they approve of such reaction, but in that case they do not necessarily consider the term counter-transference suitable (Fordham, 1956). Yet I think that transference and counter-transference belong together and hold the promise of wholeness in their mutual opposition and similarity.

Finally, the recognition of the normality of counter-transference in the analyst may have the advantage of further stimulating the analyst's awareness of his own reactions.

It is *awareness* of the counter-transference, then, that is the essential need. The necessity for awareness is denied by no analyst, and any relaxing in the effort to make the counter-transference conscious is bound to have most damaging results in all forms of analysis and, indeed, in all therapy and in any psychiatric, psychological, or similar work that is based on human relationship.

Before giving an example illustrating some dangers encountered in analytical therapy, I should like to repeat that I am using the term counter-transference not so much in connection with any particular occurrence in such relationships, but rather as describing the libidinous flow as a whole as it emanates from the personality of the analyst towards that of the analysand. Particular occurrences, such as I am going to mention, can, however, at times epitomize the nature of the libidinous flow. Equally they may precipitate developments in the analysis and thus bring latent and dangerous elements to the fore, as the case study that I am about to give will illustrate.

Emilio Servadio (1956) in his article 'Transference and thought-transference' mentions (p. 392) that 'transference in terms of communication implies that a transference situation can never be a one-sided proposition. It necessarily implies a to-and-fro emotional under-current accompanying thought exchange', and continues: ' . . . We are compelled, therefore, to use the term counter-transference as a particular case of a more general phenomenon, that is of emotional human responses in communication'.

Servadio, in the same article, actually refers to transference and counter-transference as a *universal* phenomenon, which becomes particularly relevant in the analytical setting where, to use his own words (p. 394), 'it can be closely studied in all its implications—which is seldom possible under usual extra-analytical conditions'. It is exactly because of the greater accessibility for studying certain aspects of the counter-transference and its implications that I have chosen analytical material in order to discuss problems that go far beyond the range of analytical work and are inherent in all communications between individuals. My story only serves to bring into greater relief situations that abound in all human experience. Thus many relationships, though apparently not concerned with transference and counter-transference, nevertheless carry some of the characteristics inherent in the analytical situation. This is true especially in many instances of social, medical, and pastoral work, where a strong attachment may be formed between the helper and the seeker for help. As neither is accustomed to think in terms of transference and counter-transference, certain irrational elements, which cannot be understood on an ordinary non-analytical basis, may become apparent. Thus the one who seeks for help may show signs of an unusual dependence, which the one who helps may deplore and find unacceptable. Social counsellors no less than physicians, surgeons, and ministers of the church are quite frequently seen in most awkward situations of this kind because the nature of demands made on them is not realized as transference and their even less recognized counter-transference reaction leads to anxiety and guilt, or anger and irritation, towards those whom they had set out to help. They may at times develop a stronger desire to give help to a particular person than is expected or reasonable in the circumstances. Humanitarian motives are often wrongly attributed to a helper who, through his uncontrollable drive to help, is really a victim of his unrecognized counter-transference. Likewise in certain so-called psychological and healing techniques of an avowedly impersonal character, the transference and counter-transference may not be suspected, or it may be deliberately ignored, and lead to regrettable situations, often bringing devastation instead of help.

The Entangled Therapist

As the analyst of any school has been trained to be aware of his reactions, it is obvious that he is, on the whole, in far less danger of falling a victim to unrecognized emotions. Yet it is also true that the freeing of archetypal powers in the analysis may make such unawareness even more dangerous than in cases of more superficial relationships where no such deep events have taken place. My example is connected with an unrecognized counter-transference in an analytical relationship between a younger colleague and her patient. It is seen through my own eyes as I had to deal with the effects of the other analyst's emotional fixation after she had come to me in order to seek an understanding of her painful entanglement.

The youthful and attractive woman psychiatrist who entered my consulting room on a certain morning was perhaps thirty years old. She told me at once that she had received some 'Jungian training' for several years and volunteered the information that she belonged to the introverted thought-intuition type. She appeared to be a very intelligent person, with a great deal of humour and many artistic and philosophical interests. At the same time she possessed a warm, if somewhat erratic, heart which must have made her into a devoted and much beloved therapist. She obviously gave ungrudgingly of her time and interest to her patients, and, as she had made an unhappy marriage, she had consequently sought and found a great measure of fulfilment in her work. She had already been in practice for a few years. At this moment she was on sick-leave and had come up to Edinburgh in order to consult me.

One of her patients was a man of her own age for whom she had had a great liking. He was a lonely, very introverted person himself who worked industriously in a dark office in town and had hardly any friends. He was a prolific dreamer, and Dr X found that she became increasingly interested in all his rich material. 'I began to think about his dreams and drawings all through the weekend or while I had nothing else to do,' she told me. Once she even rang him up at his office after having had a sudden inspiration regarding one of his dreams. 'I felt I just had to tell him.' The patient seems to have been at first very grateful for his therapist's interest, and he wrote her a letter telling of considerable improvement in his condition, which he put down largely to Dr X's treatment.

Shortly after this occurrence, the therapist had an impressive dream. She saw herself standing hand in hand with her patient near the entrance of a big cave. She knew that she had to enter this and lead him through its labyrinthine maze. She felt that she would be able to do so successfully, and that they would both come out together at the other end.

She dreamt this two days before their next appointment, and was so happily inspired the next morning that she could hardly bear to wait for the analytical session in which she would tell him of her 'visionary experience' as she called it. She told me later that she had never had any doubt at that time that it was her right and duty to tell him of this dream.

When the hour of the session struck at last Dr X was excited and a little nervy. She wondered what would happen if he failed to arrive. She tidied up her room and herself, lit a cigarette, re-arranged the chairs, went to the lavatory, tidied up again, and when finally the patient appeared, five minutes after the appointed time, she was most relieved. Immediately all restlessness fell from her and she felt happy and contented.

The patient had been in a depressed phase for some weeks and during the last few days he had had a particularly tough time. As soon as he had sat down he related a dream and began to give his associations. Then there was a silence. The patient asked Dr X what she thought about his dream, but she answered that she would like to speak to him about something else first. She had something very happy to tell him, she said, and proceeded to describe to him her own dream. While she did so, it occurred to her that her tale did not sound all that interesting and inspiring. After all, it had only been her *feeling* in the dream that they would find their way through the maze, and if you looked at the whole dream objectively, it said that the big therapeutic task was still before them. 'I felt that I did not carry my audience at all,' she said to me. The patient sat before her in dull, somewhat glum, silence and looked at the ash forming on his cigarette. So Dr X thought 'like lightning' (she was always good at that) and also sent an urgent prayer to heaven. In consequence, or so it seemed to her, she had an 'idea' and she broke the silence. 'This is not really the end of the dream at all,' she said to him. 'The best part I have not told you yet. Here it is: after we got right into the cave, I felt that you were very near to me, and that we were really lovers from then on.' The patient looked a little puzzled, but quite pleased really, and said: 'I suppose it means that I am your animus or something.' Dr X beamed at him and answered: 'Well, you see, this actually is a dream which I dreamt *for* you. So it is not really my dream but yours. It means that your anima is rescuing you, and that things are going well.' At first the patient was silent. Then he said very quietly: 'Can we now do my own dream, please?' Accordingly, his dream was dealt with, and the rest of the session passed uneventfully.

However, as it turned out, Dr X had not been altogether right when she had uttered such optimistic words. The first thing that 'went wrong' was that the patient did not turn up for his next appointment. This had never happened before, and the therapist got increasingly anxious while she waited for the whole of the appointed hour. She tried in vain to contact him on the phone. There was no answer, and no message reached her that day. With the early post next morning a letter arrived. She felt shaky when she saw his handwriting, tore open the envelope, and read. The patient announced, most significantly, that he had a cold and had been unable to come the day before. He hoped to resume treatment the following week. Dr X immediately sat down and wrote an answer. She said how sorry she was, and that she hoped he would soon be better. She had a friend to dinner that evening, and she told me that she was so distraite and jittery on that occasion that the friend eventually asked what was wrong. Dr X found it a relief to talk about her 'special patient', as she always called him to me, and carefully began to do so. Was he so very ill?, asked the friend. No, it was not that, she said, but he was so lonely and had a cold and could not come to see her therefore, and, 'Well, there it is,' she added, 'our job is very difficult at times, and we so easily identify ourselves with our patients.' The friend indicated that she thought Dr X must be a very kind psychiatrist, and that she wished there were more of them. When eventually the friend left, she said:

'Goodbye, my dear, and don't worry too much,' and then she smiled a little peculiarly and added: 'Don't tell me that you are in love with that chap!' 'Good heavens, no!' cried Dr X and laughed heartily.

The week passed rather too slowly for Dr X. She was much preoccupied with thoughts of her patient. She had visions of him lying in his dingy little bedroom, and felt very sorry for him. During her work with other patients her attention was apt to wander, and on one occasion she found herself addressing one of them by her 'special patient's' Christian name. In reality she had never used this name to his face, and the idea struck her that she might do so in future. The other patient, meanwhile, was very hurt when he was thus addressed by the wrong name, and momentarily Dr X forgot 'her own problems', as she put it, in order to deal with the other one's feeling of rejection by her.

When eventually the special patient returned to her for treatment, Dr X was again in a state of happy excitement. She had bought flowers for her room and received him with a hearty handshake. As he was obviously depressed and looked slightly sullen, she immediately told him that during his absence she had thought of him a great deal, and that she was quite sure he would soon get over his depression. He made no answer at first, but after a while he said: 'I have been thinking too. I have decided to stop treatment because it does not get me anywhere. I feel that it is a waste of both your and my own time and also of my money.' Then he was silent again and looked into the fire, turning half away from her.

Dr X was so utterly shattered by this announcement that she found no words for a long time. She was too shocked even to feel dismay. She was stunned into silence, felt empty and unreal. When she lit a cigarette, she noticed that her hand shook. The quiet lasted for a minute or two. Then, finally, she regained her poise sufficiently to speak. She really wanted to say: 'You can't do this to me! We are both in this business together, I shan't accept your notice just like that', but her actual words were more prudent. She said that she did not see why he felt as he did, considering his satisfactory progress and their good relationship to each other. At this the patient raised his head and asked: 'What relationship are you referring to? Surely not that between yourself and me, because that is just talkie-talk.' (This common and ghastly word cut into her like a knife, she told me. She felt that she could forgive him everything else, but never the use of this word.) She shook her head unbelievingly and asked whether he really meant this. 'Of course I do,' he answered impatiently, 'you and your precious relationships! How many patients have you got? I suppose two or three dozen, and you have this kind of "relationship" (he contemptuously spat the word at her) to them all. Where do I come in? Don't you realize that I feel the artificiality of it all, that I see through all this technique of false pretences? No,' he concluded with great determination, 'let us face facts. I don't mean a damned thing to you. I am just a job. Let's call it a day and have done with it,' and he rose to his feet and made for the door. Dr X suddenly felt a great anger rising in her and to her own surprise and satisfaction heard herself speaking very sternly to him. 'What do you think you are doing?' she asked. 'I have toiled and laboured for you and have tried to help you, and here you go and behave like a stupid child. All right, then, go away and complain about me to someone and be as unhappy as you like. There are lots of other therapists—if they will take you.'

The patient was so surprised by her irate words that at first he remained transfixed and motionless. He had raised his hand towards her as if to shield himself from her attack, and he stayed in this position even after she had finished. Then he covered his eyes with both his hands and simply burst into tears. Immediately she was at his side. Her anger was gone, and she said imploringly, 'Please, don't take it like this. I did not mean it. You must know that I didn't. I was so worried that I hardly knew what I was saying. Please, let us forget the whole thing.' She pulled him back from the door and pressed him down into the chair. He let her do so without any protest and continued to cry in a most heart-rending way. 'Wait,' she said, 'I am not letting you go like this. I am having only one more patient tonight, and I am going to send him away because you need me more at the moment.' And she went out to deal with this matter. When she returned to her patient, he had somewhat calmed down but he looked listless and exhausted. She stayed with him and they talked for a long, long time, and when at last dusk fell over a foggy November afternoon, she had the triumph of seeing her special patient smile again, and as they parted there was a great friendliness and mutual understanding between them.

Dr X went home very tired that night. She felt dejected and sad. She had to remind herself several times that all had ended well, that the patient had been friendly at their harmonious parting. So she decided not to think any more. In vain she tried to read and finally went to bed in a slightly anxious mood. 'Tomorrow,' she said to herself, 'I shall see it all in its true light and be happy again!'

But when the morning came, the grey winter light brought her no comfort. It was still the same. She felt worried and her heart was heavy. Later she described to me how suddenly an awful feeling had struck her that morning. It was that all was finished and that she had lost. It seems that at first she was quite incapable of accepting this as the truth, but it grew on her and grew until she felt desperate and bewildered. She tried her hardest to suppress the feeling, she argued with herself and wanted to forget it. But this feeling regarding her patient was in fact never to leave her again, and although she managed to shelve it temporarily, it always returned to her and she was unable to free herself entirely of its impact at any time from then on until the final break came.

'Was it predestined?' she asked me. 'Had I to fail?' The days and weeks had lost their former quality. Time flowed by like a heavy swollen river in a grey landscape. The birds had stopped singing and a cold north-easterly wind shook the barren trees. Dr X was gripped by depression as the patient's condition deteriorated rapidly. She had lost the strength to help and sustain him. He brought her his dreams as before, they worked on his material with diligence and earnestness, but the fire was waning and no Phoenix arose from the ashes.

Now and again a new glimmer of life appeared in the burnt-out building of their relationship, but every time it soon died again and left them both in their hopeless entanglement. At times the patient broke down and wept or became violent and obstinate. He again tried to leave her, she again stopped him. But the passionate zeal that she had once felt never returned. She had lost faith in herself and no longer could rally the strength and conviction to oppose him. In the end he did not come back. Dr X received a letter from a colleague that read as follows:

Dear Dr X,

'Mr A has asked me to contact you as he is rather ill and cannot at present write himself. He asks me to say that he wishes to discontinue his treatment with you as he is too ill to benefit from it. He asks you not to write to him, and in fact I myself think it would be unwise to do so at the moment seeing that the patient is in a rather precarious state of mind.

Yours sincerely,

. . .

When she had read the letter, she had the feeling of having received this same message long before. Yet she could not quite comprehend why it elicited no response in her. 'It must be because I had seen it before,' she said to herself.

The Analysis of the Therapist

Only a short time had passed after these events before Dr X first came to me for help. She was still depressed but, since it was all over now, she had felt some measure of relief within the last day or two. After she had told me her story, I asked for her own assessment. 'What do you think has gone wrong?' I inquired. She thought it must have been a case of a very strong counter-transference. She had only heard of this phenomenon a long time ago from Freudian colleagues, and in her own analysis the term had never once been mentioned. She was not sure, either, whether she made the correct use of it in applying it to her case. 'When did you first think of counter-transference?' I asked. 'Only quite recently,' was the answer. She had been reading in a text-book a description of *folie à deux* when the idea struck her that such *folie* might occur in so very intimate a relationship as that that exists between analyst and analysand. Then she had remembered the term counter-transference again and it seemed to be more appropriate in this case.

Knowledge of the term, then, had come to her from Freudian sources and she first became aware of counter-transference as something wrong. 'But surely,' she said, 'I am right in loving my patients, or is all that counter-transference too, and should I not feel anything if I want to be a good analyst?' In order to answer this question and to understand the whole intricate problem, it was obviously necessary to begin Dr X's analysis again. In what follows I shall attempt only to give a brief summary of some of our findings. In the main, the story that has already been told is so clear that it hardly calls for much comment.

First of all, it may be necessary to say a word about Dr X's original analysis. It is very tempting to direct much of the criticism of Dr X's handling of Mr A's case on to the original analyst. He had done his job well enough? Had he been skilful and knowledgeable and, in particular, had he been sufficiently advanced himself at that time to have the right of giving training to anyone else? Personally, I am satisfied that Dr X had been very fortunate in her choice, as he possessed the highest qualifications for his task, but he had been hampered by lack of facilities for training apart from the personal analysis. Like many other Jungians, he was at the time of his work with Dr X more concerned with investigations into mythology, and was comparatively less interested in questions of transference and personal relations. It is very likely, therefore, that Dr X had never been made fully enough aware of these factors, which are of such crucial importance in analytical work. It is so obvious that the pattern of Jungian analysis is all the time undergoing such essential changes that, as is the case with all truly living disciplines, it is not possible to approach our investigation in the spirit of looking for a faulty technique in the past. The dynamism of analysis allows for no such device, as any technique must hinder the natural growth of personality and relationship.

Was it then Dr X's immaturity that caused the failure of her work with Mr A? Had she been sufficiently analysed? No doubt the answer is that she was not sufficiently mature and had not been analysed enough. This fact, however, is true of every analyst and can therefore be understood in only a relative sense: perhaps Dr X was *particularly* immature at the time? Analysts are inclined to express this kind of criticism regarding each other, and they are always quite right in one sense, but it will not lead to a deeper understanding of Dr X's failing, for instance, if we confine our criticism to such general terms. We must, in fact, gain an understanding of this particular immaturity and of her failure in some detail.

231

The Cave

From the story, it is obvious that the crisis in the relationship between therapist and patient began to show some complexity with Dr X's cave dream and its revelation. She had given this 'gem of a dream', as she called it, to Mr A, and she had done more: she had added something like an active imagination on to it. The cave was a maze and she saw in it both origin and potential solution of neurosis. In the cave lay the treasure, for in it they would lose themselves and find one another, their mutual opposite and likeness, their complementary fulfilment and cure. Dr X had touched on something of such vital truth and importance, such power and magnetism that she had—at that moment—invited the very disaster that was to overtake her.

The archetype is pitiless and too great for human handling, and Dr X had told her patient something that she herself probably only half believed and half understood, but which nevertheless was wholly true and terrible. She had played with the fire of heaven and hell, and had only been aware of saying something helpful to a suffering fellow being. But she had dragged him into her own depth and had become entangled in it. The patient, on the other hand, had darkly understood, had become afraid and confused as she had opened the door to the collective unconscious. It was *her* door, but the collective is *his* also, and thus something terrible had happened to him before he was ready. It had happened from outside, from her, but it had become something inside, something in himself, for they were in truth together in this maze, as she had told him, and he had flown from it with all the self-protective fear of the un-initiated. This was the root of the whole matter.

Dr X was, in fact, never sure why she had told him her dream and her additional imagination. 'Perhaps it was to encourage him,' she said. 'Sometimes therapists know more than their patients. Or do they never?' she asked.

I agree with Dr X that they do at times, but it is here that the analyst has to prove his discipline. To know more but to say less is a necessary principle for the initiated, whose knowledge must remain a secret because all those who may learn of it unpreparedly are in mortal danger. A strong counter-transfer-ence, however, may deprive the analyst of his archetypal significance as the wise one. It may induce him to mistake his own feelings of oneness with the patient for the latter's readiness to absorb what is still not within his psychic grasp. Even the highly intuitive therapist of my story was to commit this fatal error. Intuition may at times be so much concerned with strategy that the tactical sight could get lost. Mr A, for instance, very probably really had the potentiality to see as far as his therapist, and he could eventually have partaken of all her vision, but by burdening him with contents for which he was not prepared she hindered his analysis and prevented his cure.

Analysts, like lovers, are at times in danger of hurrying their partners. As patients can be so near to us, so deeply linked to the analyst in the *opus*, we may forget our archetypal rôle and begin to regard them as our friends and equals, which, however equal the partnership in other respects, they can never be. When once asked whom he would like as an analyst, one of my wisest colleagues answered: 'I can think of several, but they all happen to be still my patients. So I must wait until they are analysed before I can go to them.' I think we all understand what my friend wanted to express.

Dr X might under certain conditions have been right to tell her dream, provided also that she had been more acutely aware of the precise situation between them and—most of all—within herself. It was her misfortune and the patient's that she was not.

Her addition to the dream was probably particularly dangerous. It showed the desire to be *the good figure* to the patient at all costs. Her guilt feelings would not allow her to leave him in his depression. He had sullenly cut himself off from her, and she would not permit this and instead tried to force him into loving her at a moment when he could feel nothing. Had he felt anything, it would most likely have been hatred. His depression was designed to protect her from this but in the blindness of an omnipotent child, parent or lover, she believed that she could bring forth his love through hers. The easy optimism with which she treated his difficulties was fundamentally not even in keeping with her own character, but was the result of the entanglement of her heart.

The new analysis of Dr X revealed many most interesting aspects connected with her unrecognized counter-transference.

The repression of negative feelings towards her first analyst, for instance, was found to have played an important part in her mismanagement of the patient. Thus the failure of an analyst can be visited unto the third and fourth generation.

Conclusion

When Dr X revealed her dream to Mr A, she committed an offence against the incest taboo. This taboo is operative in all analysis, for any transference and counter-transference must include what Freud conceived it to be exclusively, namely the transference of parental images. The widening of this concept by Jung, who sees far beyond the personal parental transference pattern, can never lead to an abandonment of the original Freudian pattern as an important factor in the patient-analyst relationship. While this relationship is to many non-Freudian analysts of an all-embracing kind, based on archetypal reality, its parent-child aspect remains a powerful factor and transfers the incest taboo to the total relationship. The cave revelation threatened the supremacy of the taboo. The cave, symbol of the great mother, so innocently connected with the life-giving anima by the therapist, was recognized in its devouring aspect as the terrible mother by the patient's unconscious, as is seen by his attempted flight from Dr X. The tragedy was the latter's partial blindness, which prevented her understanding of the deadly nature of this archetype and only let her see the good mother whose treasures lie at the depth of her darkness. Her optimism made her extol these treasures before the darkness had been lifted. It surrounded them still, but the *opus* could have turned its essence into light. The patient—knowingly-un-knowingly—saw the darkness and felt only the destructive power of the elementary mother (Neumann, 1955). He was not yet able to understand her creative potential, although she talked to him of his anima, who could have been his guide and could have made the logos in the unconscious (Adler, 1955) available to him.

Thus all potential light was swallowed by the prevailing darkness of the therapist's dream cave, which symbolizes her unacknowledged desire to devour him, and also her own imprisonment in the great mother's womb. Lest he also be thus imprisoned, he had fled, but by doing so he had incidentally—

alas, through pain and suffering—led his analyst to a new search for the light of freedom that she was destined to find out of the darkness of her confusion.

References

ADLER, G. (1955). 'The logos of the unconscious'. *Studien zur Analytischen Psychologie C. G. Jungs*, 1. Zürich, Rascher.

FORDHAM, M. (1956). Private communications.

——(1957). 'Notes on the transference'. *New developments in analytical psychology*. London, Routledge & Kegan Paul.*

HEIMANN, P. (1950). 'On counter-transference'. *Int. J. Psycho-Anal.*, 31, 1–2.

LITTLE, M. (1951). 'Counter-transference and the patient's response to it'. *Int. J. Psycho-Anal.*, 32, 1.

MONEY-KYRLE, R. (1956). 'Normal counter-transference and some of its deviations'. *Int. J. Psycho-Anal.*, 37, 4–5.

NEUMANN, E. (1955). *The great mother*. Bollingen Series 47. New York, Pantheon; London, Routledge & Kegan Paul.

PAULSEN, L. (1956). 'Transference and projection'. *J. analyt. Psychol.*, 1, 2.

PLAUT, A. (1956). 'The transference in analytical psychology', *Brit. J. med. Psychol.*, 29, 1.*

SERVADIO, E. (1956). 'Transference and thought-transference'. *Int. J. Psycho-Anal.*, 37, 4–5.

1973

After many years I re-read this paper on counter-transference with some amazement. While recognizing its thoughts and feelings as my own, I was at the same time struck by certain distortions that appeared to be in my tale, and also by some omissions, and I should like to say a few words about this in the following paragraphs.

On the theoretical side I find my definition of counter-transference (or for that matter of transference) as 'the libidinous flow as a whole as it emanates from the personality of the analyst towards that of the analysand' largely inadequate. It fails to differentiate sufficiently between conscious and unconscious elements in the relationship and, moreover, in spite of my protestations to the contrary contained in the essay, pays insufficient attention to the task of separating such elements in the counter-transference as—to re-quote Fordham—'are adapted to the patient's need' from those that are not. While it appears that I had already acquired a marginal understanding of the nature of the counter-transference, I lacked the necessary knowledge for composing a more relevant paper, because at the time of writing I had not progressed far enough in my own analytical experience.

Since I wrote the article several analysts have contributed a great deal to a deeper understanding of the counter-transference phenomenon, which is now universally recognized as an inalienable part of the analytical set-up. Nor is it any longer seen as separate from the transference but instead as forming part of the transference/counter-transference relationship. Writers such as Fordham, Racker and Lambert—to name but a few—have given new formulations and insight in this connection, so that it is not necessary to start with a description and theoretical discussion of the transference/counter-transference event, and even less with an apology for being concerned with counter-transference in the first place, which I had still felt appropriate a decade and a half ago.

Instead I intend to go *medias in res* and look once more at the case of Dr X, both from the viewpoint of her failure as an analyst with Mr A, and from that of my analytical work with her, which latter aspect I regret to find sadly neglected in the article.

Dr X's treatment of Mr A was handicapped by her own neurosis whatever else went wrong in the therapeutic situation, and there can be no doubt that her counter-transference was of a neurotic kind. To quote Lambert in his discussion of the neurotic counter-transference: 'The danger comes from unanalysed bits and emotionally insufficiently integrated early impulses and unsolved problems'. As Dr X has since died, I have, in deference to her wishes, followed my usual custom and destroyed her file.

While I distinctly remember that the relationship to her father had been unsatisfactory, I cannot, unfortunately, recall any details in this connection. Of her marriage, which was not much short of a disaster, on the other hand, I have retained many sad details in my memory. Dr X's husband had never shown her much warmth, of which she was much more in need than of his actually and generously accorded appreciation of her intellectual and artistic capabilities. Such appreciation left her cold and deprived of more essential nourishment, while the husband felt chronically rejected by her attitude in this respect. He had sought and found another love object, while Dr X gave herself up to her profession, which would, she felt, fulfil her inner needs in a deeper sense than her husband had done.

The gap in my memory in connection with her relationship to the parents, and especially to her father, is significant in so far as my own analytical orientation at the time was not sufficiently reductive, yet her amorous feelings towards her patient were obviously expressing unconscious drives connected primarily with an unsolved Oedipal situation. This point makes me feel uneasy about the quality of Dr X's own analysis, both in her original work with my colleague and in its resumption with me. I ask myself in fact how she could have remained unaware of the nature of her entanglement with Mr A unless her transference had been left in important respects unanalysed.

Although I marginally and unobtrusively mention the lack of training in Dr X's first analyst as if it were of little importance, I fail to describe the means by which Dr X's analytical understanding was supposed to be improved through her new analysis, and I fear that such improvement may in fact have come about only to a limited extent in that, while it opened her eyes to the dangers of archetypal identifications, with their resultant feelings of omnipotence, the incestuous essence of the tale, though explicitly and frequently mentioned between us in our sessions, was never sufficiently understood. For this to happen we should have had to transfer the pivot of our task to the relationship between us (that is, where it really was and rightfully belonged) instead of leaving it collusively in her broken-down relationship with Mr A, thereby falsifying the whole issue. Indeed I appear to have mistaken my rôle as one of a supervisor, *after the event* as it were, eager not to intrude in the supervisees analysis, and scrupulously avoiding what was most urgently needed, i.e., the experience of the transference/counter-transference between Dr X and myself. Such avoidance was, of course, fairly widely practised among the earlier followers of C. G. Jung, and my excuse for concentrating my interpretations on a *tertium quid* (the events that took place between Dr X and Mr A) might have sounded respectable enough at the time, but to me this makes my essay largely invalid.

Re-reading it, I am particularly critical of the frequent and at times rather flowery references to the archetype, which I seem to use as some kind of cover-up concept for such inner events as were too stark and threatening to be faced and, even more, to be personally experienced. In my account I profess myself to be awestruck by archetypal images and I attribute similar reactions to Mr A and even to Dr X, but how near this was to the truth I had not yet sufficiently recognized, because I had avoided the *awareness* of primordial events by a deceptive process of circumvention, thereby glossing over and guarding myself and my patient against the impact of collective forces.

In fact, I think I repeated Dr X's very mistake and omnipotently played around with archetypes, thus abandoning ordinary ego-happenings for the lure of self-images, which must have added to my patient's confusion, although she was bound to feel consoled by seeing the Wise Man whom she had expected me to be ending up in the same kind of quagmire as she had done. This was never mentioned by either of us, as we both remained mercifully unaware of the fact.

This fact was my own undissolved incestuous countertransference to Dr X, of which I remained unaware but which showed itself in a tendency to fuse with her, to repeat her own mistake of falling unwittingly into archetypal identification (in spite of my intellectual knowledge of the difference between identification with and incarnation of the archetype) and, last but not least, by feeling motivated to write a paper on her case that is nothing short of an *apologia pro opere meo*. Her own very pronounced transference, on the other hand, was of an openly incestuous kind and, looking back at the whole matter, I can see that her incestuous desires unconsciously expressed my own as well as hers. In addition, the negative aspects of her transference were almost wholly ignored by both of us.

The sum total of this largely unanalysed relationship, which we studiously manipulated to come to an early end with her 'unavoidably' premature departure from Edinburgh (after eighteen months with me), consisted of a continuation of her idealization of 'archetypal' *images*, of which I was one no less than her dream had been. This made the *experience* of archetypal events and their inner consummation impossible and thus left the incest motive essentially unrecognized, just as it had been when, through the deficiency of her ability to symbolize, she acted out her inappropriate desires for her patient. Unless transference/counter-transference is experienced, understood and incubated, carnal and spiritual ignorance and the lack of differentiation between personal and collective events all tend to prevent the formation of an ego and its growth towards the integration of the self. For this to come about, Oedipal as well as earlier events have to be allowed for, and I regret to say that the pre-Oedipal urges of transference/counter-transference, often deviously transmitted by both patients, were—consciously, at least—totally ignored.

Counter-transference*

MICHAEL FORDHAM

1960

In getting up to open a symposium that is to continue next month, I am reminded of another one some years ago on archetypes and internal objects. Then it was decided that a psychoanalyst and an analytical psychologist should make parallel statements on each topic without reference to each other, to see what emerged in the discussion.

I do not believe that our committee altogether realized that they had asked the same speakers to begin again and, I believe, in the same order, but here the similarity virtually ends. For my part I could not say that what I said *then* was influenced at all by reading psychoanalytic literature, for everything worth while that had been said about archetypes had been written by Jung, and it was quite unclear whether his theory had any relevance to that of internal objects. This time the picture is radically different.

Starting from a critical study of Jung's formulations, attempts have been made and are continuing to be made by several analysts to supplement his conceptions and to describe practice in relation to their own thinking. These researches have led to study of the writings of psychoanalysts who have developed concepts much nearer to our own than heretofore, and it has been possible to hold discussions with them. These I take to be one origin of this symposium.

Before enumerating some of the ways in which counter-transference has been thought about, it has become necessary to define a term that is being given several meanings at the

* This paper, and the following one by Ruth Strauss, was presented in a symposium on Counter-transference held by the Medical Section of the British Psychological Society, London, at which the speakers were Michael Fordham, Paula Heimann, Margaret Little, Ruth Strauss and D. W. Winnicott. This paper was given in the first part of the symposium on October 28, 1959, and was first published in the *British journal of medical psychology*, **33**, 1.

present time. A wide definition is required if the findings of analytical psychologists are to be included under it, partly because of the conception that transference and counter-transference are essentially part and parcel of each other, and partly because both processes originate in the unconscious. The term will therefore be used here to cover the unconsciously motivated reactions in the analyst that the patient's transference evokes; I shall maintain that some of these are illusory while others are what I have termed syntonic, subdivisions that will be defined later on as occasion arises.

When Jung claimed to have been one of the first, if not the very first, to insist that the training of psychoanalysts should include a personal analysis, and later, when he contended that the therapeutic factor in psychotherapy was the personality of the analyst, he must have had in mind the problem of what is here called counter-transference. He does not, however, use this term often, either then or later on, and this raises the question of why? The answer is not far to seek if his work since about 1912 be considered, since in it he has been primarily interested in studying the transpersonal unconscious, and so personal relationships featured not so much for their own sake as for vehicles for unconscious activity. In this investigation personal relationships were conceived to benefit because projections can be withdrawn and the contents of them built into a psychic inner world, of which the animus and anima are the representatives, related to, but mostly distinguished from, the ego. Since the term *counter-transference* was used by Freud in the setting of the personal psychoanalytic relationship, Jung probably felt its use out of place when formulating his conclusions.

He does, however, use the term twice in (C. W., 1954) *The practice of psychotherapy* in which the main body of his contribution to psychotherapeutic techniques since 1928 is collected; both passages are illuminating. One is in a footnote reference to Freud, where he states that counter-transference was discovered by Freud, protests against the idea that transference is the product of psychoanalytic technique, and emphasizes his view that it is a social phenomenon (p. 171). The second occurs in a paper delivered to a Swiss medical society in which he puts forward the concept of 'stages in psychotherapy'. Here he calls it a symptom 'or', he says, 'better a demon of sickness'—I shall come back to this later; at present I want rather to consider the context in which this reference is set.

It is during the last 'stage of transformation' that he emphasizes the importance of the analyst's psychic states. He compares the analytic relation to chemical interaction, and continues that treatment can 'by no device ... be anything but the product of mutual influence, in which the whole being of the doctor as well as the patient plays a part' (p. 71). Later he is very emphatic that it is futile for the analyst to erect defences of a professional kind against the influence of the patient, and continues: 'By doing so he only denies himself the use of a highly important organ of information'.

The analogy of 'chemical interaction' is very far-reaching; indeed, because of the considerable fusion of the personalities that occurs, a fact that can only be overlooked to the detriment of both parties, it becomes necessary for the analyst to transform himself, to some extent at least, if his patient is to get well.

In Jung's writings, and till recently in those of other analysts, there is little detailed evidence available to demonstrate how all this appears in practice, since he has rather deliberately contented himself with giving his conception in outline, illustrating it in archetypal imagery, and leaving it to the experience of analysts to work out the details as they find them in their own practices. It is clear, however, that he is sure the patient can have very drastic effects on the analyst and that this can induce pathological manifestations in him, particularly when borderline schizophrenic patients are being treated: in one place he instances a physician who came to see him with an induced paranoia, and refers to doctors and nurses who can suffer from 'short psychotic attacks' induced by the patients under their care. Apparently this has also been noticed by psychoanalysts, for Lindner (1955) described how he discovered that as he himself started to introject his patient's psychosis the patient improved. The reverse could clearly occur when an analyst has an unresolved latent psychosis, a rare but not unknown state of affairs. The whole topic has been interestingly discussed recently by Harold Searles (1959) in his paper 'The effort to drive the other person crazy—an element in the aetiology and psychotherapy of schizophrenia'.

The effect of unconscious interchanges between analyst and

patient can thus be not only normal and therapeutic but also pathological and therapeutic. In a cogent way Jung refers, as we have seen, to the 'old idea of the demon of sickness', continuing: 'According to this, a sufferer can transmit his disease to a healthy person whose powers then subdue the demon' (1954, p. 72).

From what has been said, it is evident that since Jung's discussion has been couched in terms of archetypal forms in the unconscious, conceived as a continuum with very flexible or non-existent boundaries, the theory of the ego and contiguous boundary concepts has not been developed far. Yet only when these concepts are used or implied is it relevant to speak of transference and counter-transference and so of projection and introjection, the most frequent but by no means the only mechanisms here brought into operation.

The concept of the contra-sexual components of the psyche, the animus and anima, which are at first projected on to the opposite sex before becoming the representations of the inner world, needs mention in this context because they are conceived as the 'projection-making factors' (cf. Jung, 1959).

Introducing these archetypes is also necessary because they are conceived to have a special attraction for each other, and indeed combine to form a union in the unconscious termed the conjunction (cf. Jung, 1954), of which the analyst can be aware only indirectly through his continuing self-analysis.

These end the considerations that I believe lie at the root of all procedures in analytical psychology. They lead to the idea that every activity of the analyst, be it arrangement of interviews, comment, interpretation, tone of voice, inevitably expresses some facet of the analyst's total personality, which will become more and more engaged with his patient as the analysis proceeds. For this reason care needs to be taken in assessing the importance of techniques. It is claimed that those based on ego structures cannot cover the whole analytic procedure because they can or do exclude unconscious effects mediated through the animus or anima as the case may be; the word 'effect' seems to me preferable to influence.

Among Jung's close followers technique has got rather a bad name, for the understandable reason that it can be designed to influence the patient in the interest of theory, and then can become a defensive abstraction that must often, if not always, be classed as counter-transference. The idea can be illustrated by being considered in relation to Jung's view of psychoanalytic theory, for this he regarded as a technique used against the irrationality of the archetypal unconscious. It is not my object to discuss this proposition, nor to claim that Jung's idea is correct now. I believe that it was in the early days, and is still a prominent feature of therapeutic techniques designed to manipulate patients with a view to removing symptoms.

I now want to suggest how the papers published by members of the London Society are related to what has been said. Plaut's idea of the analyst incarnating the archetype for the patient is based on the introjection of an archetype active in relation to the patient; it is the archetypal predisposition in the analyst that makes the 'incarnation' possible. Moody (1955), who related how he 'found himself' reacting to a child in a therapeutic manner, described a procedure dependent upon the same process, while Stein (1955) in his paper on 'Loathsome women' elaborated the subject of the animus-anima conjunction and how it affected him.

It is perhaps not altogether surprising that it should be an analytical psychologist, Kraemer (1958), who published a case illustrating how a psychotherapist could suffer from illusions about a patient by misusing her dreams to justify a counter-transference. Jung's general thesis does, I think, open the door to the development of such illusions, and this may have been apparent to you. This illustrates again the lack of an adequate account of the ego's part in analytical procedures; there is little discussion of the effect of repression.

It is with a view to introducing the repressed parts of the ego that the term illusion has been useful to me.

Illusory Counter-transference

It is conceived that illusions spring from projections arising out of the repressed unconscious, the anima, and also indirectly from the animus-anima conjunction. Repressed elements are particularly important in stabilizing the illusions.

The term illusion seems to me better than symptom, though this is what it is, because it gets away from the idea that a counter-transference need necessarily be valueless. The illusory form can be a serious and indeed is the worst obstruction to the development of analytic procedures; it can become organized into manipulative techniques aiming to deny what the patient is, with a view to compelling him to change; and he can then be made to conform to a frame of reference quite different from his need at any particular time.

On the other hand an illusion can be corrected if the defences mainly responsible are successfully overcome. A boy aged eight, who talked only to his family, came to see me. I can remember that he looked quite pleased to come with me from the waiting-room where he was with his mother, but when he came into the room he stood bolt upright and looked away from me; he appeared stubborn and resistant and would not use any of the toys available. I concluded that he was angry at coming to see me so I made this interpretation, but with no effect, so I was left in doubt about the accuracy of what I had said. I later discovered from his mother that the boy was indeed angry, but it was because there were three people in the room—I conducted the first interview with a psychiatric social worker present. The illusion I had held was that only two persons were present. But it is evident that the interpretation, part of which was correct, did not operate entirely negatively, for it led to the right answer in the end. I think that a trained analyst may be expected not to entertain illusions that make it impossible for the analysis to proceed. But the kind of illusion that can be modified and can be corrected, as in my example, will occur however well an analyst is trained, and to expect their eradication is idealistic.

Reflecting on possible counter-transference illusions led me to realize that they covered the whole of psychopathology. It also appeared that what was and what was not illusion depended to some extent on the conception of analysis entertained by the analyst, on analytic ideals, and on the concept of reality held by him.

As I am going to comment further on ideals, perhaps this is the place to state that the transpersonal analytic ideal held by analytical psychologists is most often expressed as a personality who does not need to formulate techniques, but who will operate correctly and therapeutically with his patients. This personality does not need rules of procedure, but can use dreams, fantasies, affects, reflexions, etc., with safety because they are integrated into himself and adapted to the patient's needs.

245

It will be evident that fixed counter-transference illusions must feature most in the training of analysts. In training, analytic ideas are formulated, in relation to the candidate's transference to his analyst and supervisor, and these enter into the trainee's counter-transference to his patient. It is perhaps an indication of the difficulty of our topic that it is not easy to get collaboration between training analysts in attempts to study what goes on in these parts of training. It would be interesting to know whether psychoanalysts have had any more success.

A check on becoming possessed by the personal ideal analyst —made up in candidates mostly from their past experience of parent figures brought into relation with the way their own analysts have conducted, or are believed to have conducted, their analyses—is to observe analytic rules based on theory; theory in turn is based on the transpersonal ideal. The transpersonal ideal, in contrast to the personal one, lies behind the supervisor's aim of showing the trainee where he or she is subject to illusions about a patient and where he uses wrong or inadequate interpretation of a patient's observed material. But the counter-transference illusions of a candidate can also be unconscious: it is not that he wrongly interprets observed material but that the observations have not reached consciousness. They are therefore not accessible to the supervisor and are most likely to become conscious first in the candidate's analysis. That is one reason why analysis of candidates is needed during training.

My main aim in introducing the subject of training is to underline the importance that some analytical psychologists, of whom I am one, attribute to counter-transference illusions and the place they take in analysis. A central feature of training consists in showing the candidate not only that he is liable to illusions, but also the fruitfulness of finding their place in himself by keeping in touch with the unconscious processes in himself; how this will continue to happen anyway as a result of his analysis; and how his continuing self-analysis forms one of the bases of learning. I want to suggest that one function of clinical and theoretical discussions and writing papers is to continue the processes that began in training when counter-transference processes were being discovered, often for the first time. This idea introduces the syntonic counter-transference.

Syntonic Counter-transference

It is not, I believe, in the sphere of illusion, in the sense in which it is used here, that analytical psychologists have anything of particular interest to say about counter-transference, but rather when it comes to applying the main content of Jung's concept of analysis. I have already referred to the studies made by others, and I now want to develop one of my own, which grows out of the idea that the unconscious acts as an 'organ of information', i.e. a perceptual system, comparable to the receiving set of a wireless.

It would be easy to close this subject by introducing typology and say that I am referring to intuition; this could be done were it not that introjection and other affective states are clearly part of the process of discovery.

Let me start to develop the concept by giving an example of what I mean by thinking there is a counter-transference that can be called syntonic.

A female patient was showing very marked features of projective identification; her interviews became entirely preoccupied with what was going on inside me and her conviction of her accuracy. At the same time she would intersperse her assertions with questions. Now there were many reasons for not answering them, but I found myself refraining from doing so from another motive; indeed there grew up in me a conviction that to do so would be a blunder. I will assume that you will think it valid if I say that I was unable to find a source for this affect in myself. I refrained from making any interpretation for several months, until one day she was talking about her father and, in describing her behaviour with him and his with her, it became apparent that she was re-enacting her relationship with him in the transference: a main feature of his behaviour was that he did not answer her questions.

The feature of this incident to which I want to draw attention is that the analyst becomes aware of inner processes for which it is not possible to account completely, but which later become sensible when considered in terms of the patient. I have taken this example because it is rather more easy to describe than others that occur every day. If one waits for a long time and the patient provides the explanation, it is much more convincing than if the whole process occurs quickly and an interpretation

247

is made. I think, however, that this process lies at the basis of many if not all therapeutic interpretations; thus, giving a good interpretation is an expression of a syntonic interchange in which psychic contents pass unconsciously from the patient into the analyst. Intellectual or intuitive inference is only of minor importance because it is the affective process that gives rise to certainty in the analyst; this can then be conveyed to the patient.

I am not sure whether these ideas about counter-transference were influenced by parallel interest amongst psychoanalysts, and perhaps it does not matter very much, but what I had described and formulated as a syntonic counter-transference was based on very similar evidence to that submitted by Paula Heimann (1950), while Money-Kyrle's paper on 'Normal counter-transference' (1956) also develops a comparable idea to mine: there he says that interpretations depend upon the very rapid operation of projection-introjection mechanisms, that is upon affective rather than intellectual processes. To relate this theory to that of analytical psychology it is necessary to add the absolute unconscious in which the boundary concept does not apply and the space-time frame of reference does not operate. Applied to the analytic situation this means there is always an underlying continuum between analyst and patient, which only gets diminished as analysis proceeds; it is never eliminated.

How elements in this continuum become separated out and become conscious is not known, but image formation plays a large part in it, and at this level projection and introjection play an important part.

Now let us return to the example and see whether the episode can be understood in the light of these considerations. There was a period before anything became conscious at all, but the patient and I were behaving according to a prescribed pattern without realizing it. Then the father archetype was unconscious and there was no boundary between the patient and myself. It can be conceived that, during this period, as the patient's ego defences against realizing the state of affairs were stronger than mine, the archetype had been driven in the direction of my ego and I began to react syntonically to it. The next part of the process was that the patient's affectively charged pattern became introjected by me and began to become conscious, i.e., I was becoming aware that I was reacting on an irrational basis. Next, the patient produced the information necessary for me to understand the affective component in why I didn't answer her questions, and then I could project the pattern back into the patient and make an interpretation in relation to her. An adequate one would be, 'Now I see why I don't answer your questions; it is as it was with your father. You made me like your father by the very persistence of your questions, to which you did not expect an answer.' But this disposes only of the personal content, not the archetypal substratum. The interpretation clarified a boundary so that her experience of her father could then be differentiated from my experience of mine. I became orientated and could begin, with certainty, a new phase in the analysis; and when I then came up against vigorous resistances these did not shake me in what I was doing.

This formulation helps to make it understandable why analysts need to take notice of their irrational experiences: realization of a syntonic counter-transference can start with a sense that the analyst is doing or feeling something that he cannot at first explain; it will later become understandable when the unconscious content becomes related to the main ego nucleus, which can perceive and moderate its activity.

There is another consideration to which reference must be made before closing. When the analyst's ego is trained to relax its control, then another centre can be sensed and symbolized, which Jung has called the self. To it the ego can relate as a part to the whole, which, like Clifford Scott's notion of the body scheme, is cosmic—the cosmos being the total analytic situation; as part of the whole the ego can allow for the activity of an unconscious that it cannot understand but that is, as it were, understood by the self; and this makes a great deal of difference.

There are some who will regard this as an illusion, but analytical psychologists will not agree and though I have added the concept of the self here as if it were a kind of elegant appendage, it controls and has controlled all my thinking about counter-transference (cf. Fordham, 1957). The idea was, it will have been noticed, introduced earlier when the whole personality was conceived to become engaged with the patient.

In this paper it has been my aim to give in outline the kind of framework inside which one analytical psychologist works.

Though many of the examples and references are from the writings of others, I have not, I think, said anything that does not relate to my own experience.

References

FORDHAM, M. (1957). 'Notes on the transference'. In *New developments in analytical psychology*. London, Routledge.*

HEIMANN, P. (1950). On counter-transference. *Int. J. Psycho-Anal.*, **31**, 1.

JUNG, C. G. (1954). *The practice of psychotherapy. Coll. wks.*, **16**.

——(1959). *Aion. Coll. wks.*, 9.

KRAEMER, W. P. (1958). The dangers of unrecognized counter-transference. *J. analyt. Psychol.*, **3**, 1.*

LINDNER, R. (1955). *The fifty-minute hour*. New York, Rhinehart.

MONEY-KYRLE, R. (1956). Normal counter-transference and some of its deviations. *Int. J. Psycho-Anal.*, **37**, 4 and 5.

MOODY, R. (1955). On the function of the counter-transference. *J. analyt. Psychol.*, **1**, 1.

PLAUT, A. (1956). The transference in analytical psychology. *Brit. J. med. Psychol.*, **29**, 1.*

SEARLES, H. (1959). The effort to drive the other person crazy—an element in the aetiology and psychotherapy of schizophrenia. *Brit. J. med. Psychol.*, **32**, 1.

STEIN, L. (1955). Loathsome women. *J. analyt. Psychol.*, **1**, 1.

Counter-transference*

RUTH STRAUSS

1960

In the discussion on counter-transference, Dr Heimann seemed to suggest that Freud's motivation for the use of the couch need not be regarded as defensive. I am inclined to think, however, that there is some defensiveness in his decision, for he admits that he did not like to be looked at over long periods of the day. He thus expressed awareness and acceptance of his need to use certain ego defences in order to create the best condition for the work to be done, from the patient's point of view as well as from his own.

Jung, on his part, deliberately broke away from the practice of using the couch, and in providing the opportunity for patient and analyst to look at one another he was fully aware that the analyst was exposed to what he has called the infectious nature of the unconscious (1954). However, from the beginning the analytic situation was to Jung primarily a two-person situation arranged with the aim of continual interaction of patient and analyst. It is, as it were, a clear statement on the analyst's part, from the first interview onwards, that he is prepared to be a partner on equal terms, if and when the patient is ready to accept it.

It appears, at first sight, as if the two-person situation were contradictory to Jung's view that analysis introduces archetypal elements and that, as a result, the transference contains non-repressed archetypal forms. But the occurrence of these images, whose carrier the analyst is bound to be, can only be of value to the patient if they are expressed as a personal experience with the analyst.

Let me give an instance of this. A patient who felt distressed

* Presented in the second part of a symposium on counter-transference held by the Medical Section of the British Psychological Society, London, November 25, 1959, and first published in the *British journal of medical psychology*, 33, 23.

and blocked could only talk a little. What she could say was that it was my unfeelingness and unconcern that made it impossible for her to communicate with me. The following session she brought a picture showing a rock surrounded by the sea. This was meant to illustrate my relentlessness and her despair. She explained that she was the waves lapping gently around the rock—myself. Waves and rock were transpersonal images that emerged spontaneously from the unconscious conflict constellated by the analytic situation. As long as the conflict could not be understood in its personal context no progress was possible. I shall come back to this example later to take up some of the aspects with which we are particularly concerned here.

At present I wish to discuss a specific aspect of the analytic situation at its first stage, namely, the position of patient and analyst, from the point of view of their opposite position and, on the other hand, of the common ground from which they approach the patient's problems.

The fact that the patient has been accepted for analysis, be it for therapeutic or didactic reasons, implies to him that the analyst has agreed to help him to become better, and that the analyst has the power to do so. In the first stage the patient cannot accept the idea of having an effect on the analyst, and therefore has dreams in which the analyst may appear, for example, as the dentist, or the patient may remark that he feels as if he was with the dentist. He may say that he is in the hands of the analyst, or that he feels ashamed at having to undergo analysis. By all this he expresses his feeling that this situation is painful or undesirable, but must be endured. He needs the analyst to act, to carry the whole of the responsibility, since the patient cannot or must not have any influence or effect on the analyst lest progress or ultimate success should be jeopardized.

In contrast, the analyst is aware of the persistent and continual affect between patient and analyst. He accepts it as an intrinsic part of analysis, without which no useful work can be done.

The patient is afraid of or bewildered by the unknown, the unconscious, which feels at that stage to be the bad object inside him. He expects the analyst to know. The analyst is, however, prepared to use the manifestations of the unconscious, of which the transference—personal or archetypal—is primarily the vehicle. By virtue of his knowledge and training, the analyst recognizes the transference as the indicator of the patient's unconscious experiences, conflicts and fantasies about the relationship. He will also take note of his own inner processes, some of which at least will be related to the patient's experiences.

I do not want to suggest by this that the analyst is, or should be, groping in the dark in the same way as his patient, although this is also a familiar enough experience to me and other analysts. The decisive difference is that within the analytic situation a process of mutual interaction is facilitated, which, as mentioned before, the patient is not prepared to allow to happen at the initial stage. Later, when he becomes aware of the possibility of mutual affects between him and the analyst, additional defences, hitherto unnoticed, will come to the fore.

As for the common ground between patient and analyst, we have, in fact, through experience and training, more knowledge regarding the patient's disturbances and needs, which analytical psychologists recognize as well as psychoanalysts. Further, the responsibility does rest on the analyst. The commitment to help the patient has been expressed by the fact of taking him on. Among other aspects of a different quality regarding the common ground held by patient and analyst, I want to point to one in particular—the quest for wholeness. This may be expressed on the patient's part by an unmanageable greed or envy, or by intense despair over not being the only patient; by making the analyst into the source of all wisdom, the prophet, or the persecutor. The quest for wholeness is above all understood and shared by the analyst. This has far-reaching implications to which I shall refer later. In fact, on account of this the analyst is ready to give what Margaret Little, if I have understood her correctly, has called 'the analyst's total response to the patient's needs' (1957). Speaking as an analytical psychologist I would say that the ultimate reason for having chosen the profession of an analyst is due to the quest for wholeness. This complex, urge as well as aim, corresponds with Jung's concept of the self.

In this connection I felt a certain similarity between Michael Fordham's remark, 'When the analyst is trained to relax his control, then another centre can be sensed and symbolized which Jung has called the self', and Freud's early instruction to analysts to keep an evenly hovering attention.

Since the subject of this symposium is counter-transference, I am chiefly concerned with the analyst's position. From the somewhat schematic description I have already given, it may have become apparent that I am interested in a specific aspect of the analyst's position, namely, its ambiguity. This involves the analyst's potential strength and weakness from which the classical view of counter-transference springs. His problem is neither to lose the awareness of the common ground nor to give up the position that constellates the opposites. But, of course, either may happen at any time; the less so, the more the analyst can deal with his own unconscious conflicts and fantasies. The common ground, one aspect of which is the quest for wholeness, seems one of the main stumbling blocks to the procedure of analysis because of its danger of becoming fascinating and idealized.

At this point I want to come back to the picture of the rock and the sea. My patient felt stuck and I was petrified, in the sense that I could not show her any feeling. Her accusation that I was cold and unfeeling seemed correct and I felt guilty about not being able to do anything for her. Szasz, in his recent paper on the 'Communication of distress' (1959), has expounded some stimulating ideas on this particular problem. Looking at the picture, I realized that I had responded to her unconscious need by being the rock. The rock was everything that the sea was not. The rock was solid, shaped and static; the sea was fluid, formless and in motion. I also knew then that the rock could do no harm to the sea. In fact, it would be the sea that would eventually wash away bits of the rock.

My patient's picture reflected her conflict over sustaining the pain of separation, however threatening and remorseless this seemed. She felt that merging with me would create that union that is one aspect of wholeness.

My dilemma, or 'mistake', or fixed attitude, was caused by my unconscious fascination by the ideal of wholeness. Hence my feelings of guilt, which prevented me from realizing that I had to sustain the position of being the rock, unfeeling, until this position could be resolved. However, my guilt feelings functioned also as a signal that I had failed my patient somewhere. Her picture helped me to realize where. I had lost sight of the importance of one of the two positions that the analyst must sustain, that of being his patient's opposite. The result of my changed attitude was that my patient could dare to show me her hate without being afraid of destroying me.

The analyst's slipping from the opposite position seems to me to be the one mistake that lets the patient down. This is so whether it is the opposite in the patient's fantasy (in which case it is complementary to the patient's ego), or whether it is the real opposite, which the patient's ego needs to learn to sustain. I have called this collusive mistake 'siding with the patient'. This results in (a) the syntonic counter-transference, to use Fordham's term (1957), and (b) identification with the patient's defences and ideals. Both syntonic counter-transference and identification are inherent in what I have called the common ground of patient and analyst.

The temptation to side with the patient, rather than with his potential self, arises as an issue at different stages in analysis. On the analogy of Dr Winnicott's discussion of the Hippocratic Oath, one may call this failure mental adultery.

I myself have come up against the crucial problem of 'siding with the patient' in my own experience and in supervision. Perhaps it is gaps in the training of analytical psychologists that make them particularly susceptible to this predicament, in contrast to Dr Heimann's experience with trainees and young analysts, who seemed to suffer from not allowing themselves to feel with (or for) their patients, since they were chiefly concerned with applying theory when giving interpretations. The training of analytical psychologists in earlier days tended to approach the patient's psychopathology in accordance with Jung's teleological view. While it is still recognized that this view has validity, analytical psychologists at a later date understood more fully how much of analysis consists of dealing with repair of early damage. Hence young analytical psychologists, who used to find it difficult to deal with their patients' defences, are in a better position today.

Dr Winnicott has brought up other relevant and stimulating aspects of the different approach of psychoanalysts and analytical psychologists, when discussing the importance of diagnosis in relation to counter-transference. He found himself in agreement with Fordham's views when dealing with psychotics or borderline psychotics, but doubted their validity for neurotics, that is, in classical psychoanalysis.

On this I want to make two comments:

(a) Analytical psychologists do not frequently come across clear-cut neurotic cases. This may well be due to the fact that borderline cases feel particularly attracted to analytical psychology. I agree with Dr Winnicott that this constitutes a severe problem in training.

(b) In my opinion the difference between analysis of neurotics and of borderline psychotics is more a question of degree than of kind. According to my experience those patients who must be considered as neurotics need to have the experience of merging with the analyst in order to relive the pain of separation and thus to grow strong enough to give up those fantasies and defences that have cut them off from their present reality. Breaking through barriers to the level of primitive relationship, in Dr Winnicott's words, I have reached—with neurotic patients as well—layers that contain the psychotic bits fused with those of archetypal, that is, non-repressed, nature.

To exclude any misunderstanding, I want to state that I am in full agreement with those who aim at eliminating mistakes, but it seems to me an illusion to assume that analysts will ever be free from mistakes. Moreover, if this be considered an ideal, it brings us up against the danger of 'siding with the patient', by being identified with his ideal, since he expects the analyst to be faultless. Therefore it seems to me essential to treat mistakes in the same way as any other manifestation of the unconscious. I think that Dr Winnicott's remarks on the specific problem of the analyst's ego being more, or less, structured have their place here too. The more flexible the analyst's ego the greater will be his readiness to use his own mistakes constructively. How the analyst can use his mistakes will, of course, depend on the patient's ego development—whether he has to work them through by self-analysis or whether he can let the patient participate in this process.

Dr Heimann seemed to regard the latter as an unwarranted burden for the patient. Michael Fordham (1960), in his example, expressed the opposite attitude when suggesting as an adequate interpretation—'Now I see why I don't answer your questions . . . ' He was then allowing his patient to gain sight of the working of his own mind, mentally and emotionally. By making a statement like that he was communicating his concern to the patient. According to my experience it has been of particular value to the patient whenever I could bring my own mistakes into the analysis.

Summarizing what I have said so far, I want to recapitulate the specific aspects of counter-transference with which I have been concerned:

1. Counter-transference as operative from the first interview onwards.

2. Counter-transference as a means of meeting the patient's needs and expectations by the analyst, yet sustaining the ambiguous position which consists of

(a) the opposite position;

(b) the common ground of patient and analyst.

3. Counter-transference as a stumbling-block illustrated by giving up one of the two positions, with special regard to 'siding with the patient'.

4. The analyst's attitude to treating disturbance caused by counter-transference phenomena.

If I cannot agree with Dr Winnicott's suggestion of using Dr Little's term 'the analyst's total response to his patient's needs' in order to narrow the meaning of counter-transference to those phenomena which, he hopes, can be eliminated, it is not because I prefer muddle to clarity, but for reasons that I have attempted to develop in my paper.

Since I do not believe that mistakes can be eliminated altogether, I feel that making use of mistakes, treating them as material equally valuable as any other manifestation of the unconscious, will contribute to the dynamics of analysis. I do not think that counter-transference in its narrow sense can be usefully split off from the analyst's total response. In fact, I would rather say that mistakes can be part of the 'analyst's total response to his patient's needs'.

Assessing the significance of transference/counter-transference problems in relation to the analyst's personality, I want to consider it together with the question of whether the sex of the analyst matters for the analytical process. Invariably when choosing an analyst the patient will be conscious of the analyst's sex, and sometimes this will be decisive. Yet, according to my experience, fundamental problems and conflicts of the patient will emerge and be worked through in the course of analysis, irrespective of the analyst's sex. Similarly, the personality of the analyst, as experienced in his preferences and vulner-abilities, will not be as such decisive for the successful process of analysis, depending upon the analyst's awareness of an ability to handle his counter-transference. In contradistinction to what has just been said, this will not be relevant for the outcome of analysis as far as the non-transference/counter-transference elements, which may also be an essential part of the analytic situation, are concerned. For successful analysis involves the growth of a two-person situation into a mature two-person relationship where ego boundaries are developing.

Additional Note

Since this paper was read a great deal of literature on counter-transference has been published.

As far as analytical psychologists are concerned, the relevant papers have been collected in this volume. Psychoanalytic authors, in particular Searles (1965) and Racker (1968), have expressed views on the phenomenon of counter-transference in many respects similar to those stated by me. For example, the two aspects of the interaction between analyst and patient, i.e., (a) 'the opposite position', and (b) 'the common ground', seem much in accordance with Racker's terms 'the com-plementary and the concordant identifications' and their ramifications.

References

FORDHAM, M. (1957). 'Notes on the transference'. In *New developments in analytical psychology*. London, Routledge.*

——(1960). Counter-transference. *Brit. J. med. Psychol.*, **33**, 1.*

HEIMANN, P. (1960). Counter-transference. *Brit. J. med. Psychol.*, **33**, 9.

JUNG, C. G. (1954). 'The practice of psychotherapy', *Coll. wks.*, **16**. London, Routledge.

LITTLE, M. (1957). '"R"—the analyst's total response to his patient's needs'. *Int. J. Psychol-Anal.*, **38**, 3/4.

RACKER, H. (1968). *Transference and counter-transference*. London, Hogarth Press.

SEARLES, H. F. (1965). Collected papers on schizophrenia and related subjects. London, Hogarth Press.

SZASZ, T. (1959). The communication of distress between child and parent. *Brit. J. med. Psychol.*, **32**, 3.

WINNICOTT, D. W. (1960). Counter-transference. *Brit. J. med. Psychol.*, **33**, 17.

Technique and counter-transference*

MICHAEL FORDHAM

1969

PART I

Introduction

Analytical psychologists as a whole have paid little attention to
the subject of technique. Yet without developing a clear
picture of what analysts do—and that is what technique implies—data obtained in the analytic situation cannot be
fruitfully compared, no scientific studies can be made and
communication between colleagues becomes difficult, if not
meaningless.

Besides Jung's publications, a number of books dealing with
the practice of analytical psychology have appeared (cf. Adler
(1961), Baynes (1955), Harding (1965), Wickes (1959) *et al.*).
Sufficient account has therefore been given of Jung's specific
contributions to psychotherapy. They may, however, be termed
macroscopic and invite a next step: the microscopic study of
analyst-patient interaction. It is a step that meets with difficulties and resistances expressed through anxiety lest study of the
analytic situation, with a view to bringing analysts' activities
to light, might interfere with valuable spontaneity in their
relation with patients.

As an amplification, reference has more than once been
made to the alchemical analogy of the *vas bene clausum* (the
well-sealed vessel), suggesting that such living matters cannot
with safety be discussed outside therapeutic interviews (cf.
Kirsch, 1961). This is untrue, and, if some effort is not made to
bring details out into the open, they are handed on in private
and a secret tradition develops that is not made accessible to
critical evaluation; instead, it forms a core of unresolved

* First published in the *Journal of analytical psychology*, 14, 2.

transference and counter-transference matter, kept private because of the infantile anxieties attached to it.

In London, interest had been directed to elucidating what analysts do in detail (cf. Moody (1955), Plaut (1956)), and I myself contributed by making a study of the transference, giving particular attention to the counter-transference (Fordham, 1957, 1960 and 1964). That psychoanalysts have contributed in ways that have brought them very much nearer Jung's view of interaction between analyst and patient (cf. Racker, 1968, especially) has been valuable, and I shall make use of their work in this essay.

Jung's Contributions

Since the studies conducted in London stem mainly from Jung, I shall begin by reviewing his observations on technique and how they developed over the years.

In his early publications he showed his grasp of experimental method and, later, of that of psychoanalysis, but it is in his correspondence with Loÿ (Jung and Loÿ, 1914) that this early position is most clearly stated; there he discusses psychoanalytic technique and writes that though 'there are general principles and working rules for individual analyses . . . the . . . analytic procedure develops quite differently in every case' (p. 272); thus early on he was aware of the need for flexibility in applying rules and of the individual character of the procedure.

In this correspondence he also lays stress on the therapeutic influence of the analyst personally—a theme that has been widely discussed—but it was in 'The therapeutic value of abreaction' (1921) that he made a most significant statement that applies to analysis, though he first considers abreactive treatment. He says that it is not so much suggestion that is therapeutic as the influence of the therapist himself: 'I would rather call it . . . his human interest and personal devotion. These are the property of no method nor can they ever become one; they are moral qualities which are of the greatest importance in all methods of psychotherapy' (p. 132). He then goes on to apply this idea to the psychology of the transference conceived as 'the patient's attempt to get into psychological rapport with the doctor'. He not only analyses the situation but meets the patient's need for a realistic relationship. This

261

requires honesty, for: 'How can the patient learn to abandon his neurotic subterfuges when he sees the doctor playing hide-and-seek with his own personality, as though unable, for fear of being thought inferior, *to drop the professional mask of authority, competence, superior knowledge,* etc?' [p. 137, italics mine].

This emphasis on personality and individuality is one root of the belief that technique is to be avoided. It was conceived as something that had little to do with personal qualities, did violence to the individual nature of the analytic process, and, worst of all, could become disembodied. These are necessary features of techniques of the natural sciences and so they are inappropriate.

It is of interest that Jung refers to the display of professional authority, competence and superior knowledge, qualities that a patient rightly expects his therapist to have acquired. That these introduce asymmetry into the analytic situation from the start is well known and it will continue, though in diminishing proportion, as the analysis proceeds (cf. Fordham, 1957, p. 79f.). Jung here warned of dangers in the use of technical skills through a special case of the therapist using them defensively. It is not a generalized attack on technique, for in his essay 'The relations between the ego and the unconscious' there are clear indications that he approves of the acquisition of techniques; he refers there to the 'synthetic hermeneutic method' and to 'the technique of differentiation between the ego and the figures of the unconscious' (1916). In 1931 he wrote of the 'principles of my technique' (p. 46), which aims 'to bring about a psychic state in which my patient begins to experiment with his own nature', and in another paper written at the same time: 'As is well known, one can get along quite well with an inadequate theory, but not with inadequate therapeutic methods' (1931a, p. 38).

Furthermore, he always gave reductive analysis relative importance though developing other definable procedures of his own: dream analysis and, though he tries to avoid applying the idea of a method to it, active imagination also; he further recommended the therapist to acquire a wide knowledge of mythology and comparative religion to use in the method of amplification—he surely did not mean these to be used to build up a therapist's defences!

Yet again and again he emphasizes the defensive uses to

which technique can be put. The root of this theme stems from his relation to Freud: it was Freud, he believed, who emphasized technique and placed his authority behind it so that psychoanalysis became identical with its method: Freud, he said, insisted on ' . . . identifying the method [of psychoanalysis] with his sexual theory, thus placing upon it the stamp of dogmatism' (1930, p. 324). To this he took vigorous objection—so here is an important source of Jung's critique of the uses to which technique can be put, and also, it may be noted, of Freud's theorizing. It may be noticed here that the two are conceived to be indivisible.

I would like to say in parenthesis that though Jung needed to take this stand, his concern about the future of psychoanalysis has not been borne out by its subsequent development, while ironically there has grown up among analytical psychologists a strong tendency to develop the very dogmatism against which he took such a strong stand (cf. report on the Second International Congress for Analytical Psychology 1962, Anon. 1963, p. 167, and Harding 1963).

I myself do not think of this tendency in such an unfavourable a light as Jung did. To fight for a discovery or important element of theory or technique can, in my opinion, very easily lead to a need for dogmatism, provided the theory or technique is worth fighting for.

To return to Freud, Jung divined in him a basic assumption that 'took over the rôle of a *"deus absconditus"*' (1963, p. 148f.), and gave a compulsive one-sided character to psychoanalysis. He struggled against it and thought he had resolved his own conflict by developing a theory of opposites that could lead him to say: ' . . . the structure of the psyche is so contradictory or contrapuntal that one can scarcely make any psychological assertion or general statement without having immediately to state its opposite!' (1943, p. 77).

Jung seems to have conceived technique as a method based on theory. Whether this was in his mind when he expressed caution about theorizing (cf. for instance, 1938, p. 7) cannot be gone into here. In my view what he says is a plea for weighing the relevance of theoretical statements. Whether a theory be true or false, whether it is useful or no, does not depend upon whether its opposite can be stated, but upon which of two mutually exclusive alternatives is the more true or useful in any particular context. Only when a theory becomes a conviction does a technique, based on it, become the exponent of a one-sided position and only then is the way open for it to be used as a rigid defence against irrational and unconscious dynamisms. Since Jung introduced many theoretical concepts of his own he could not in principle have been against the method but only against identifying explanation with the scientific procedures of psychoanalysis as a whole.

There can be little doubt that Jung was ambivalent about theorizing. Sometimes he seems to want a general theory that will explain psychic events, but he often emphasizes that there is none, with scarcely concealed satisfaction: there is, for instance, no general theory of consciousness, no general theory of dreams (1944, p. 43). It may be that his somewhat nostalgic wish for a general theory led him, as a compensation, to over-emphasize the irrational, unpredictable nature of psychic life: '... we have to reckon with a high percentage of arbitrariness and "chance" in the complex actions and reactions of the conscious mind. Similarly there is no empirical, still less a theoretical, reason to assume the same does not apply to the manifestations of the unconscious' (*ibid.*).

The Actual Present

Another strand in his thinking, at the time when he was separating from psychoanalysis, is particularly relevant: he criticized the tendency to investigate infantile memories at the expense of the 'actual present' (1913, p. 166f.). The issue he raised has proved of immeasurable importance and under-scored the emphasis he develops on the interaction of analyst and patient, placing it in the centre of the analytic situation. This was well stated when, developing his earlier position, he wrote: 'By no device can the treatment be anything but the product of mutual influence, in which the whole being of the doctor as well as that of the patient plays its part' (1929, p. 71), and then: 'For two personalities to meet is like mixing two chemical substances; if there is any combination at all both are transformed' (*ibid.*). Here is surely the root of his alchemical analogies and the concept of the dialectical procedure later brought into clear focus.

The Individual and the Collective

In 1935, he reapproached the individual nature of personal analysis. When discussing psychotherapy as a whole, he stated that there are two trends in the human psyche: one leads towards collectivism in social identifications, the other towards individualism.

In the case of individualists, reductive analysis is the treatment of choice as a corrective to individualism. (Let it be noted that technique is here linked with a therapeutic procedure.) It is only when individuality is underdeveloped that the non-technical dialectical procedure applies. 'Since individuality . . . is absolutely unique, unpredictable, and uninterpretable the therapist must abandon all his preconceptions and techniques and confine himself to a purely dialectical procedure, adopting the attitude that shuns all methods' (1935, pp. 7–8).

The attitude expressed in his statement has exercised very considerable influence and has led analytical psychologists to claim 'unprejudiced objectivity' or 'enlightened subjectivity', to rely solely on intuition or to speak apologetically, of using rules thus qualifying procedures resulting from their application (cf. Fordham, 1968). In this confusion, which I consider unnecessary, they can gain some support from one of Jung's formulations, but not very much. In passages on method in *Psychology and alchemy* (p. 43ff.) he seeks to avoid 'preconceived opinions' and then goes on to describe his methods: techniques of establishing the context of dream imagery, either through associations obtained from the patient, the use of dream sequences (which can be taken as their equivalent) or amplification by using ethnological parallels. These techniques are clearly to be used: when writing of the patient's struggle for wholeness he says in the same volume (1944, p. 3): ' . . . while the patient is unswervingly seeking the solution to some ultimately insoluble problem, *the art and technique* of the doctor are doing their best to help him towards it' [author's italics].

There can be no doubt that Jung uses both theories and techniques not only to reduce excessive individualism to collective normality but in all sorts of ways, even if it be only to ' . . . make it a rule never to go beyond the meaning which is effective for the patient' (1931, p. 46). My reading of his position in 1935 is that he was overstating his case to highlight a worthwhile issue. In later essays, for instance his essay on the transference (1946) and in his last technical contribution to psychotherapy (1951), he is far less extreme—after all, he developed a theory of transference and this cannot be done without modification of the position he took up in 1935. If the whole situation is conceived as individual and unpredictable there can neither be a description nor a generalized theory of the relation between analyst and patient.

In this perplexing situation, which stems from emphasis on the irrational, a formulation that Jung presented in 1942, in his paper 'Psychotherapy and a philosophy of life' (published in 1943), seems to me particularly enlightening. It shows where he thought technique could not or rather ought not to be applied. Starting from his earlier view, he says that in those cases where a collective solution is not possible, and so when individuation begins, the moral, ethical and philosophical assumptions of both patient and analyst come under review in the therapeutic situation. If the patient is to expose his convictions on these matters the analyst must do the same without reservation; it is in this situation that a personal confrontation takes place, leading to further self-realization by analyst and patient alike. Technique then becomes undesirable, and 'explanation' becomes a defence whereby ' . . . the possibilities of individual development are obscured by being reduced to some general principle . . . ' (1935, p. 11).

He goes further to imply that, by force of circumstance, method is at an end, for the analyst's theoretical views, on which technique is based, may well either prove broken reeds or need radical modification if the patient is not to be damaged by them. The moral conflict with the patient leads on to the important stage of transformation in which 'the doctor is as much "in the analysis" as the patient. He is equally a part of the psychic process of treatment and therefore equally exposed to the transforming influences' (1931, p. 72).

Personal Note

My own formulations could not have been constructed without Jung's ideas, and that is why I have worked over those that have been meaningful to me. From him I took the alchemical analogy, though in a way that initially made me give excessive importance to the analyst's internal life: to his particular qualities rather than his ability to manage them. This led on to pursuing a subjective investigation and to understanding, contrary to my expectation, that the analyst's affects were responses to the patient and that then they were indeed a source for understanding the patient rather than himself; in this way I got out of a subjective bias. Thus arose the concept of a syntonic counter-transference (Fordham, 1957), developed as I started to grasp that what I had thought of as part of myself was an introjected part of the patient.

My present position now depends upon another development: a concept of individuation outlined in *Children as individuals*. The concept (1969), which grew out of earlier work (Fordham, 1955), is close to that worked further forward by Frieda Fordham (1969), who showed how individuation in infancy was consonant with Jung's basic definition. This position was also implied in 'The importance of analysing childhood for the assimilation of the shadow' (1965). Concisely, I hold that individuation processes can be shown to occur in all the stages of life that Jung differentiated (1931a) and that the non-rational open-minded attitude, which Jung adopted for individuation cases in later life, enters into and plays a significant part in an analyst's behaviour with all patients.

PART II

Technique

In the natural sciences technique has come to mean the skill of the scientist in using instruments of various kinds, whether mathematical or experimental. They are not subject to subjective or personal influence. Statistical techniques follow a logic of their own and an experiment, though designed by a person, operates without his himself having subsequent influence upon it. Can this concept be applied to interchanges between human beings at all and in particular between analyst and patient? That is to say, can there be a technique of analysis that has no relevance to the analyst as a person? This is surely the state of affairs that Jung, though he seems to be half hoping for it, discards when he says it is not available to the analytical psychologist (1944, p. 43). In spite of this, it would be possible to interpret what he says to mean that when applying reductive techniques a scientific procedure is relevant but not when applying the dialectical procedure.

It will be apparent, however, that if the dialectical procedure be relevant to all analytic procedures (I was going to say 'techniques') then the analyst's personal reactions, far from being excluded, must be included in all of them. Therefore, if it is possible to refer to 'analytic technique', some modification of the 'scientific' concept, as I have formulated it, must be made rather than hankered after. Yet, while it is apparent that modification is required by the nature of the analytic situation, I mistrust excessive reliance on personal qualities. If there are dangers attached to the use of depersonalized or transpersonal 'scientific' techniques, there are perhaps greater ones related to relying on the individual personal qualities of the analyst. He easily becomes idealized and so opens the door to such abuses as intrusive display of his personality or acting out his counter-transference.

Since technique enters into teaching, the subject may be developed by reflecting on a relevant and important feature of training. Technique, it will be conceded, involves reliable knowledge that can be communicated to candidates who under optimal conditions acquire it. As our knowledge of technique progresses and as we know more and more about the dynamics of the analytic situation, so our training improves and trainees start off from a better position as analysts. However, during supervision of candidates for membership of the Society of Analytical Psychology in London, it often becomes clear that they cannot grasp and manage the problems their patients present because their personal conflicts and anxieties prevent them from doing so.

Many years ago, a candidate, a psychologist trained in reporting, revealed this particularly well. He could tell me in a sufficiently organized way how his patient behaved, what he said, and how he, the candidate, replied. Together we then worked out interpretations that he could use in detail and we predicted the results. After several successful applications of this procedure, it became apparent that he was not following up his achievements and ceased to be keen on proceeding as we had been doing; supervision then became more pedestrian, with his reporting, my commenting on case material, and his using what I suggested in various ways.

One feature in all this became clear to me: the candidate could not follow up the advantage he appeared to have gained. A number of possibilities for this state of affairs presented themselves, of which the following may be selected:

(a) his analyst had not been able to analyse the affective consequences of the exercise undertaken as part of supervision, because

(b) the affective implications of what occurred were far beyond the candidate's development. So the project we developed was accomplished only by splitting himself into an observing and a thinking person. Thus he remained unconscious of his involvement in the process and this blocked further use of what he had worked out in supervision.

From experiences in supervision besides this one, and also as the result of analysing candidates' counter-transferences to their patients, it became clear, once again, that an analyst must necessarily work within the range of his own affective possibilities. To push him ahead of what he can grasp affectively, even though he can comprehend the problem intellectually, of necessity raises his defences. It can lead on to exacerbating the false self, the very result that Jung rightly criticized. That the candidate refused to follow up the achievement was thus, in one sense, to his credit.

It is such experiences that seem to bring into doubt the relevance of the scientific method. However, it can be held that they merely indicate the interference of counter-transference affects, and so it would follow that had the candidate been further analysed he would have been able to pursue effectively the experiment that I initiated with him. He would be able to formulate interpretations and follow them up with others, or pursue other methods relevant to the material produced by his patient.

In training analytical psychologists the concurrent analysis and supervision of candidates is designed to prevent the misuse of technique and to ensure that what is learned is related at all points to the personal capacities and gifts of the trainee; thus the aim is to ensure that all transactions between analyst and patient remain personal in the sense that Jung used the term.

Having these ideas in mind, is it possible to formulate a concept of technique? I follow Jung in holding that analytic (or synthetic) technique cannot be defined as independent of human beings, as is usual in the natural sciences. It must include the personality of the analyst and refer to a differentiated part of the self that basically, by deintegration (cf. Fordham, 1957), is made available for the treatment of patients. Technique then cannot be defined unless it is thought of as including the person of the analyst. I suggest that if it be conceived of as the distillate of habitual behaviours by an analyst with differing kinds of patient, the problem can be made more manageable.

Technique, which I shall identify mainly with interpretation, then comes to depend upon the analyst's having achieved a sufficient range of experience and maturity. In addition he needs to have learned, in the personal setting of the analysis of patients, in supervision, seminars (later in discussion with colleagues), in reading and private reflection, how to refine his experience. As a result he will have acquired the capacity to communicate with patients and abstract his experience with them into theories so that colleagues can understand, profit from and add to them. This formulation obviously covers only a part, though an essential one, of the total interaction between analyst and patient, for it only states the range of the analyst's ego development. But it is upon this that technique as defined must depend.

The definition requires qualification as follows: since the analytic situation is in essential respects unique and unrepeatable—hence the need to establish the individual context of any content under review—even the interpretation of the most familiar situations will contain variations in wording or phrasing and their affective content will differ from case to case. Variations in tones of voice and differing emphases, not to mention facial and other bodily movements, are inevitable and desirable so long as their relation to the patient is noticed and understood. It is important to grasp that, though technique is essentially a scientific procedure, many interventions may be fruitfully compared to the work of an artist, who uses his technical mastery in the service of a creative and individual achievement.

Since communications about technique to a third person or to a group or in a published essay alter the analytic events, often in significant respects, it can be claimed that to teach, to communicate techniques, to discuss technical procedures or to arrive at conclusions about what procedures are correct and what incorrect are all useless. Against this position, which I regard as due to idealization of technique and a wrong understanding of its nature, it can be held that, without great loss and with much gain, a moderate degree of abstraction and generalization can be used from which great advantages accrue. It becomes possible to compare notes with colleagues and to formulate techniques having validity in the social context that enrich and develop analytic practice with individual patients. In addition, more detailed matters can be gone into: studies can be made about the relevance of interpreting part of the patient's conflict or the whole of it, of activity or passivity on the part of the analyst, of timing interpretations and the quantity of them, of the meaning that the analyst's interpretations as a whole may take on in the light of the patient's positive or negative transference.

The problem that Jung opened up by stating that some patients need to become better adapted, while others need to work out individual solutions, can now be reconsidered. The difference between what Jung said and the ideas I have begun to develop is as follows: if *all* valid techniques are personal interactions between analyst and patient, then the individual element becomes an essential part of all interpretative and other analytic procedures. But this does not mean that all cases are the same; indeed, Jung's distinction still stands, as it were, macroscopically. It is only when the detailed microscopic analysis of the analytic situation is gone into that his distinction comes to be seen as quantitative rather than qualitative.

All patients are basically individuals: some are more or even over-adapted, others are less or grossly unadapted. A technique of interpretation is intended to increase the capacity of the patient for reflection about himself, first in relation to his analyst, and, as a consequence, to his wider environment and his inner world. It has no other aim: it does not aim to remove symptoms nor render the patient normal or adapted, though if these results are in the patient's interest they will take place. All this

271

leaves the patient to make use of technical procedure in his own individual way.

It may be added that when an analyst uses a technique he is affirming by implication that he has been over this ground before, that he is familiar with it and can respond easily and comfortably to his patient. The likeness of the analyst's experience with that of his patient leads, because of his familiarity with what is going on, to a capacity to project himself, i.e., put himself into his patient's place, or to introject, i.e., experience the patient's feelings inside himself: these twin processes form the basis for flexible and complex identifications, necessary if he is to relate intimately (empathize) with his patient. By letting projections and introjections happen freely and relying on their taking place sufficiently, the raw material for interventions is provided (cf. Money-Kyrle, 1956). It is, to use an alchemical analogy, the *prima materia* of analysis.

The unconscious processes of projection, introjection and identification happen during listening to the patient. It is then that the analyst keeps himself open-minded, he 'puts aside preconceptions', and empties his mind as far as possible. Freud defined this attitude first in a classical phrase, 'evenly hovering attention'. When practising this 'technique', information is being collected and the analyst is finding out, through the activity of his attention based on unconscious processes, what is near the surface in the patient at the time.

On the basis of conclusions drawn from what the patient is saying *today*, an analyst makes technical interventions designed to clarify, explore and interpret the patient's communications. In this next step he draws on the whole of the knowledge of his patient that he has accumulated over months or years of analysis. The analyst distils the to-and-fro processes of projection, introjection and identification till he arrives at a position from which he can make an interpretative intervention in which he is flexibly involved. Under these conditions his intervention can be appropriate, he will estimate the patient's anxiety and make interpretations at suitable enough times; if he makes 'mistakes' these are of the order that can be retrieved (cf. Heimann, 1960 and Strauss, 1960). The activities just described are part and parcel of 'routine therapy'. They only work with patients mature enough to use insights and are the expression of technique whose range increases with knowledge, experience and the analyst's personal development. The alchemical analogy to this seems to be the use of a '*theoria* for effecting chemical changes' (Jung, 1944, p. 285).

In 'routine analysis' it looks as if a part of the analyst has been set aside to act as an instrument much like the experimental instruments in the natural sciences. But this is only apparent because the unconscious processes, upon which the part relies, do not obtrude themselves. It follows that routine analysis of patients is conducted as if the analyst were using a 'scientific' technique with which he is thoroughly familiar. Under these conditions it is just as if he is conducting a sequence of experiments whose results he can predict and in which he is not personally involved. This state of affairs covers but reinterprets psychoanalysis as it has been developed over the years by many psychoanalysts (cf. Greenson, 1967). It depends upon establishing a therapeutic alliance that will hold through the interpretation and working through of resistances in the positive and negative transference.

The account of this procedure, which is necessarily brief and has been developed and elaborated in considerable detail elsewhere, implies that the analyst deploys his technique without the intervention of any counter-transference at all—an ideal that is, however, never reached.

Before proceeding to consider counter-transference—a term not much used by Jung—and its relation to technique, there is one feature of the analytic situation that needs attention: it is the analyst's style, which expresses the individuality of the analyst. In the course of time each analyst develops his own characteristic way of analysing patients, which is distinct from that of any other. It can be and has been held that the individual style is the central core of all analytical procedures. On this basis, formal training becomes undesirable because it is essential for a trainee to find out in his own way, in relation to his patients, how to conduct analyses. Supervision and lectures and seminars on technique then come to be thought of as undesirable.

It is difficult to contradict this idea because style is by definition individual and ultimately incommunicable, but even if the analyst's style is an essential feature of his practice, and I agree that it is, there is no reason to suggest that analytic training, in which a personal analysis is a central feature, can fail to expand the range and provide useful contributions to the development of his style.

It may fairly be claimed that Jung's special contribution was to a field where individuality was primary, but he did not say that techniques and methods were to be eschewed. This idea, already discussed above, is not the whole of Jung's thesis and so the generalization based on a part of it and made to cover the whole analytic situation cannot be justified by referring to his work.

Counter-transference

During the conduct of routine analysis, technique holds the patient, who ultimately, in spite of what he may project into his analyst's use of it, will be grateful to him. Counter-transference is easily managed by the analyst and can be the part of the analysis that makes for empathy with his patient's conflict situations.

Analytical psychologists have developed a special interest in the counter-transference. It stems from the idea of the dialectical procedure and from Jung's assertion that the analyst needs to be just as much in analysis as the patient. For this reason it can sometimes be thought that the analyst's having emotions about a patient means that there is a counter-transference present in need of analysis. I cannot agree to this idea because the analyst can experience uncomplicated affects of two kinds: there are personal 'human' interchanges that occur most at the beginning or end of the interview, though they may also happen at any time that seems desirable. Then there are the more intense loves and hates, which can be directly relevant and so adapted to the patient's needs (in contrast to his wishes).

Suppose a patient is truly deprived and worth love, then loving is appropriate; the same applies to hate of a patient when he means to be destructively violent. The only difference here between analyst and patient is in their differing consciousness. Since an analyst knows about his affects, he need not act on them but understands them as indicators and useful parts of the analytic situation. He knows that love and hate by analyst or patient can indicate either their basic unity or the inimical nature of their two personalities. Each can also contain realistic estimates the one of the other. The situation is the equivalent, in day-to-day work, of the confrontation that Jung conceived in moral, ethical and religious terms. Having laid emphasis on affective communications based on health, I shall now go into the counter-transference in more detail.

The classical view of counter-transference, still frequently held as I have already mentioned, is this: it is undesirable and ideally takes no part in the analyst's technique. Its effects are held to be negative because an unconscious process is defended against and distorts the analyst's interventions. For instance, if the analyst is *not* analysing a patient in reasonable comfort and if the patient's behaviour, his illusions or delusions, disturb him in ways that are not to be defined and understood, then a negative counter-transference may be present. If he then finds himself making mistakes, they are probably due to his counter-transference.

The following are examples of the undesirable effects of counter-transference. (1) An analyst may reject the patient's transference by saying, 'I am not like that' *when* the patient's projection requires interpretation. (2) He may defensively play a rôle that means he imagines that what he does or how he feels *necessarily* has a bearing on the patient's transference. He may then start to believe erroneously that expression of his good behaviour and good feeling will *of necessity* benefit the patient, when well-meaning interventions are felt by the patient as impingements that interfere with the development of the patient's transference affects. These illusions and others like them can be grouped as counter-transference in its negative sense. A list of them would comprise the sum total of all the analyst's psychopathology; indeed, nothing an analyst says that is based on unconscious fantasy or impulse, and is defended against and so gives rise to illusions or delusions, can be brought into relation with technique.

But is counter-transference always undesirable? In 1957 I first suggested that it need not be so; I extended the use of the term and divided it up into illusory and syntonic parts. The illusory elements cover the negative elements in the counter-transference. Syntonic elements are basically different because, through introjection, an analyst perceives a patient's unconscious processes in himself and so experiences them often long before the patient is near becoming conscious of them.

The significance of his experience may or may not be recognized by the analyst. But in neither case is it of any use in the analytic process till the patient produces enough relevant material for the analyst to communicate what he has long 'known' to the patient. Only when the patient is on the edge of reaching an affect that the analyst has reflected inside him can the syntonic counter-transference be used. Before this the introject acts as a foreign body that often defies understanding.

It was these states that led me to use the term *syntonic counter-transference* and to think of the processes it represents as related to technique (cf. Fordham, 1957, 1960 and 1964). Since then I have come to think that the clinical experiences subsumed under this heading seem better considered in terms of an introject that has failed to become re-projected. The two unconscious processes, projection and introjection, are thus considered valuable processes, and, together with information gained by listening and observing, form the basis upon which technique rests. A syntonic counter-transference is thus part of a more complex situation. So conceived it helps to avoid two pitfalls:

1. Because the introject is of little use at the time, it becomes negative, since it deflects the analyst from his aim of working at the level the patient has reached. It is relevant only to what is right under the surface and well defended by the patient. Conceiving analysis as including not only the unconscious content being resisted but also the resistances themselves, it can be asked why does the analyst have the experience? If through introjection an analyst gets indirect experience he often cannot understand, could it not be that he defends himself against the patient's own defences by knowing beforehand? Since he has no evidence of the source of his experiences, the conclusion I would draw is that he has ceased to listen to what his patient has been saying, because of his unconscious hostility to the defences that the patient seeks to communicate to him. In other words he treats the patient as if his defences do not exist. This illusion can lead to brilliant 'intuition', flair and the like that sometimes produce exciting results. It does not belong to analysis of the patient because the defences are ignored.

2. The introject may result in internal identification with it

of the analyst's ego; then we may arrive at 'incarnating' an archetype, a phrase used by Plaut in 1956. He postulated alternatives: either the analyst educates the patient or incarnates the archetypal image. His formulation, at the time very useful, like that of the syntonic counter-transference, has unfavourable aspects—in particular it leads to the impossibility of the patient integrating the content of a projection. Here again there is often a concealed counter-transference illusion.

Each concept therefore highlights, or rather names, a state of affairs that all analysts can locate in the total analytical situation, but looked at in terms of the projection-introjection sequence the syntonic counter-transference can, like the incarnating of the archetypal image, be recognized as part of the unconscious communication process upon which technique rests. If either be considered in isolation, it implies at best a temporary breakdown in communication to be located in the projective part of the analyst's work. Just as the introjective processes in counter-transference were most easily seen in identification with them, so was it with projective processes. A projection leading to identification results in an experience by the analyst that a part of himself is a part of the patient. This means that an alliance is made between the parts and so affective understanding of the patient is furthered; this Racker (1968) calls, appropriately, 'concordant counter-transference'.

It is of interest that both these concepts, which rely on the study of events within the analyst, should be invented by analytical psychologists; they seem to have arisen from anxiety about the analyst's making projections and consequently overlooking the need for them. It is, I think, relevant to state that though there is little in Jung's publications against it and indications that he knew about the need for projection, nothing has been said overtly about its positive value. Jung's assertion that projections are part of the process of becoming conscious seems to have been overlooked and not applied to the analyst's work of interpretation. So the current attitude among analysts has been that projections ought to be taken back into the self and so integrated. Consequently there arose a tendency to exclusive subjectivism, i.e., if an analyst detected a projection from himself it was treated negatively and the tendency became established to aim at preventing projections. This view, however, can refer only to projections that create fixed illusions or delusions—it does not include those that are part of affective communication.

Gradually I came to realize that the practice was wrong, and, as a step in reversing this false position, I formulated the idea of the syntonic counter-transference. But because of the prohibition on projection I did not dare to think that the introject needed projecting and so I remained in a guilt-ridden subjectivism.

My inability to see the importance of projection (and I do not think I am alone in this) arose also from insufficient recognition of the essential infantile component in counter-transference. It is indeed only quite recently that I have understood that patients represent to the analyst parental figures in his unconscious. The angry attacks of patients are therefore treated as admonitions and condemnations that the infant part of the analyst needs, while their love and admiration are fed on by him and sustain him. Accordingly his infant part seeks to evoke these responses from his patient. Analysts have tended to defend themselves rigorously against these counter-transference responses because of the ideal analytic schema which ordains that an analyst ought either to be in the position of a parent or at least the equal of his patient all the time. If he is not, then the analyst easily rationalizes the situation and condemns himself to masochistic silence in the service of an ideal that abjures a projection it cannot prevent. An alternative seems to have been to rely on inappropriate 'spontaneity', which is then given infantile omnipotent characteristics as intuition but is really concealed projection.

The useful introject occurs while listening to the patient and, if kept at a distance from the analyst's ego, provides material through which an interpretation can be formulated. Then an internal dialectic can occur and if the analyst can also project himself, and particularly the infantile parts, into the patient and combine these with knowledge gained from the patient, a valid interpretation can result. The internal part of the dialectic may be almost instantaneous or prolonged, but it requires projection before an effective interpretation can be made. This situation was, I believe, indicated by Jung in the diagrams of crossed projections in 'The psychology of the transference'

(1946, p. 221) but he seems to have taken a more negative view of it than is being developed here. His presentation further lays emphasis upon culture and history so that the infantile roots of it become obscured from view.

An Analytic Episode

The following example illustrates the concepts considered here by showing the failure in interchange between a patient and myself. It was corrected, if incompletely with moderate ease. This helps to throw the processes under discussion into relief. The example will introduce aspects of counter-transference evoked by and evoking psychotic-like patterns.

A woman who had been virtually deprived of sex information till adolescence had been puzzled about its effect on her in later life. One day she told me that her eldest son, aged about five years, had been playing a game in a bath. There was a big toy fish whose belly was split open. The boy put small fishes inside. The mother thought this an opportunity not to be missed and started a rather long to-and-fro interchange about babies and how they got out—not, it will be observed, about the alternative understanding that the fishes might represent penises that are put inside the mother. The discussion continued till the boy jumped up, excited, and asked her to let him see her little door down below. She said 'Yes', and after a pause added 'sometime' and changed the subject.

For a long time her own infantile sexuality had seemed problematic and I could not fully grasp its significance to her. I could feel into her situation and her unconscious anxieties and I knew very well what it was about intellectually, but neither she nor I could make headway in the transference because my ideas about it seemed to her plain nonsense or even delusions. On this occasion I pointed out that it seemed she had unintentionally seduced her son and then had to frustrate him, using a deception in the process. I offered this interpretation with rather careful choice of words because of previous unproductive clashes.

After a pause and some further remarks by me, relating this situation to her own childhood and comparing her behaviour with that of her own parents, who were very rigid in their views about sex, I stated, with some irritation, that whatever their demerits they had not needed to resort to such manœuvres. This was expressed mildly so as to give as few grounds as possible for what I feared would be felt as a damning criticism. It led to a very unexpected retort: 'It is you that want to look.' I felt bewildered, but recognized that some reply was required. As I could not produce one, I tried to locate the source of my state in myself first, but without success, so there was a short pause before I replied: 'Maybe, but you remember that once you told me your husband only had to look at you to get an erection.' This made her silent and reflective.

The patient often has to be analysed through projective identifications, of which her remark was one, and when working well with ordinary skill it would have been possible for me to let her develop this 'thought' into reflections about my emotions, perhaps speculation about my childhood; and sometimes she could work back to herself and, albeit rarely, find the situation in her childhood to which the transference referred. In this sequence interpretation could then have been used to relieve anxieties and resistances that otherwise appeared insuperable, without the warding-off activity that became necessary for me. My reply was defensive and so obstructed the on-going personal interaction systems expressed in delusional forms.

All this was clear to me at the time, or shall I say within five minutes. But, reflecting on this episode afterwards, it became evident that my interest in the subject had made me stop listening in a way that included unconscious processes. Consequently my interest in the problem she presented led me to remain unconscious of the transference implication in her story. Had I been able to project myself into what she was saying, I believe I should have succeeded in making in essence the following interpretation: 'Are you not telling me this because of a wish that I had behaved as you did to your son, when, earlier on in the analysis, you gave me openings for doing so, and are you not reproaching me for my failure to take them up, as your parents also did and so avoided your sexual interests and impulses when you were a child?'

This speculative interpretation is based upon analysis of my own counter-transference. I was predisposed to reproach myself and did so. This had blinded me to her reproach of me, which was the one she levelled at her own parents, whose positive virtues had made the faintest criticism of them almost impossible. Their failings were put down, and with justice too, to the culture pattern in which they were brought up; but by this mature understanding she preserved them from the infantile attack that she needed to launch. 'Looking' featured in what she had been told about her father, who used to sit beside her cot and gaze at her.

This example illustrated nicely the way in which my patient had represented her infantile sexuality in symbolic forms, which had kept her as a child unaware of the instinctual sources from which the symbols sprang. The interpretation might have opened up avenues of investigation along these lines but it was not made because I had introjected her reproach and probably also the feeling of her parents that such matters should not be mentioned.

There is one element in my interpretation that relates to the projective-introjective components in communication. If an analyst says 'you' to a patient it is worth remembering that the pronoun refers to a projection: 'I' likewise refers to the patient's projection introjected by the analyst. If this dual process is not borne in mind the situation easily leads to confusion and is a source of conflict centring on the meanings of the words 'I' and 'you'. It is the basis of many quarrels of children when they get into confusion about what each has said to the other.

What I have described illustrates the difference between being conscious or unconscious of a counter-transference. My patient's unpredicted behaviour had made me retreat into myself—syntonic counter-transference—and wait till I could find a way of managing what I had found out on previous occasions was a delusional transference. This has, in the past, frequently led to delusions of my own about myself as well as my patient. Then, her unpredictability had been far less manageable.

My recovery from it was, on this occasion, only so rapid because I had reached the point where, after many past failures, I could recover. The obstructing counter-transference was partly due to my establishing a masochistic 'policy' of not responding because I knew I could not spot the differences between her projection and my own position. When I could not, I thought as follows: 'Well, perhaps . . . ' then the way had become open to masochism. The next step would be to identify with the introject, which happened when I believed that what she said was true. Then I had arrived at incarnating the projection. By following this up I discovered a delusion inside me and began to arrive at the technique of managing this patient's delusional transference, an essentially impenetrable psychotic-like state that needed to be reprojected.

Technique in Psychotic States

In chapter seven of *The psychology of the transference* Jung says: 'The decomposition of the elements indicates dissociation and collapse of existing ego consciousness. It is closely analogous to the schizophrenic state, and it should be taken very seriously because this is the moment when a latent psychosis may become acute, i.e., when the patient becomes aware of the collective unconscious and the psychic non-ego' (1946, p. 265).

In this passage there is no indication of how often the psychotic transference occurs. He makes it clear that the patient in this state need not be clinically psychotic but that the pressure of affect disturbs the analyst far more than during 'ordinary analysis', and induces regression to levels comparable to that of the patient. At this point it may seem justifiable to abandon technique and start relying on intuition. Jung, however, is quite clear that this is not enough. The therapist ' . . . must hold fast to his own orientation; that is he must know what the patient means' and 'must approach his task with views and ideas capable of grasping unconscious symbolism' (*ibid.*, p. 268); then he adds: 'The kind of approach . . . must therefore be plastic and symbolical, and itself the outcome of personal experience with unconscious contents'. This is why 'we are best advised to remain within the framework of traditional mythology' (*ibid.*). All this can be taken as part of what I have included in the definition of technique, which should therefore apply to the transference psychosis as much as to the transference neurosis.

So that there can be no ambiguity, I must state that I do not use mythological knowledge in analytic sessions. How Jung used it in therapy is not at all clear from reading his publications, in marked contrast to his convincing demonstration of its value in deepening understanding of dreams and fantasies outside analysis. My own personal experience of it in analysis was far from satisfying in that it too easily introduced intellectual defensive systems into the therapeutic situation.

When Jung writes in the same context, which implies the use of mythology: ' . . . Whenever possible I try to rouse the patient to mental activity and get him to subdue the *massa confusa* of his mind with his own understanding'. This is in line with what analysts, I conceive, try to do all along—but how? If this be translated to justify setting the patient to learn about myths by reading books, this can easily result in the very warding off of the transference of which he accuses Freud (Jung, 1946, p. 171).

This interesting issue is not essential to my thesis, discussion of which can better be furthered by asking: is it possible to refer to a technique of managing a transference psychosis in the same way as a transference neurosis? If we follow Jung the answer seems to be Yes, but because of my reservations I think that the problem needs more sorting out and here I have found the work of psychoanalysts impressive.

Some claim that they can approach this area by using interpretative techniques alone and that affective involvement with the patient is not a special feature (Rosenfeld, 1965). Others, such as Margaret Little (1957 and 1960), Searles (1965), and Winnicott (1947 and 1960), consider that the analyst's affects are so important that psychoanalysis in its classical sense cannot be conducted. Little holds that the analyst's 'total' response to the patient is essential. She conceives that it is important to rely on and use the countertransference and that to rely on technique as defined by the majority of psychoanalysts is insufficient (cf. supra, p. 273, Little, 1957, also Bion, 1955). She notes the elements of surprise and arbitrariness and these clearly prevent the deployment of controlled technique, which relies on the analyst's predicting the outcome of his interventions.

However, what seems at first surprising, chaotic and uncontrollable can perhaps be subjected to analytic observation and brought within a describable framework. Jung had already done this, but Searles's researches into the psychotherapy of schizophrenia, in which the 'therapeutic alliance'—as previously understood—is out of the question, is of special interest.

His work complements and expands Jung's description by showing how it feels personally. He states openly that the therapist's comfort, his hate and love of the patient, are good and reliable indicators for therapeutic action. For instance, he defines a first stage in psychotherapy of psychotic patients in which the therapist feels unrelated to his patient. From this he infers the cause: the patient is reacting to him as inanimate, an animal, a corpse, an idea or something essentially *not human*. During this period the therapist experiences definable affects, but first and foremost he needs to see that he himself is at ease. Having achieved this over a prolonged time, he begins to hate the patient and this ushers in a totally destructive transference of a delusional kind.

In both situations he conceives that the counter-transference becomes an indicator of the transference. Next there is a phase in which love begins and the analyst becomes deeply involved in it. Are these experiences to be classed as counter-transference or are they 'healthy' responses by the analyst? They are experienced in a modified form in many thorough analyses; indeed, if Jung's essay be taken as a paradigm of a complete analysis, they may be expected to occur always.

In my view Jung's thesis justifies an extended use of the term 'counter-transference' to cover these experiences (cf. Fordham, 1960), yet he does not use the term except with reference to Freud. This was probably because he interested himself in meeting the psychotic-like needs of his patients and his re-activeness did not correspond with counter-transference illusions. At first sight there seems to be an essential difference between the therapist's response to the psychotic transference and his responses to a transference neurosis in routine analysis. There is less mental control exerted by him than when he is being an analyst using technique in its classical sense, and he needs to rely on his affects much more than on his mind. But his affects are not disruptive to the progress of analysis and are urgently needed by the patient. Searles means, if I understand him, that without the analyst's remaining comfortable, without his hate or without his love, the patient cannot begin to make any sort of transference relationship; this is apparently not so when there is a transference neurosis.

On these grounds it becomes questionable whether the therapist's work with a psychotic transference can be thought of as technique. Nevertheless Searles succeeded in mapping out the course that affects regularly take, and thus he has gone far towards defining a technique of therapy for psychotic patients. It is of interest to look in passing at other situations that Searles states can occur and need to be recognized; the patient needs the therapist to do his thinking for him, he nullifies all the efforts of the therapist to be helpful, the patient treats the therapist as ill or seeks to help him in his diseased state. If anything is to be done, the analyst needs to work inside these delusional reversals of the part of an analyst in analytic therapy.

Researches into the psychopathology of clinical psychoses and borderline states have given most impetus to the study of counter-transference. Because of the unremitting pressures that these cases exert on the analyst, there have been tendencies to introduce proceedings based on the acting out of affects, or through unconsciousness to introjection of the psychosis (cf. Jung, 1946, p. 171f, and Meier, 1959, p. 32). Each can now be seen as those manifestations of counter-transference that have here been defined as incarnating it or behaving syntonically. On the other side, under these pressures the aim of furthering and deepening analytic work has been abandoned and it has been changed to mobilize ego defences (cf. Federn, 1953, *et al.*).

It is not my intention to discuss the analytic psychotherapy of psychotic disorders, though there are indications that they can be better understood by more penetrating understanding of counter-transference. I have wanted rather to show how the study of counter-transference in these cases has led on to extending the idea into the framework of classical analysis itself. Searles showed how a psychotic transference seems to attack the classical technique and so, if I am correct, the first step must be to analyse the structure of technique in the neuroses. The difference between the transference/counter-transference set up in the minor disorders and the psychoses then seems to be quantitative rather than qualitative.

If a careful study of the analytic situation be made this is often quite easy to demonstrate. There is a modicum of truth in the delusion of a patient that the analyst is ill and urgently needs the help of the patient, which the analyst could fall for by incarnating the delusion and conclude that he was really getting treatment for himself; this means he has regressed to an infantile position. But in any analytic situation there lies the potential for this to occur. The technique of asking the patient to produce his ideas, feelings and affects with as little restraint as possible initiates a transference situation, but it also provides the ground for the analyst's feeling like an infant being fed in various ways: being given good food that he can digest and enjoy or being stuffed with food he does not want or cannot make use of, and this can lead on to regression to persecutory levels. He may be expected to be conscious of these affects and in the counter-transference neurosis they are manageable; but when the transference becomes delusional his own persecutory and depressive feelings become much stronger and less easy to manage. In this situation he will hope to react, if not with technique, at least with affective flexibility. It is true that often he ceases to be an analyst in the usual sense but this is due to the strength of the affects rather than their nature.

Having recognized this state of affairs, it becomes clearer that the counter-transference can become an indicator of the patient's transference. So the analyst has acquired an instrument that he can use. Counter-transference becomes one— but not the only—source of information about the patient's transference. So long as the analyst is conscious of the part his unconscious processes (and defences are among them) play in his interaction with his patient, his ego can analyse and use this information as part of technique, whether it be in neurotic or psychotic states. This conclusion provides a basis for working out in day-to-day analysis what Jung formulated as the dialectical procedure.

References

ADLER, G. (1961). *The living symbol*. London, Routledge.

ANON. (1963). Report on 'The second international congress for analytical psychology', *J. analyt. Psychol.*, **8**, 2.

BAYNES, H. G. (1955). *The mythology of the soul*. London, Routledge.

BION, W. R. (1955). 'The language of a schizophrenic', in *New directions in psychoanalysis*. London, Tavistock.

FEDERN, P. F. (1953). *Ego psychology and the psychoses*. London, Imago.

FORDHAM, F. (1969). 'Several views on individuation', in *Analytical psychology: a modern science*. Library of Analytical Psychology, vol. 1. London, Heinemann, 1973.

FORDHAM, M. (1955). 'The origins of the ego in childhood', in *New developments in analytical psychology*. London, Routledge, 1957.

—— (1957). 'Notes on the transference', in *New developments in analytical psychology*. London, Routledge.*

FORDHAM, M. (1960). 'Counter-transference, I', *Brit. J. med. Psychol.*, **33**, 1.*
—— (1964). 'The ego and the self in analytic practice', *J. Psychol.* (Lahore), **1**, 1.
—— (1965). 'The importance of analysing childhood for the assimilation of the shadow', in *Analytical psychology: a modern science.* Library of Analytical Psychology, vol. 1. London, Heinemann, 1973.
—— (1968). 'Review of Henderson's *Thresholds of initiation*', *J. analyt. Psychol.*, **13**, 2.
—— (1969). *Children as individuals.* London, Hodder & Stoughton.
GREENSON, R. R. (1967). *The technique and practice of psychoanalysis.* London, Hogarth.
HARDING, E. (1963). 'A critical appreciation of Jackson's "Symbol formation and the delusional transference" ', *J. analyt. Psychol.*, **8**, 2.
—— (1965). *The parental image.* New York, Putnam.
HEIMANN, P. (1960). 'Counter-transference, II', *Brit. J. med. Psychol.*, **33**, 1.
JUNG, C. G. (1913). 'The theory of psychoanalysis', in *Coll. wks.*, **4**.
—— (1916). 'The relations between the ego and the unconscious', in *Coll. wks.*, **7**.
—— (1921). 'The therapeutic value of abreaction', in *Coll. wks.*, **16**.
—— (1929). 'Problems of modern psychotherapy', in *Coll. wks.*, **16**.
—— (1930). 'Introduction to Kranefeldt's "Secret ways of the mind" ', in *Coll. wks.*, **4**.
—— (1931). 'The aims of psychotherapy', in *Coll. wks.*, **16**.
—— (1931a). 'The stages of life', in *Coll. wks.*, **8**.
—— (1935). 'Principles of practical psychotherapy', in *Coll. wks.*, **16**.
—— (1938). Foreword to the third edition of Frances Wickes's *Inner world of childhood*, in *Coll. wks.*, **17**.
—— (1943). 'Psychotherapy and a philosophy of life', in *Coll. wks.*, **16**.
—— (1944). *Psychology and alchemy. Coll. wks.*, **12**.
—— (1946). 'The psychology of the transference', in *Coll. wks.*, **16**.
—— (1951). Fundamental questions of psychotherapy's in *Coll. wks.*, **16**.
—— (1963). *Memories, dreams, reflections*, ed. Jaffé. London, Routledge.
—— and LOŸ, R. (1914). 'Some crucial points in psychoanalysis', in *Coll. wks.*, **4**.
KIRSCH, H. (1961). 'An analyst's dilemma', in *Current trends in analytical psychology*, ed. G. Adler. London, Tavistock.
LITTLE, M. (1957). ' "R" the analyst's total response to his patient's needs', *Int. J. Psycho-Anal.*, **38**, 3–4.
—— (1960). 'Counter-transference, V', *Brit. J. med. Psychol.*, **33**, 1.
MEIER, C. A. (1959). 'Projection, transference, and subject-object relation', *J. analyt. Psychol.*, **4**, 1.
MONEY-KYRLE, R. (1956). 'Normal counter-transference and some of its deviations', *Int. J. Psycho-Anal.*, **37**, 4–5.
MOODY, R. (1955). 'On the function of counter-transference', *J. analyt. Psychol.*, **1**, 1.
PLAUT, A. (1956). 'The transference in analytical psychology', *Brit. J. med. Psychol.*, **29**, 1.*
RACKER, H. (1968). *Transference and counter-transference.* London, Hogarth.

Technique in Jungian analysis

ROSENFELD, H. A. (1965). *Psychotic states: a psychoanalytic approach.* London, Hogarth.

SEARLES, H. F. (1965). *Collected papers on schizophrenia and related subjects.* London, Hogarth.

STRAUSS, R. (1960). 'Counter-transference, IV', *Brit. J. med. Psychol.*, 33, 1.*

WICKES, F. G. (1959). *The inner world of man.* New York/Toronto, Farrar & Rinehart.

WINNICOTT, D. W. (1947). 'Hate in the counter-transference', in *Collected papers.* London, Tavistock, 1958.

—— (1960). 'Counter-transference, III', *Brit. J. med. Psychol.*, 33, 1.

Comment: on not incarnating the archetype*

ALFRED PLAUT

1970

Introduction

Fordham's paper, 'Technique and counter-transference' (1969), is a thorough survey of an area in analytical psychology (extending into dynamic psychology in general) as well as a statement of an original point of view. It has given me a much-wanted stimulus to review and clarify a phrase that in discussions has become connected with my name and goes back to a paper I wrote fourteen years ago (1956).

The paper was the third in a symposium called 'Jung's contribution to analytical thought and practice', and my title was 'The transference in analytical psychology'. It is important to recall this for the following reasons: (a) In 1956 nothing, or next to nothing, had been published on the subject of counter-transference by analytical psychologists other than Jung (who, as Fordham said, did not use the term much). (b) My contribution had to be brief. (c) The second thoughts that I am about to present can touch on only one or two facets of Fordham's comprehensive survey, i.e. where they overlap or show up discrepancies.

Two further observations are: first of all, the phrase I am supposed to have coined (Fordham, *ibid.*, p. 109), i.e. 'incarnating an archetype', does not in fact occur in the paper to which it is attributed. True, in summarizing, the words 'to incarnate the animus' do appear, but the words *animus figure* (i.e. a teacher) precede it in the text. Furthermore, I wrote in three places of incarnating an (archetypal) *image* (italics mine). Obviously archetypes are concepts and therefore cannot be logically conceived as becoming flesh and blood ('incarnate').

* First published in the *Journal of analytical psychology*, 15, 1.

Jung (1947, p. 213) is very well aware of this: 'The archetypal representations (images and ideas) mediated to us by the unconscious should not be confused with the archetype as such'. Why then have the misquotation and the quotation caught on? Instead of fighting a paternity suit I shall go into the psychological origins and consequences of this phenomenon.

It is striking that the word 'archetype' as such does not appear in Fordham's paper (other than where I am quoted) and does not seem to play a part in his technical considerations. If this key-concept has been omitted, one may ask what has taken its place.

General Considerations

I agree with the general trend of Fordham's paper, and there is much common interest in the issues involved. What are they?

1. Our theoretical and technical equipment must be constantly reviewed. This may not lead to discoveries, but it ensures at least that the equipment remains in serviceable condition.

2. We have to remain mindful of the difficulties that are peculiar to psycho-dynamic science, to use Guntrip's term (1968).

3. The third point to which I refer in my paper, 'What do you actually do?' applies. Jung (1934, pp. 32–3) in his 'Archetypes of the collective unconscious' makes an interesting observation concerning meaning: 'Interpretations make use of certain linguistic matrices that are themselves derived from primordial images. From whatever side we approach this question, everywhere we find ourselves confronted with the history of language, with images and motifs that lead straight back to the primitive wonder-world'.

I should like to add that in my submission all ideographic phrases have an inbuilt obsolescence, i.e., they wear thin with usage and have then got to be broken down into ever smaller and more precise units. Research in physical sciences certainly confirms this microscopic aspect, and in my view (which seems to be shared by Fordham) this is also the case in dynamic psychology. Another view of research, in analytical psychology, is that our knowledge of archetypes can be enlarged (but not fundamentally changed) only by re-discoveries both in documents and literature of the past, and social phenomena (e.g. student unrest) in the present, but not necessarily by clinical research. There are snags in both approaches, which happen to be very similar and could be summed up by Jung's statement (1929, p. 109), 'Psychology has still to invent its own specific language'. He certainly does not under-estimate the magic of words figuring as explanations. The danger for any writer is that he coins his own favourite phraseology containing analogies and metaphors that are but stages on the way to new concept formations. The result is what Bion calls the 'Tower of Babel situation', i.e., it leads to a confusion of tongues.

4. Results: in all theoretical discussions we have to remember that we are unable to show with any degree of reliability the superiority of results based on one theory or technique over against another. Jones (1936) subdivided results into 'therapeutic' and 'analytical'. As regards the former, it is, for example, not possible to show that an analytical psychologist using Jung's 'participation mystique' as a point of reference will get better or worse results than a psychoanalyst who uses 'projective identification' as his point of reference. The patient and his family must be the arbiters of 'therapeutic' results. As regards analytical results, assessments are liable to lead to arguments between analysts rather than to elucidation of theory. At all events, patients do have second or third analyses by different analysts. This means that we have to see each other's failures and/or limitations. Recognizing the tentative nature of our theoretical and technical claims imposes a degree of modesty.

If I read Fordham's paper (*ibid.*) correctly, his aims are wisely confined to clarification and particularization of concepts and mechanisms bearing on technique, which thereby becomes more communicable and teachable. Let me use a metaphor to describe my views of Fordham's position: one can demonstrate how to make an omelette and what ingredients are required. After a few trials the recipe becomes repeatable by a novice in cookery with creditable results. This does explain the physical and chemical principles involved in the making, but not the omelette as such. To the consumer the explanation of an omelette is probably irrelevant, but either the witnessing of its creation may be miraculous to him (like an archetypal image) or he may simply be interested in the sensuous aspects of eating. (The latter is comparable to 'therapeutic' results, which concern all analysts and patients.)

When the mystique is taken out of cookery more people can become reasonably good cooks, while plenty of room remains for inspired creators of new recipes. I shall return to this metaphor later.

Special Points

1. *Evocative words and phrases. Some examples:*

Fordham (*ibid.*) writes about the analyst's 'style', which is individual and ultimately incommunicable. We know also that Jung used the term 'personal equation' in order to express the analyst's personality as an important factor that influences all his psychological observations. Few analysts are aware of the fact—and we have no evidence that Jung was conscious of it— that the personal equation has a history that began in 1796 at the Greenwich Royal Observatory and reached its climax some 70 years later.[1]

It influenced experimental psychology, resulting in the complication- and in the reaction-experiment (Cf. Boring, 1950), which makes exciting reading. The point is that by 'personal' and 'equation' an apparent paradox was introduced: the adjective 'personal' was individual and subjective, the noun objective (mathematical). In Jung's usage of the term the former receives the greater emphasis and accounts for his liberal standpoint towards various 'schools' of analysis, while the phenomena of the objective psyche became conceptualized in his theory of archetypes. At any rate 'personal equation' in Jung's usage emphasizes an analyst's constant predisposition rather than a particular counter-transference. Fordham's 'style' has no scientific overtones since it takes its origin from writing, literature and art. Yet it may be taken to express that global word, 'personality'. It is, to say the least, an indication of what a person is, as expressed in de Buffon's statement, '*Le style est l'homme même*'.

In Fordham's paper 'style' is given a place corresponding to

[1] It is possible that in Jung's student years the term was still so widely known that all one had to do was to put it in quotes for every educated person to know what one was talking about.

that of an individual's handwriting: expressive of the personality perhaps, but writing as such (provided it is legible) is obviously more important for communication than for the individual formation of letters. Unless we are graphologists 'style' lacks the scientific overtones of 'equation'. There is a shift of emphasis in the direction of lesser importance, and the greater weight of the personal element becomes attached to the phenomena of counter-transference and the mechanisms (projections, introjection, re-projection) by which it operates.

In coining a new phrase or in using a word in a new context, it is therefore important to show how it differs from previously existent ones; in other words, to show what it is not. A residue of analogy or metaphor always remains, awaiting later microscopic examination. The verb 'to distil' in Fordham's paper is a good example, appearing more than once, e.g., 'the analyst distils the to-and-fro process of projection' or 'It [the counter-transference] lies at the root of technique and is indeed the *prima materia* out of which technique is distilled'.* This verb is, of course, an analogue evocative of physical science in the first example and alchemy in the second. Neither is an explanation of a process in purely psychological language.

Returning to my own verb 'to incarnate', I realize that it is loaded with religious overtones. I regard the allusion to religion, i.e., the miracle of the spirit becoming flesh, as the true psychological reason for repeated (mis-)quotation. By psychological I do not mean psychopathological, but rather that in science there is no place for miracles. Recognizing this danger, I wrote that I was referring to a certain attitude towards a transferred image, that it had nothing to do with a rôle-taking technique, and remarked on the dangers inherent in this attitude by referring to provisos for *comparative* safety. All to no avail: I had stirred up an archetypal image by referring to the incarnation. Obviously I had touched on 'the primitive wonder-world' by which we are still affected. In it spirits can become incarnate, outside it concepts have to remain abstract.

2. *Theoretical points*

I should like to submit that, when one deals with a concept that together with others makes up a theoretical framework,

* This quotation is from the summary that appeared at the end of Michael Fordham's paper, 'Technique and counter-transference', when it was published in the *Journal of analytical psychology*, 14, 2.

all the other concepts are implicitly or explicitly involved. It follows that one cannot write about Jung's contributions concerning the transference (and counter-transference) and elaborate these within the framework of analytical psychology without touching on related concepts. Here are a few examples:

(a) *On psychic energy*

Concerning the energic point of view Jung (1928, p. 4) writes: 'The idea of energy is not that of a substance moved in space; it is a concept abstracted from relations of movement. The concept, therefore, is founded not on the substances themselves but on their relations, whereas the moving substance itself is the basis of the mechanistic view'.

I think we can see that the gist of Fordham's paper is congruent with this (as we now say) dynamic principle of Jung's idea. Everything moves when processes are given priority. When archetypes (no matter how much energy they contain) become images, they may also become too substantial and immobile, because they are fascinating. Herein lies the danger of not recognizing delusions and of reinforcing these rather than analysing the delusional projection.

(b) *Introjection and counter-transference*

If the archetypal images gain delusional strength, e.g., in psychotic states, the patient may either project these into the analyst or ascribe them to himself. Jung refers to the latter as introjection (1917, pp. 69–70). Both projection and introjection are in that sense undesirable, but as they do occur the question is how to deal with them. In my earlier paper I followed Jung's line when I quoted that if the analyst can wait for it a certain 'subterranean undermining of the transference' will occur. But, of course, this may never happen or the analyst may not be able to wait. In which case he may do better to realize that he cannot keep the introject at the necessary distance from his ego, and he would then do better to re-project, as Fordham counsels.

Herein lies the possible advance in technique: the analyst is as much in need of projection as the patient. However, this advance cannot be divorced either from theory or from the analyst's personality. Not everybody has the same capacity to wait hopefully for a movement in the patient's unconscious, and whether he can do so or not depends on how the introjected content affects him.

(c) *Object-relations and archetypes*

The reason why Jung wrote so little about introjection (of objects via infant-mother relation) seems to me attributable to his introverted psychology, which made the *a priori* aspect of archetypal images the mainstay of his theories. It would also seem that he continued to regard introjection much in the way in which he did earlier when he wrote *Symbols of transformation* and related introjection to Schopenhauer's view (1912, p. 136): 'A movement perceived from outside can only be grasped as the manifestation of an inner will or desire'. Fordham's usage on the other hand would correspond to the reference Jung (*ibid.*, p. 136n) makes to Ferenczi 'which denotes the exact opposite: taking the external world into oneself'.

The question, so far as I can see, remains how these extremes will be brought together in practice, i.e., in a specific patient-analyst combination; if the analyst is able to share the transferred archetypal image and can allow it to come close to his own ego, recognition of this state of affairs may be sufficient. But I think it is safer to assume that the analyst's ego is often too 'weak' to rely on such recognition when affects are aroused. He would then be wiser to re-project. It strikes me that Winnicott's (1951, pp. 229–42, and 1962, pp. 166–170) concept of transitional phenomena could help to bridge the gap between 'the incarnation of an archetypal image' and 'the re-projection of an introject': if the analyst can allow himself to become the patient's 'first not-me possession' he may well find in this developmental concept the technical equipment for which we are looking. (I realize that this proposition would require a clinical example, which, however, goes beyond the confines of my comment.)

I should still consider that in selected cases there is a place for the analyst to incarnate an archetypal image, to allow for the 'primitive wonder-world'. But because of the religious, numinous overtones of 'incarnation' I should be quite happy to use secular language (see cookery) and say that the analyst may allow himself to become edible, provided he is reasonably sure of surviving. I realize that by jumping from an archetypal (Jungian) fire I may have, so to speak, jumped into a (Kleinian) frying-pan. But the jump is deliberate and the metaphor serves in two further ways: firstly, it shows the relationship that exists between the mental mechanism of introjection and the physiological process of eating and digesting. Secondly, it refers to the common denominator between my cookery and Fordham's distillation-image, in that both are based on our detailed awareness of the transforming influences of counter-transference on the analyst. There is no reason why specific patient-analyst combinations should not become the subject of systematic research, with benefit to all parties concerned while the language of psychology is still developing.

Finally, I agree with the desirability of differentiating transference from counter-transference; if counter-transference is given a special, positive place in theory and technique, as Strauss (1960) and Fordham have given it, it becomes a most useful indicator of the transference. When I wrote my earlier paper the positive aspects of this differentiation had not yet been described.

References

BORING, E. G. (1950). *A history of experimental psychology*. New York, Appleton-Century-Crofts.

FORDHAM, M. (1969). 'Technique and counter-transference', *J. analyt. Psychol.*, **14**, 2.*

GUNTRIP, H. (1968). *Schizoid phenomena, object relations and the self*. London, Hogarth.

JONES, E. (1936). 'The criteria of success in treatment', in *Papers on psychoanalysis*. London, Baillière, Tindall & Cox, 1950.

JUNG, C. G. (1912). *Symbols of transformation*. In *Coll. wks.*, **5**.

——(1917). 'On the psychology of the unconscious'. In *Coll. wks.*, **7**.

——(1928). 'On psychic energy'. In *Coll. wks.*, **8**.

——(1929). 'The significance of constitution and heredity in psychology'. In *Coll. wks.*, **8**.

——(1934). 'Archetypes of the collective unconscious'. In *Coll. wks.*, **9**, i.

——(1947). 'On the nature of the psyche'. In *Coll. wks.*, **8**.

STRAUSS, R. (1960). 'Counter-transference, IV', *Brit. J. med. Psychol.*, **33**, 1.*

PLAUT, A. (1956). 'The transference in analytical psychology', *Brit. J. med. Psychol.*, **29**, 1.*

——(1970). 'What do you actually do?' *J. analyt. Psychol.*, **15**, 1.

WINNICOTT, D. W. (1951). 'Transitional objects and transitional phenomena'. In *Coll. papers*. London, Tavistock.

——(1962). 'The aims of psycho-analytical treatment', in *The maturational processes and the facilitating environment*. London, Hogarth.

Reply to Plaut's 'Comment'*

MICHAEL FORDHAM

1970

Just as my paper 'Technique and counter-transference' (1969a) stimulated Plaut (1970) so has his 'Comment' stimulated me in a number of ways, some of which I believe it will be profitable to develop.

To start with a disclaimer: the almost complete absence of the term *archetype* in my article is not due to its being 'omitted' but is the result of considering technique as a manifestation of ego functioning.

Let me next answer a reproach: am I wrongly attributing to him the term 'incarnating the archetype'? In his original paper Plaut (1956) refers more than once to 'incarnating it', referring to the archetypal image. While he may be right in reproaching me for inexact attribution and for not including the term 'image', it remains that the phrase 'incarnating the archetype' has been widely used as a shorthand and I must record in my defence two observations: 1, I did not put the phrase in quotation marks, and 2, in the phrase 'incarnating the archetypal image', the word 'image' is redundant because an archetype could not be embodied without there being an image.

I believe that I was also in order to interpret (i.e. to 'misrepresent') a formulation that was obscure in a number of respects. Clear definition is not always necessary or desirable and it is not my intention to criticize so long as it be recognized that the formulation is imprecise and that it will provoke differing understandings and interpretations by others. That interpretations of such formulations often appear to the originator as 'misunderstandings', 'misquotations' and the like, is more or less the rule, so I need only say that to me the religious association to incarnating was not important; I recognize, however,

---

* First published in the *Journal of analytical psychology*, 15, 2.

that in saying so I must state my difficulties more clearly than I have done in my paper. There I compressed my thoughts unduly and so I welcome this opportunity to expand them.

In the first place Jung's case, which Plaut cited, showed that the patient could distinguish Jung from the daemonic image as in an ordinary transference. When Plaut quotes Jung as saying 'There is no way of getting out of the toils of the unconscious except for the doctor . . . to acknowledge himself as the image' (1917, p. 90), Jung means, as I understand it, that there is no point in denying that he was representing the projected image to the patient and that it would be merely interfering to use either interpretations of a reductive kind or defensive common sense. Plaut refers to the latter when he says that he could think: 'Oh, yes, there is quite a lot in what she says' or 'I am nothing of the kind . . . ' (p. 18).

I would understand that Jung would think somewhat as follows: 'This is an archetypal experience that transcends both the patient and myself, it is religious in nature and represents a religious need of the patient'. He would communicate the substance of this idea to the patient, as he says in another context (cf. 1916, p. 131). Thus Jung does not do anything like incarnating the daemon but continues with interpretation. Yet this passage, as if to introduce the subject of incarnating, precedes Plaut's three main points: 1, That the archetypal image must be recognized and distinguished from the patient's conscious demands. This is clear to me, though the distinction is not so easy and sometimes not possible or desirable. 2, That the unconscious affects the analyst is also in line with my experience.

It is the substance of his third point, where he refers to incarnating and the need for distinguishing the ego from the archetypes, that I would find obscure for the following reasons: Plaut chooses as an example the animus figure (a part of the woman) to be incarnated. As a man he cannot 'become what the patient's unconscious asserts' (1956, p. 18) because the animus in her own unconscious cannot by definition be a part of him; only if he introjects this image can sense be made of his thesis. Once it is introjected, then its relation to the ego becomes relevant (I assume he means the conscious parts of the ego). This is the basis on which I assumed that Plaut's thesis involves introjection. I would also say so if the image was any archetypal image at all, but for a somewhat different reason: the image, though collective basically, has individual characteristics and its associative connections are significantly and usually drastically different in any two people. I added identification because of the word 'become' in Plaut's phrase, 'Then I would *become* . . .'. I recognize that Plaut states that incarnating occurs 'without identification' (p. 19) but this does not convince me, though it is just possible that we are using terms in different ways. Only if he had said 'become *for the patient*', in the sense of its being the patient's experience, can I conceive that there would be no identification, but then there need be no introjection either.

In spite of these formal objections, I think I know very well what Plaut was aiming at, as I hope I showed when I used his idea in an earlier paper (Fordham, 1957, p. 98). In analytical psychology there was, at the time, a view that the transference of infantile characteristics, though inevitable, was undesirable; they needed to be dissolved by the application of explanatory principles or reductive criticism. On the other hand, when it came to archetypal forms, education was often applied. At that time I was coming to understand that the centre-piece of analysis was the interpretation, living through and integration in the transference relationship of affects having infantile and archetypal characteristics. Their interpretation, I observed, need not have the supposed critical reductive aim but was rather a means of elucidating and clarifying affective processes and all their associated connections. These affects may form the basis of a 'wonder world', which Plaut wishes to preserve; I don't think there would be much disagreement between us on this score, so I can go on to say that incarnating, whatever it meant in detail, laid emphasis on the affective interpersonal transference relationship. More recently Davidson (1966) compared it to active imagination and this develops interestingly my earlier remarks on the relation between the two (in Fordham, 1957).

That I now think the experience can be expressed in relation to the functioning of projective, introjective and identification processes is because they go a long way to explaining inaccessible transference processes, especially where a transference of delusional intensity predominates. With these ideas I have found it possible to extend the applications or interpretations, I believe beneficially.

Technique in Jungian analysis

Next: I am not at all easy when Plaut says that an analyst would 'be wiser to reproject' (p. 93) nor that 'there is a place for the analyst to incarnate an archetypal image'. Projection and introjection are unconscious processes, and are not usually under *control* of the conscious parts of the ego; much less so during good analytic interviews where the analyst's attention is focused on his patient. Afterwards and sometimes, as in the example I gave, where the part of the interview I recorded became a subjective experience, it is possible to work on the disorder. If therefore he thinks that an analyst can, as a matter of technique, project or introject then I would like to know how it is done. According to my view, what he proposes is magic in its formal sense; by which I mean that a manageable model is made of the real unmanageable situation. Manipulation of the model with the aim of achieving some desired result may or may not prove successful. Whether the desired magical effect is produced or no is not a matter of technique, for the result is unpredictable.

Then on to the subject of 'distillations'. Interpretations rely on the analyst's capacity to distil (mostly unconsciously) the data they provide. Distilling, I suggest, could mean sorting out false perceptions from the true ones that accord with observations—the others, the false ones, do not.

To approach the subject of antecedents: the term 'style' is not new—it can be found in the literature and papers that have been written on it (cf. Rosen 1961). I meant to use it in an ordinary sense, and it was evidently precise enough for Plaut to understand what I meant, though he used it in ways that I did not intend. No doubt it will be used and given meanings not thought of by me and I may object. His linking it up with the personal equation and personality seems to me unwarranted, because I think the personal equation is the stuff of one analytic relationship; but, all the same, if he finds it useful it will be interesting to see the results of his thoughts.

Next, Plaut claims that the 'positive aspects of the differentiation (between transference and counter-transference) had not yet been described' when he wrote his paper published in 1956. This statement is not surprising in view of the rather inadequate level of communication between analysts at that time, but the idea of positive counter-transference has a history. The discovery had an indirectly positive result in that the distinction led to instituting training analysis in the early days of psychoanalysis. It was implied in Jung's 'The therapeutic value of abreaction' (1921) and developed into the idea of the dialectical process. It was rather specifically expressed in 'The psychology of the transference' (1946) though the term *counter-transference* was used only in a footnote. By 1956 the sense of it was being discussed and Moody had published an interesting example of the value of acting out the positive counter-transference in 1955. In 1957 my concept of the syntonic counter-transference had been published and had been discussed in the Society of Analytical Psychology over a year before. Among psychoanalysts the subject was being gone into intensively and in 1950 Paula Heimann published a paper 'On counter-transference' in which she specifically wrote on its positive aspects. One year later Margaret Little had written 'Counter-transference and the patient's response to it'.

No doubt Plaut, like myself, was ignorant of the developments taking place in psychoanalysis. I thought my idea of the syntonic counter-transference was original and I was only later to discover that Paula Heimann was seven years ahead of me. Since then I have paid close attention to psychoanalytic writings and I owe much to them. In estimating the importance of projection-introjection systems in the normal counter-transference, for instance, I owe much to Money-Kyrle and I have lately learned a great deal from Racker, whose book was published after a late draft of my paper had been completed.

In his 'Comment', Plaut raises another question of interest to me. He thinks that a clue to a solution of his uncertainty may be found in the analyst's being ready to let himself become the 'first not-me possession' and he links this with Winnicott's idea of 'transitional objects'. Now one of the essential features of the transitional object is that it is *not* a person. It is a bit of fluff, a rag or a doll, etc. It therefore seems to be wrong to express it in this way. Yet the process of discovering that the mother (as breast, arms, etc., etc.) is not me and yet belongs to me, though not clearly defined or known about, is different from the transitional object as I understand it from Winnicott's writings and my own observations. In my understanding, the transitional object is a very early self representation (Fordham, 1969) so it would be confusing to assume that when the analyst is felt to be a 'not-me possession' he has become a transitional

Technique in Jungian analysis

object. All the same, Plaut's proposition is pertinent, especially as Jung laid emphasis on 'not-me' archetypes.

References

DAVIDSON, D. (1966). 'Transference as a form of active imagination'. *J. analyt. Psychol.*, 11, 2.*

FORDHAM, M. (1957). 'Notes on the transference'. In *New developments in analytical psychology*. London, Routledge.*

——(1969). *Children as individuals*. London, Hodder & Stoughton.

——(1969a). 'Technique and counter-transference'. *J. analyt. Psychol.*, 14, 2.*

HEIMANN, P. (1950). 'On counter-transference'. *Int. J. Psycho-Anal.*, 31, 1.

JUNG, C. G. (1921). 'Therapeutic value of abreaction'. In *Coll. wks.*, 16.

——(1916). 'The relations between ego and the unconscious'. In *Coll. wks.*, 7.

——(1917). 'The psychology of the unconscious'. In *Coll. wks.*, 7.

——(1946). 'The psychology of the transference'. In *Coll. wks.*, 16.

LITTLE, M. (1951). 'Counter-transference and the patient's response to it'. *Int. J. Psycho-Anal.*

MOODY, R. (1955). 'On the function of counter-transference'. *J. analyt. Psychol.*, 1, 1.

MONEY-KYRLE, R. (1956). 'Normal counter-transference and some of its deviations. *Int. J. Psycho-Anal.*, 37, 4-5.

PLAUT, A. B. (1956). 'The transference in analytical psychology'. *Brit. J. Med. Psychol.*, 29, 1.*

——(1970). Comment: on not incarnating the archetype. *J. anal. Psychol.*, 15, 1.*

RACKER, H. (1968). *Transference and counter-transference*. London, Hogarth.

ROSEN, V. (1961). 'The relevance of "style"'. *Int. J. Psycho-Anal.*, 42, 4-5.

Transference/counter-transference: talion law and gratitude*

KENNETH LAMBERT

1972

A Clinical Problem

After about two years of his analysis, I was listening to a patient who had in the past occasionally made me sleepy. He was talking in an extremely monotonous, ruminative way, fitting various aspects of his psyche together as if it were a jigsaw puzzle and bringing in my interpretations as new bits for the puzzle.

The effects on me as his analyst were on this occasion considerable. I began to fall into a dazed state in which I could neither listen nor make any effort of attention. The temptation to surrender to this feeling of inadequacy was strong, but my commitment to analyse my patient enabled me to make the effort to think about my condition. I decided to try out saying that I thought that, perhaps, what he was saying was not what he really felt, but that there was something else he had to communicate that was much more important.

He did not respond at once, but then began to remember that, when his father was trying to show him how to mend his bicycle and later a motor-car, he (the patient) could never understand or grasp what was quite a simple process. His father, exasperated, would say 'Don't stand there like a stunned gosling'. This patient had had a unique experience of being 'stuffed' as an infant and child by two maternal figures who never gave him the chance to experience need, cry for it and succeed in getting it met. They anticipated every wish long after the early weeks of his infancy in a most intruding way. It was likewise later with his father who, in his vain

* First published in the *Journal of analytical psychology*, **17**, 1.

attempts to instruct his son in the practice of fixing things, could only tell him to look at him doing them and never considered letting the son experiment and try out simple operations with his own hands. Later my patient said that it felt to him as if he were being forced to look—and that it seemed like a plank entering his head through his eyes, or like a plank from a lorry entering the windscreen of a following car that the patient was driving and being wedged into the car without hurting him or the passengers.

Thus the patient had never consciously experienced the feeling of abandonment but only the feeling of being over-intruded upon and stuffed. As a result he pursued a do-it-yourself policy of stuffing himself with books and theories and then thinking things out alone in a ruminative way. He had studied a textbook of psychoanalysis at university and now took my interpretations away with him to think out and fit into the textbook framework. His relation to me was to keep me at a distance and treat me as a book. Then he would check up with me when my interpretations produced puzzles that would not fit the book.

It will be seen, therefore, that the dazed and helpless feeling experienced by me was obviously relevant to his 'stunned gosling' feeling. Was it that I had identified with the 'stunned gosling' feeling that he had split off while he did his ruminations? Was it that he had reversed the original process and had become the stuffing parents while making me into the stunned gosling? Was he paying me out, as if I were his parents, tit for tat, by becoming a stuffing, stunning bore?

There is something to be said for each of these three interpretations. Anyway, the raising of the issue in a non-punitive way began a process of considerable alleviation, leading him into experimenting with a looser, less self-stuffing and more relational situation with me. And in me the feeling of being stunned has gradually modified, while signs of more relational feelings of gratitude have appeared in my patient.

This kind of experience is well known to analysts and forms the basis of the contention of this paper that the phrase transference/counter-transference, thus linked, is useful for emphasizing the fact that transference and counter-transference hang together, whether we are conscious of this or not.

Transference and Counter-transference in the history of Analysis

Interestingly enough, this study of the link between transference and counter-transference represents a rather late-developing insight in the practice and literature of the analytical schools. As is well known, the subject of the transference was, at first, treated mainly in isolation. Even more so was it the case with counter-transference. According to Racker, it was 1910 when Freud first recognized some of the importance of the counter-transference and then mainly in terms of its dangers. After that, in so far as psychoanalytical literature is concerned, there is a silence of forty years, with the exception of an article by Hann-Kende in 1936. The subject was not re-opened until the end of the forties by writers like Lorand, Winnicott, Heimann, Margaret Little, Annie Reich, Gitelson, Weigert and Money-Kyrle.

The recently published volume—No. 73 of the International Psycho-Analytical Library—entitled 'Transference and counter-transference' by the late Heinrich Racker (1968) and containing papers written by him mainly during the fifties, represents to my knowledge the first systematic study of transference/counter-transference by a psychoanalyst, together with a fully worked out description of counter-transference in therapy.

Meanwhile, in analytical psychology, Jung began to emphasize, by the end of the twenties, the importance of the personality of the analyst and his work upon himself. He did not link this to counter-transference, though in 1946 in 'The psychology of the transference' he notes that Freud had already discovered the phenomenon of the counter-transference although mainly in the context of its possible deleterious effects upon the health of the analyst (1946, p. 171). He also explicitly states in one place that 'the counter-transference is evoked by the transference' (1929, p. 72), but does not mention the reverse. His main emphasis, however, is always upon the personality of the analyst as of major importance in the therapeutic situation. Later analytical psychologists like Stein, Fordham, Kraemer, Moody, Plaut, Strauss, Williams, Jackson, Whitmont, Krantz, and others, writing in the fifties and sixties, have developed and expanded this theme. Thus, by now, if we compare the work of, say, Michael Fordham and Heinrich Racker, we find a striking capability developing for cross-fertilization and agreement between the two schools about the main points involved. In addition, perhaps we should mention the part played in all this in London by the two symposia on 'Counter-transference' that were held by the Medical Section of the British Psychological Society in 1960 when the speakers were two Jungians, Michael Fordham and Ruth Strauss, and three Freudians, Paula Heimann, Margaret Little and Donald Winnicott (Symposia, 1960).

Today, eleven years later, it is becoming generally agreed that the phrase transference/counter-transference is a meaningful mode of expression. As Michael Fordham expresses it at the end of his paper 'Technique and counter-transference', work with psychotic and borderline cases 'has converted counter-transference from an unwanted and undesirable intrusion into a useful instrument in the hand of the analyst' and he adds, 'transference evokes counter-transference and vice-versa' (1969, p. 116). This elaborates his statement in the 1960 symposium that 'transference and counter-transference are essentially part and parcel of each other . . . and both processes originate in the unconscious' (1960, p. 1).

Racker's parallel study sets out more of the detail of the inter-relationship between transference and counter-transference which he sums up in the following, at first sight, paradoxical phrase 'transference is a function of the patient's transferences and the analyst's counter-transferences' (1968, p. 125). This is a variant on the original phrase of Hann-Kende who defined counter-transference as 'a function of the transferences of the patient and of the analyst' (1936).

Jung's Analogies

In this paper, I am seeking to define a specific area in this vast subject, in which I think analytical psychologists can benefit from Racker's work. Accordingly, in attempting this, I wish to note, but not discuss, a number of the areas of patient-analyst interaction that have been described by Jung in terms of analogies and in other ways. I refer to 1, the mutual influence of two whole persons in the dialectical procedure (1935, p. 3); 2, the transformation of the two personalities

306

resulting from their combining as if two chemical substances were being mixed (1929, pp. 71–2); 3, the overcoming of the demon of sickness whereby a sufferer can transmit his disease to a healthy person whose powers then subdue the demon (1929, p. 72); 4, the wounding of the physician that gives him the measure of his power to heal (1929, p. 72); 5, the inter-crossing transference relationship or marriage quaternity (1946, pp. 222–5) and 6, the activation of incest fantasies between analyst and patient (1929, p. 62). It will be shown that there are constant similarities between Racker's studies and those of Jung, though Racker's work embraces a more elaborated and detailed study of the personal interactions involved.

Racker's Work: The Analytical Situation

I would therefore now like to concentrate the discussion on ways in which Racker's work gears in with and informs our own. To begin with, I think he is right, when assessing the transference/counter-transference situation, to define first the nature of a therapeutic individual analytical situation. Thus he emphasizes that in it two persons are involved—each with a neurotic part and a healthy part, a past and a present, and a relation to fantasy and to reality. Each is both an adult and a child, having feelings towards each other of a child to a parent and a parent to a child.

This simple statement is open to various interpretations. It could tempt the superficial thought that what is sauce for the goose is sauce for the gander—as many patients defensively think. This, however, does not apply even to relationships that are not specifically therapeutic, for many of these are in fact asymmetrical. This is where the nature and purpose of the relationship demands greater responsibility and awareness, at least in some aspects, on the part of one member of the relation-ship than on the part of the other. I refer, of course, to the parent-child relationship, the teacher-pupil, the employer-employed and in certain areas either way in the husband–wife relationship. Without this greater consciousness on the part of one of the parties the relationship will go seriously wrong and come to a halt.

The analytic relationship is one of these. It requires a

considerably greater capability and know-how for the augmentation of consciousness on the part of the analyst in the first instance. As Racker puts it, this difference is both quantitative and qualitative. The requirement is uncomfortably severe— for, to analyse effectively, the analyst needs to be not only conscious of, and emotionally comfortable with, his own personal infantile and child dynamics in relation to his patient, but also conscious of the way in which the very analytic set-up itself induces in him not only responsible attitudes towards his patients but also regressive ones. All this involves a kind of openness to himself and his internal objects that may result in both himself and the patient experiencing a long analysis in a beneficial way and in the patient in particular becoming increasingly able to deploy his personality within and, in time, outside the analytic situation.

The analyst, therefore, in setting up a therapeutic situation commits himself to what Racker calls a 'predisposition' (1968, pp. 133–4)—a predominating tendency to function as an analyst and to understand what is happening in his patient and himself.

I would add myself that I consider the analyst to be under an obligation to work towards seeking an agreement from his patient about establishing the kind of situation in terms of place, number and length of sessions, fees and holidays that can promote a situation where the transference/counter-transference can best be understood and used for therapeutic purposes. The responsibility is considerable because his patient, at the beginning of an analysis, is often unconscious of the reasons for the therapeutic set-up suggested by the analyst. Of course, it is not always possible to achieve this, but there are times when success in securing it depends upon the analyst's inner conviction alone.

The Neurotic Counter-transference

We now pass on to the types of transference/counter-transference that can arise out of the analytic set-up and the analyst's predisposition. Corresponding to Fordham's distinction between illusory and syntonic counter-transference we find Racker distinguishing between the neurotic counter-transference (pp. 91 ff.) and counter-transference proper. As I want to concentrate on the counter-transference proper and its relationship to the transference, I shall not elaborate much on the neurotic counter-transference in this paper. Suffice it to say that for Racker it arises if the analyst becomes identified with his own infantile and child feelings in relation to the patient (1968, p. 106).

An extension arises if these infantile feelings focus more upon the opinions of the patient's relatives—or society—or the analyst's colleagues. In this case we have what Racker calls the neurotic sub-transference (1968, p. 114). The crucial point here does not rest upon the analyst's reacting to his patient from the infantile, the childlike and the primitive within himself, for these features are bound to be part of a total response to his patient. It rests, rather, upon whether the analyst identifies with these reactions and hence develops delusionary or disproportionate anxiety, anger, dependence etc. in connection with his patient as well as pathological defences against these feelings. The danger comes from unanalysed bits—early impulses and unsolved problems that have not been emotionally sufficiently integrated.

One of Racker's contentions is that the very set-up of analysis, with its interdiction upon many kinds of behaviour, including genital behaviour, can activate in the analyst a wide range of sexual and aggressive feelings towards his patients—if female as if towards his mother, if male as if towards his father. All kinds of oedipal feelings and oral, anal and phallic complications can be activated. Anger, hatred, rivalry, unconscious manipulation of the patient's relationships, submissiveness, manic excitement, depressive and paranoid responses can all serve to blind the analyst to the realities of the patient's position and damage his capacity to respond appropriately to the patient's need.

I cannot forebear from quoting Racker's generalized example. A male analyst becomes very angry with the avarice of a female patient. Intellectually he may be able to understand that she defends herself from him because he is felt by her to be the thieving analyst. An archaic, internal object, the rapacious mother, is being projected on to him. Emotionally, however, he may fail to respond adequately because at that time, or perhaps always, he is overcome by oral resentment towards the patient who, by rejecting him, has become for him his own robbing mother or perhaps the withholding breast. The neurotic counter-transference in this case renders him impotent as an analyst. On the other hand, if he can recover enough to have an emotional identification with the patient's threatened ego, he may be able to turn the neurotic counter-transference into what we shall soon be discussing as a complementary counter-transference (vide 1968, pp. 124–5).

The other danger of a neurotic counter-transference is that the analyst may graft upon or induce in his patient his own neurosis—an example being that of a young analyst, convinced that he should be independent when he has not yet reached that point, forcing his patient to act a false independence when this is the last thing the patient should be attempting to do (vide 1968, pp. 125–6).

Comparing Racker's concept of the neurotic counter-transference with Fordham's concept of the illusory counter-transference, we can see that they agree over the illusory aspects of the counter-transference, but it is not certain whether the two concepts overlap in all respects. Racker's emphasis upon neurotic affect appears to be broader and, indeed, reminds me of Jung's patient's dream of her former analyst clinging to her like a madman on the wrong side of the frontier (1934, p. 144). Jung's alarming example, assuming that the dream really is about the analyst, forces us to hope that analysts are better analysed today and hence not so liable to such disasters. For me this would be the last word I wanted to say about this, were it not for the fact that in writing this down I made one or two slips of the pen and wrote down *neurotic transference* instead of *neurotic counter-transference*.

Wondering why, I thought that my disapproval of neurotic counter-transference had made me think that it is only a transference made onto the patient and not a counter-transference at all. I came to the conclusion that this would be an uncharitable confusion. There is a quantitative and qualitative difference between a patient's transference to one normally more-or-less stable analyst, and the response of an analyst who sometimes under stress and erosion from a number of disturbed patients may react neurotically to their transferences from time to time. Neurotic counter-transference is a more apt description and represents, normally speaking, a professional hazard. It is a neurotic counter-response to a transference from a patient rather than a neurotic transference on to a patient who has done nothing to provoke it—not that this latter event is not a hazard as well.

Counter-transference Proper

We can now pass on to the central point of this paper, which is to examine Racker's contribution to the counter-transference proper—corresponding in many ways to Fordham's syntonic counter-transference—but again a wider concept than Fordham's.

Racker is concerned with the understanding of counter-transference from the point of view of the inner experience of the analyst and how his handling of it influences the transference of the patient. He therefore discriminates between two modes of it—one that is relatively steady and quiet—comfortable, perhaps, as Michael Fordham would put it: the other disturbing, dramatic, less comfortable. The first he calls the *concordant* counter-transference, the second the *complementary* counter-transference. The two are inter-connected and are based upon the development of the pre-disposition of the analyst to identify with his patient through comprehension.

The Concordant Counter-transference

In the concordant counter-transference, the analyst identifies his ego with the patient's ego, and each part of his personality with the corresponding part of the patient's personality (1968, p. 134). Racker explicitly confines this to ego, superego and id and excludes internal objects as such, although of course internal objects have close connections with all three structures. The analyst who has made these identifications can become conscious of them to the extent of his own personal analysis and self-analysis.

About the process involved, Racker, like Fordham, holds that the identifications are made through projection and introjection, by which he means the resonance of the exterior in the interior, leading to (a) the unconscious recognition that what belongs to another is one's own (through introjection I feel that this part of you is me) and (b) the unconscious equation of what is my own with what belongs to another

311

(through projection I feel that this part of me is you). The name 'concordant counter-transference' stresses the manner in which the analyst goes along with his patient's dynamics through empathy and sympathy.

An interesting aspect of this concept lies in Racker's view about how the concordance arises. It is the result of the analyst's predisposition to empathy with the patient, whereby it turns out that an important aspect of the relation remains always in the following form: the analyst is the subject and the patient is the object of knowledge and concern. This annuls the 'object relationship' between the patient and the analyst whereby there are two persons interacting. Thus there arises instead, as Racker puts it, the approximate union or identity between the various parts (experiences, impulses, defences) of the subject and the object (1968, p. 136). On this level, the patient and the analyst are in minimal tension over against each other and are in a state of maximal union.

I think we can see very clearly that the therapeutic set-up envisaged here includes the level of the very early primitive states of the infant's primary identity with his mother. It provides a containing place for the anxieties of the very ill patient who is not only in reality wishing to regress to the state of an 'as if' primary identity with the mother-analyst but is actually beginning to be able to do so. And it is this very happening that can spontaneously generate in the analyst a growing concordant counter-transference.

Between the analyst and the patient, there come into play the four mechanisms of defence against anxiety in early infancy as described by Fordham in *Children as individuals*, namely projection, introjection, identification, and idealization. These experiences form the basis of the ability of the analyst and patient to develop between them a growing comprehension of the patient's problem, a process that is entirely in line with Jung's view that what he calls the incest fantasies are 'positively dragged into the light of day by the analytic method' (1929, p. 62).

The basic point here is that the concordant counter-transference arises, extends, and deepens uniquely within the analytic setting as such. Outside analysis, it may be observed in maternal care for the infant and young child, in the sympathy some teachers have for adolescents, and perhaps in states of being in love. Nevertheless the limitations of such types of concordance are well known, leaving it fairly clear that the range and depth of the concordant counter-transference in the analyst can be quantitatively and qualitatively much greater.

We may add that the analyst's capacity for concordance rests upon the experience of a good enough handling of himself by another when in a state of dependence. The motive power is gratitude, and the good enough handling enables a person to have concern for another that is real—not contrived. With the analyst, it is the experience and memory of his own analysis and the capacities for self-analysis started off by it that are determinative. Furthermore, it is likely that, whatever other fundamental aspects of counter-transference there may be, we shall find that it is out of his concordance that the analyst does his decisively creative work. We must add, however, that concordance is a growing process in a successful analysis and seems to become deeper as a result of another kind of counter-transference.

The Complementary Counter-transference

This other aspect of counter-transference is what Racker calls the 'complementary counter-transference'. It arises from the fact that, despite the annulment in the analytic situation of the object relationship in principle, there can yet appear a number of the aspects of an object relationship. The analyst is still and always remains a total human being with a capacity for making object relationships: he may experience libidinal need, etc. (1968, p. 105). Again, he makes transferences onto or projects onto his patient as if the patient were an internal object of his own, or he identifies with certain internal objects of the patient. Strong emotions of anxiety, anger, guilt, withdrawal, submissiveness and depression on the one hand, or love, gratification and manic excitement on the other, may seize him or continuously disturb him. In other words he may repeat infantile attitudes. Or again he may experience resistance to certain emotions in both his patients and himself—for instance to certain kinds of aggression. Furthermore, these feelings, as Fordham has pointed out, may be very intense indeed, the nearer to psychotic areas of experience the treatment gets.

Out of all this a number of possible responses arise. At one end of the spectrum we find thoroughly neurotic counter-transferences. In the middle there arises the possibility of the analyst reacting to the experiences not so grossly but still in fact neurotically acting out within the analysis. At the other end, the analyst may be able to employ his counter-transference experience to give himself information about the patient's transference. This then renews his concordant counter-transference, out of which he can make a therapeutically effective interpretation. The counter-transference involved is named 'complementary' and develops when, for a number of reasons, the patient treats the analyst as a projected internal object, with the result that, in a complementary way, the analyst feels treated as such and experiences emotions appropriate to such treatment (1968, p. 135). This is counter-transference proper, whereas, if the analyst were to respond to such treatment as if his patient were one of his own internal objects in projection, we should be dealing with a neurotic counter-transference. The mechanism involved in complementary counter-transference proper is the analyst's unconscious identification with an internal object in the drama of the patient's inner life.

A Case History

At this point I should like to give a clinical example of a man in his early thirties who had a very depressed mother, whom he experienced as an anxious, stuffing and over-impinging mother. She was also a fundamentalist evangelical woman who firmly believed in the impending end of the world. She always said that her son would not live beyond the age of eighteen in the world as it is, for by then the Second Coming would have taken place. His father, though intensely deprived of parental care from an early age, presented as the exact opposite. He was an active, highly optimistic and successful big business man, who was scarcely ever at home. He, too, was a keen Christian but quite different from the mother. He was liberal and progressive, firmly believed that the world was getting better and sincerely felt the success of his vast business enterprise and the setting up of the Kingdom of God to be intimately connected.

The boy denied all anger and unhappiness save that of

loneliness, was somewhat accident-prone, and liked to escape from home with boy friends or into the country for bird-watching, which, however, he liked to do alone. At university he met a gay manic girl who seemed to be life itself for him. She became the focal point for the projection of his whole feeling for life. After a struggle with his father, who had wanted him to become a business man, he had himself become a very capable intellectual with a reasonable, bland and somewhat sentimental presentation of himself to the world—a presentation with which he tended to identify.

He married the girl, who very soon broke down into a state of semi-psychotic anxiety. She was, like him, an only child, though in her case the parents were more overtly disturbed than his, and the mother psychotically so. She went into analysis and grappled with it in an intense way. She also encouraged him into analysis, to which he finally agreed, driven now by an intense anxiety over the whole situation—not only over his wife, but also over his mother-in-law, whom he feared he had damaged to the point of psychotic breakdown by his taking her daughter away from her into marriage.

He found relief in entering into analysis and developed a mild superficial positive transference. I liked him and was able to go along with him with a developing deepening and positive concordant counter-transference. At the same time, I began to become conscious from time to time of the presence of some annoyance inside myself. At the time I at first thought that it was about his bland presentation of himself, of which he was at first quite unconscious. Then I thought that it was anger at his very 'reasonable' and quietly obstinate blocking of my interpretations. The typical response was 'Yes, I quite see that, but . . .', and then would follow a gentle puzzled demolition of what I had said.

I also thought that the annoyance was due to the fact that my patient rather cut me out or kept me at a distance, while he invested all his life and emotions in his wife, who had to be the image of his anima. It was this that sometimes produced a sort of deadness in his talk and behaviour in the consulting room, and occasional sleepiness in me, despite the content of his communications which was, normally speaking, very interesting.

Later on, I felt that he was projecting onto me the parental internal objects, while I was feeling by identification some of his life-long confusion, resentment, and anger against his parents for being both depressed and over-optimistic; for being over-impinging and stuffing and at the same time absent and depriving; for forecasting the end of the world before he was eighteen and at the same time believing that everything was getting better and better. In other words, for him my interventions felt as confusing and angry-making as did his parents' efforts, and I could feel his anger within myself. At the same time I thought I could feel the anger his internal parent figures felt at his treatment of them. I was thus feeling the angry conflict within his inner world—an anger that had always been covered up in the actual life of his family. I also understood my sleepiness to be a reaction by withdrawal to the way in which he kept withdrawn from relationship with me and his internal parental objects.

The situation later became tragic, for his wife, who had made progress in her analysis, one day made an angry punishing suicidal gesture in which it appears that she took an overdose, possibly in an accidental way, and died. He was of course overwhelmed with grief, anger and despair, for his whole life felt to him to be invested in her. Then it was that out of the analysis of his grief and mourning processes, there gradually emerged the deeply self-destructive pattern in his own psychology. It was not a matter of a gross suicidal impulse but a subtler impulse to destroy himself as a person and give himself over to addictive behaviour, to become a wanderer on the face of the earth, to become a psychological recluse, though presenting a superficial bonhomie. Indeed, he had a dream in which somehow he had got involved in a marriage ceremony, surrounded by over-ostentatious celebrations, with a girl who he knew would be a hard superficial mother. He was horrified and wondered how he could get out of it.

All this was, of course, part of the working through of his mourning, but it contained more. It contained the shadow side of the idealized positive feelings about life that he had thought he had seen in his wife when he married her. The girl in the dream was not his wife but represented a negative side of his anima. In contrast to this, his wife, especially as her analysis proceeded, had become a deeper and less shallow person and, despite her self-destructive impulses and ultimate accidental death, had in a way affirmed life. The idealized positive anima figure he had tended to project upon his wife. She became less able and less willing to meet this and indeed she felt anger towards him over it although, when depressed, she could feel that she stood in the way of his happiness through her illness.

By this time the anger in me had been superseded by genuine sympathy for his tragedy, and the complementary counter-transference had more anxiety and depression in it as the feeling in his internal parental objects changed. Indeed, it was also true that he experienced at this time real sympathy and consideration from his actual parents as well.

The mastery of these counter-transference feelings made me able to feel for the whole of him more fully, with the result that I could make some helpful interpretations. The withdrawal symptoms that I had experienced in feeling sleepy, which represented negative counter-transference feelings to his originally negative transference, began to move towards a more positive counter-transference on my part, and this was re-sponded to by a more genuine positive transference on his part—less superficial and bonhomous. He was able to feel genuine gratitude as part of his attitude towards me and to realize a bit the psychological danger he was really in. At the same time he realized a very full feeling of wanting to take revenge on someone for his wife's death. Just as his wife had felt strong feelings of taking revenge on her parents and her analyst and her husband, but had taken it out on herself, so he was trying, like her, to find ways of taking revenge on his parents, his dead wife, and myself—on life as a whole perhaps, even if it were by subtly destroying himself as a person.

Shortly after feeling the benefit of the interpretations over his danger, he visited the flat where he had lived with his wife and spent the weekend with friends there. They were life-accepting people and he felt grateful. In anticipation, out of his envy, he feared to go home to his own lonely flat, but as he approached it he got a good sense of his dead wife's presence as an inner object and he felt good. He also felt grateful to her for her affirmation of life, but at the same time envious for what he fantasied was the peace of death. This led on to a discussion with me about death as a fulfilment and death as a deprivation.

To sum up, this whole analytical process started with the

patient's need and my disposition to function as analyst. This produced a certain superficial positive transference in him and a superficial positive counter-transference in myself of a concordant sort. Of course it was not fully concordant. This would be an impossibility at the beginning of an analysis. Gradually the counter-transference developed negative elements in response to the urgent inner problem of the patient, which arose out of the conflict between his ego and his internal parental objects. His anger at them, bad treatment of them and withdrawal from them were unconsciously directed against me and activated counter-feelings in me. In other words, his transference deepened for being more negative and my counter-transference deepened for becoming more negative and complementary.

After this I became able to master the feelings and understand better. The area of my empathy extended and a positive concordant counter-transference became possible again on a deeper level, in such a way that my interpretations could be received as beneficial rather than confusing or persecutory. In other words, the resultant increase in true positive transference on his part could lead to greater openness to therapy. Later, his life and relationships and work began to open out and develop in a very creative way as his capacity to benefit from therapy developed.

This particular illustration refers to what Racker calls the counter-transference *position*, which remains in being over a period of time, and which he compares with counter-transference *thoughts*, which are passing thoughts about the patient that suddenly swim into consciousness and may be used for understanding the particular situation at the moment (1968, p. 142). I give an example.

Counter-transference Thoughts

A patient who hated her mother, and from time to time has the greatest difficulty in communicating with me, was talking to me in a very halting and broken up way that nevertheless had a droning effect. On this occasion, I became seized, in a very objective way, with an inability to concentrate on her words. I was helpless—and furthermore I became aware of a series of fantasy images and thoughts that would permit no gainsaying or suppression. Though they were so insistent, I felt I could not attend to them and grasp what they were about for fear of losing all touch with my patient.

I turned my attention to the situation and could just get myself to wonder what was going on. Suddenly the thought struck me that I was feeling what it was like to be her. She was trying to communicate with me and having a titanic struggle to do so because of counter-thoughts and impulses. My thought no doubt sprang from the memory that she had in the past spoken of a cynical voice that mocked and shouted at her whenever she tried to communicate or be cooperative.

So I waited for an opening and then said, 'I think that while you are trying to talk to me, there is something going on inside you that is quite different from what you think you are trying to say.' She paused and then said, 'I was thinking that I would like to make bread. The husband of my friend makes bread. My mother even taught me to make bread. No, she didn't! She made the dough herself and then gave it to me and let me imprint ready-made shapes onto it'.

This communication had me wide awake and naturally made me think to myself about the implied criticism of me. She went on and suddenly said, 'I wanted to throw the dough away onto the floor and have nothing to do with it. My mother was always right.' I said, 'That's what really goes on underneath, when you are trying to be the good cooperative patient. You think that I, like your mother, want you to be just that. You want really to throw onto the floor all this analysis stuff you feel I have started off, like the dough.' She replied, 'Yes, you are always right in what you say.' I said, 'Yes, it's a pattern that often develops between us. You produce material and I interpret lots of things and you really feel it's a lot of nonsense. It's all too like your mother. Because of this, there is a lot of you that feels fed up to the teeth with the whole thing, and would like to find your own way of doing it, i.e., making your own dough.'

I could say this out of a renewed concordant counter-transference, after having learnt from the very striking complementary counter-transference that arose from identifying with what was going on between her internalized mother figure and that ego of hers that was trying so hard to be cooperative, in denial of her strongly truculent feelings. The piece of reconstruction just described was made possible by a combination of transference/counter-transference experience with knowledge of events in the patient's past. Thus the emotional experience in the past was made vivid in the present and indicated to the patient the extent to which her experience of the present was saturated by the remembered emotional experiences of the past (cf. Lambert, 1970, p. 27).

The Talion Law in Transference/Counter-transference

We are now ready to move on to the dynamic part played by the 'talion law' in the transference/counter-transference relationship and particularly in relation to the complementary counter-transference. I think that the last two case examples will have illustrated the point, but I propose to state the essential points in abstraction.

1. The transference/counter-transference relationship, because the infantile and child parts of both analyst and patient are involved, tends to be profoundly influenced by the talion law. This, of course, is the primitive situation of 'an eye for an eye, and a tooth for a tooth'. In terms of the psyche it refers to the feelings that are aroused by love and hate, by cooperation and aggression—feelings that may be denied but are really there (1968, pp. 137–42).

2. Racker puts it simply by stating that positive transference is answered by positive counter-transference; negative transference is answered by negative counter-transference and, by implication, vice versa.

3. In the actual analytical situation, however, I think that there are two types of progression in relation to the talion law:

The first is where the predisposition of the analyst to care for and understand the patient creates a superficial positive transference. This is answered by a deepening positive concordant counter-transference in the analyst that may render the patient secure enough to risk experiencing his latent hostile feelings as negative transference. This in turn activates negative elements in the analyst's complementary counter-transference, and here we get to the central point in the therapy from the point of view of the patient's relationship to his internal objects.

Two things can happen. In one case the analyst cannot

understand his negative complementary counter-transference. He then either tries to suppress his feelings of hostility towards his patient, or he expresses it by more or less subtle and possibly unconscious ways, or he does it openly. In any case, the patient, who had projected his hostile internal object upon the analyst and unconsciously feels the analyst's hostility, introjects it again, not modified but enhanced. The outer world has only confirmed his delusionary inner world. This is the 'vicious circle' of delusion that results from the straightforward operation of the talion law.

In the other case, the analyst manages to understand the complementary negative counter-transference and also to master his feelings in such a way as to be able to make useful interpretations out of a renewed concordant counter-transference. If he does so he may succeed in making a breach in the patient's vicious circle either in part or wholly, either temporary or long-lasting (1968, p. 138). If he does so, the relief of the patient may be such and his gratitude so great that a step towards a genuine and deep positive transference in the patient is made, together with an enhancement of his capacity for trust (vide Plaut, 1966, p. 113–22). This promotes further openness to therapy.

The second type of analytic progression that we often find is that in which, though there is a predisposition on the part of the analyst to understand, the patient at once brings a strongly enduring negative transference straight into the treatment, expressed by continuous hostile negation or masked by a compulsive positive over-estimation of the analyst. Then the analyst is involved from the first in negative complementary counter-transference and is landed with a lot of hard work mastering this and turning it into understanding and beneficial interpretations. The breaching of the vicious circle is liable, as we all know, to be long and arduous. On the other hand, any positive transference that thus develops is likely to be deep-seated and fruitful.

We may notice here that these considerations brought in by Racker are quite close in spirit to Jung, who seems to have considered that on a deep level a positive transference is important in successful therapy. We may consider that the kind of positive transference envisaged is not an idealization or a one-sided denial of the negative, but is related to a repaired capacity to trust and to modify persecutory and paranoid delusions. Then the patient may be free to accept the reality of the analyst in his good and bad aspects, as well as his own good and bad aspects, and also the good and bad aspects of analysis itself. At this point something like health is being established, but it rests upon the ability of the analyst to contain the operation of the talion law and to modify the vicious circle caused by the fact that the outer world is seeming to the patient to confirm his worst fears.

Case Illustration

The patient was born three months after his father's death to a mother who was in grief and depression. She found she could not bear nursing the child and at the age of six months put him in a home for babies and small children. He was there for nearly two years until he was adopted by his maternal uncle and his wife—a childless couple. He had pneumonia by the time he was rescued and for a time he became unmanageable. The adopting mother was very patient and understanding, though perhaps a somewhat rigid person. She did very well and won the love of the child. The father was a formidable leader in his profession and rather jealous of the child.

As might be expected, the child grew up isolated, though extremely intelligent and gifted. He was always up against any group he belonged to—prep. school, boarding school, the R.A.F. and society, though only in a certain way. He feared their impingement upon him and his hatred of them for reminding him of his traumatized life in the babies' home. He feared their retaliatory action against his nonconformity, and at first he would get beaten up and ragged until he fought through to a unique isolated position in the group. On the other hand, he learn to mollify them by being very interesting and amusing. As he became a man, he really was very disturbed and suffered sexual inhibition, eating obsessions, two broken marriages, violent rages against women, difficulties over working and a tendency to addiction to drugs.

Coming into analysis seemed like being adopted again, though not as a pure repeat, and so he spent some time 'cocooned', to use his words—and contained by my concordant counter-transference. During this time he became able to work

322

and to employ some of his creative literary talents, to work through a promiscuous phase and to dare to enjoy becoming a father and being a husband in his third, this time apparently stable, marriage. This was due to the negative elements beginning to come out against me as establishment or fascist, which I could then interpret out of my complementary counter-transference.

Meanwhile, the fits of violent temper-tantrums against his wife became modified. They were always based upon the feeling that she did not understand how much he had to put up with and what a struggle he had to contain his infantile needs. As could be expected, it was with groups that his difficulties were considerable, although his work-group life was reasonably creative. While thinking that he loved large parties or gatherings at home, he discovered that in fact he hated and feared them and that his friends felt he resented their impingement. After a good deal of personal analysis he experienced therapy in groups, where he feared to make his needs known or to express his anger. At one group session he sulked and would not join in. The group was not hostile to him and individual members went to him to invite him to join them. He still sulked. Finally the whole group decided to go to him as a body and take him into their midst. In other groups he had had to be the 'enfant terrible'—who defied and entertained them and who would jolt them by his unexpected behaviour. But all the time he was on the look-out for confirmation of his early trauma but wondering whether they would turn out helpful and interpretative.

In this patient the vicious circle of persecutory anxiety had often been increased by his environment in the earlier years, but a combination of individual and group analysis has succeeded, through the mastery by the analyst and the groups of their negative counter-transference in such a way as to modify by their concordance the vicious circle in which he was fixed. Though surprised, he has been very grateful to those who basically did not retaliate and a considerable opening out of his personality has ensued.

Gratitude

In this paper, reference has been made to gratitude on the part of patients—and it is to Melanie Klein that analysts owe a debt of gratitude for her work in drawing their attention to the experience of gratitude as an essential feature in personal development (1957). It belongs to the movement of the generations. In normal development, when the infant's experience of having his needs met enough by his mother is satisfactory, gratitude spontaneously appears among the many other experiences of his parents as good and bad. It is out of this gratitude that children in growing up can in turn do something for their children, who are also the grandchildren of their parents.

In the analytic situation, where the repair of damage done to normal development is part of the therapeutic process, a similar pattern appears. Out of the transference/counter-transference, with its uncovering of the operation of the talion law, an appropriate interpretation that is truly non-punitive can activate gratitude in the patient who is worried by his destructiveness and persecutory feelings—especially when these feelings are maiming the patient's capacity to make use of his analyst's interpretations. It may be considered that this non-punitive handling of destructiveness can activate gratitude at the deepest levels—deeper even than those activated by patience in listening, steady concern and putting at the disposal of the patient the accumulated knowledge and skill of the analyst.

If we consider the motivation of the analyst, we may think that it depends upon a sufficient experience of gratitude in himself for an appropriate handling of the talion law in the transference/counter-transference situation on the part of his own analyst and others concerned in his analysis and training, as well as by his colleagues, as he gains experience as an analyst.

Conclusion

I should like to conclude by indicating points where Racker's work amplifies and makes more explicit the formulations of Jung as listed above.

1. *The mutual influence of two whole persons in the dialectical procedure.* Racker's studies represent a detailed analysis of how the dialectical procedure or the analytic set-up promotes a

longitudinal process in the interplay between analyst and patient in transference/counter-transference. The analytic predisposition of the analyst may lead to the patient's positive transference. This can activate the analyst's positive counter-transference of a concordant type, which in turn leads to the patient's risking expression of his negative transference. This may be met by the analyst's complementary negative counter-transference, which may be transformed by him into a deeper concordant counter-transference. Gratitude for this can activate in the patient a deeper positive transference leading to therapeutic advance.

2. *The transformation of the two personalities resulting from their combining as if two chemical substances were being mixed.* Racker shows how the personality of the analyst reverberates to the unconscious drama of the patient both in concordant and complementary counter-transference. His knowledge of the patient in this way is deepened and a creative interpretation can, in time, profoundly influence the patient's personality. We may add that the potency of both analyst and patient can be enhanced by this creative work.

3. *The overcoming of the demon of sickness whereby a sufferer can transmit his disease to a healthy person whose powers then subdue the demon.* Racker illustrates this in detail by showing how through identification, introjection, and re-projection the analyst can take into himself the inner drama of his patient, understand it and give it back to the patient in a form whereby he can understand, assimilate and integrate it in a more creative and repaired form.

4. *The wounding of the physician that gives him the measure of his power.* For Jung the subduing of the demon of sickness can take place, 'but not without impairing the well-being of the subduer' (1929, p. 72), cf. Adler's note on 'the wounded healer' (1961, p. 117). Racker opens the way to a further understanding of how the analyst feels in his own person the impact of the patient's love, greed, hate, aggression and destructiveness. It is his reaction to this and his understanding and the overcoming of the talion response that give him therapeutic potency.

5. *The intercrossing transference relationship or marriage quaternity.* Racker's contribution here may be taken in terms of his analysis of the interplay between concordant transference, with its 'annulment of the object relationship', and complementary

325

transference, which rests upon the presence of object relationships between the analyst and patient all through the analysis. The connection with the marriage quaternio stems from the fact that the interplay between endogamous relationships and exogamous relationships is implicit in the interaction between concordant and complementary counter-transference.

6. *The activation of incest fantasies between patient and analyst,* Racker's analysis goes into considerable detail on how the incest fantasies of infancy and childhood are activated by the analytic set-up so that both patient and analyst are involved. The success of the treatment depends naturally upon the analyst's having been made aware of these processes in his own analysis.

Finally, despite the work done by Racker and the usefulness of it to analytical psychologists, there remain a number of unsolved problems. Perhaps the greatest is to understand the conditions that render nugatory all efforts of the analyst to overcome the working of the talion law and to break into the vicious circle in which the patient has got fixed so that he remains quite unable to distinguish between his inner world and outer reality.

References

ADLER, G. (1961). *The living symbol,* London, Routledge & Kegan Paul.
FORDHAM, M. (1957). *New developments in analytical psychology,* London, Routledge.*
——(1969). 'Technique and counter-transference'. *J. analyt. Psychol.,* 14, 2.*
——(1969). *Children as individuals,* London. Hodder & Stoughton.
FREUD, S. (1910). *The future prospects of psychoanalytic therapy.* Standard Edition XI, London, Hogarth.
HANN-KENDE, F. (1936). 'Zur Übertragung und Gegenübertragung in der Psychoanalyse', *Int. Z. Psychoanal.* 22.
JUNG, C. G. (1929). 'Problems of modern psychotherapy', in *Coll. wks.,* 16, London, Routledge & Kegan Paul.
——(1934). 'The practical use of dream analysis', in *Coll. wks.,* 16. London, Routledge & Kegan Paul.
——(1935). 'Principles of practical psychotherapy', in *Coll. wks.,* 16, London, Routledge & Kegan Paul.
——(1946). 'The psychology of the transference', in *Coll. wks.,* 16. London, Routledge & Kegan Paul.
KLEIN, M. (1957). *Envy and gratitude.* London, Tavistock Publications.
LAMBERT, K. (1970). 'Some notes on the process of reconstruction', *J. analyt. Psychol.,* 15, 1.*

PLAUT, A. (1966). 'Reflections about not being able to imagine', in *Analytical psychology: a modern science*. Library of Analytical Psychology, vol. 1. London, Heinemann, 1973.

RACKER, H. (1968). *Transference and counter-transference*. London, Hogarth.

Symposia on counter-transference (1960). *Brit. J. med. Psychol.*, **33**, 1.

Index

Interpretation (*contd*)
definitions of, 38
development in idea of, 39–40
methods of, 115
timing of, 43
types of, 40
Interventions, 41, 42
Interview, 117
activity outside, 121–4
frequency, 121, 131
recorded, 138
simplicity, 146
Introjection, 28, 137, 248, 272, 276–8,
294, 299–301, 311, 312
Involvement, 6
Irrational experiences, 249
Isaacs, S., 162
'I-thou' attitude, 178, 179, 185–7

Jackson, M., 5
Jacobi, J., 111, 120
James, J., 204
James, W., 204, 208
Jealousy, 195, 198
Jellinek, E. M., 202
Johnson, A. M., 96
Jokes, 9, 10
Jones, E., 13, 47, 291
Jung, C. G., active imagination, 188,
189, 191
alchemic interaction, 56
alcoholism, 200, 203, 206, 208, 213
analyst's attitude and role, 3, 7, 43,
137
Anna, case history, 172
'Answer to Job', 33, 143
causal elements, 130
confession, 25–7
counter-transference, 97, 221, 234,
243, 306
daemonic image, 298
dialectical relationship, 144
early model of psychotherapy, 24
energy, 294
fantasy, 161, 176
individualism, 265
infantile sexuality, 129
interview frequency, 121
perfection, 207
personal and transpersonal unconscious, 113
personal equation, 292
personality of analyst, 112
professional authority, 262
projections, 128

psycho-analytic theory, 244
psychotic states, 282
reconstruction, 64–5
reductive analysis and synthesis, 164–
5
self, 249, 254
spiral, 55
synthesis, 70
technique, 47–51, 261
termination of psychotherapy, 101–2
transference, 111, 115, 119, 123,
131–3, 135, 145, 147, 148, 152–9,
178, 306
transformation, 28

-K factor, 30
Kaye, H., 18
Kessel, N., 202, 211
Kirsch, H., 260
Klauber, J., 63, 64
Klein, M., 42, 62, 161, 163, 185, 323
Kleinians, 173
Knight, R., 204
Kraemer, W. P., 219, 244

Lambert, K., 18, 62, 64, 236, 303, 320
Laurie, P., 200
Leibowitz, J. O., 201
Libermann, D., 166, 170
Life, 119–21
and transference, 120
philosophy of, 120
Limitation, 35
Linder, R., 242
Little, M., 215, 219, 253, 283, 301
Living the shadow, 125, 126
Love, 32, 57, 58, 274, 284
'Love-in', 7
Loy, R., 152, 153, 155, 261

McLuhan, M., 68
MacQuarrie, J., 179
Malan, D. H., 5
Manic-depressive disorder, 200
Meier, C. A., 285
Meltzer, D., 36
Memory, infantile, 264
prenatal, 215
theory of, 63
Menninger, K., 204
Milner, M., 13, 16, 174
Mind, theory of, 4, 5
Mistakes, 104, 211, 256, 257, 272
Money, symbolic significance, 183